PORSCHE
911

GUIDE TO PURCHASE & D.I.Y. RESTORATION

LINDSAY PORTER & PETER MORGAN

Foulis

Haynes

Other Haynes Publishing Group titles of interest to the enthusiast:
Porsche 911 Owners Workshop Manual (264)
Porsche in all its Forms (P169)
The Porsche 924/944 Book (F764)

First published 1988
Reprinted 1988, 1990 & 1994

Published by: G.T. Foulis & Co., an imprint of
Haynes Publishing,
Sparkford, Nr. Yeovil,
Somerset BA22 7JJ, England.

British Library Cataloguing in Publication Data
Porter, Lindsay
   Porsche 911: guide to purchase & DIY restoration. — (Guide to purchase & DIY restoration).
   Automobiles — Maintenance and repair
I. Title II. Morgan, Peter III. Series
629.28'722   TL152

ISBN 0-85429-475-9

Library of Congress Catalog Card No.
87-83503

Printed in England by J.H. Haynes & Co. Ltd.

Contents

Foreword by Roy Gillham

It was with great pleasure that I received Lindsay Porter's approach asking if I would consider writing a foreword to this long awaited book on the restoration of a car the like of which we shall never see again.

Loved since its inception, and increasingly wept over by the owners of the pre-1976 non-galvanised models as they see the tin-worm take hold and spread, the 911, whether under restoration, requiring restoration or in pristine condition, has a dedicated following throughout the world.

One of the main functions of the international group of Porsche Clubs is to give guidance and assistance to that sturdy band who relentlessly toil to keep their early 911s not just roadworthy, but in Concours condition. Anyone who has been fortunate enough to attend any of the Annual Concours events organised by Porsche Clubs throughout the world will testify to the time, effort and finance put in to the restoration of the earlier 911.

Through this book, which contains so much detail and guidance, the toils of the Porsche 911 restorer will undoubtedly be made easier and the goal reached that much sooner.

Roy Gillham
Executive Director
Porsche Club Great Britain

Introduction and Acknowledgements

The Porsche 911 is one of the most admired, sought after, lusted for and highly desired cars ever built. Or at least that's what opinion polls tell us about the car. They also tell us that the 911 is the car that creates more envy than any other – and it's the one that is more likely to be vandalised than any other. So, the moral seems to be, lock up your Porsches! At least, when you are not experiencing the unparallelled delight in actually *using* your 911!

Unfortunately, some current examples are also among the most expensive production cars on earth, making the ownership of a good condition Porsche 911 beyond the reach of most people; at least, until this book came along. The aim of this book is to show the owner or potential owner what to look for when buying a car and, most importantly, the correct techniques for a home restorer to use when putting a deteriorated example of the marque back into one piece. It is also hoped that the book will be useful to those having some or all of the work carried out for them, because correct techniques and the correct order of proceeding are described in detail. Indeed, a small number of the techniques described in this book are emphatically *not* for the home restorer to undertake because of

their technical complexity or the need for special skills or equipment. Nothing daunted, we've touched upon them here so that you, the owner or potential owner can know what is being done (or what *should* be done!) when the experts get hold of your car.

One of the best things about the Porsche 911 is the wide availability of parts, even for the earlier cars. Porsche themselves still produce a vast range and if you must have original parts, you won't mind paying the exceptionally high prices demanded. Fortunately, there are a number of independents specialising in Porsche parts and you can often save an awful lot of money by buying through them. It would be fair to say, however, that you should satisfy yourself that the standards of non-Porsche parts are sufficiently high. Do so by buying only through a highly reputable independent specialist.

Getting the information together for this book has proved extremely time-consuming and has involved the services and expertise of a good number of people. I took virtually all the photographs used here at a number of specialist restoration centres, including Autofarm, at Tring in the South-East of England, where there is a huge turnover in Porsches, parts and

services. Indeed, they must be the UK's largest independent Porsche specialist and their reputation matches their size! Many of the body shop pictures were taken at Dave Felton's workshop near Leek in Staffordshire, where the most painstaking and skillful workmanship I have ever seen takes place. Dave refuses to give quotations for work because jobs take 'until they're done', but I would venture to suggest that his Porsches' bodies are better than even Porsche know how to make them! A lot of the pictures were taken at Classic Car Restorations in the South-West Midlands where nothing was too much trouble to see that the work was done properly and the pictures we wanted produced on time.

The restoration writing and 'Buying' sections of this book (but not the 'Modifications' section) were carried out by probably the best person in Britain for the job. Peter Morgan is a Chartered Engineer who has totally restored his own 911 and was for some time the Technical Editor of 'Porsche Post', the magazine of Porsche Club Great Britain. He has done a fabulous job!

My colleague Miranda Horobin worked long and hard to write the 'Specifications' and 'Heritage' chapters of this book, proving once again what a meticulous and what an

accomplished and versatile soul she is! I must take responsibility for other sections of the book and, for better or for worse, for its overall form. My heartfelt thanks are due and gladly given to all those who have contributed in ways large and small to the book's completion.

Lindsay Porter
Bromyard, Herefordshire.

Attempting to produce a single text to cover all the many detail changes that have affected the 911 through its long production run is a big task. Combine that with the need to satisfy not only the 'thoroughbred' enthusiast but also the interested but non-skilled owner and it is inevitable someone somewhere will feel something is missing. There are many tasks which are beyond the scope of the average amateur mechanic and these are pointed out, but not described in detail. Generally, I have tried to give enough information to give an understanding of the principles used throughout the construction of the 911, even if in some cases, the renovation is not covered in depth.

In the preparation of my part of the text for this book I have called upon the experience of many friends within the Porsche Club Great Britain. My parts of the text have been largely written around the early to mid-seventies 911 and I have sought many details on other models from many respectable individuals, both inside and outside professional Porsche circles. I would like to thank everyone who helped me for their support. A special commendation goes to my wife Anne, who showed outstanding patience as I spent night after night, either on a word processor or checking out some procedure or other in the workshop.

Peter Morgan
Cambridge.

Using this book

The layout of this book has been designed to be both attractive and easy to follow during practical work on your car. However, to obtain maximum benefit from the book, it is important to note the following points:

1) Apart from the introductory pages, this book is split into two parts: chapters 1 to 6 dealing with history, buying and practical procedures; appendices 1 to 7 providing supplementary information. Each chapter/appendix may be sub-divided into sections and even sub-sections. Section headings are in italic type between horizontal lines and sub-section headings are similar, but without horizontal lines.

2) Step-by-step photograph and line drawing captions are an integral part of the text (except those in chapters 1 and 2) – therefore the photographs/ drawings and their captions are arranged to "read" in exactly the same way as the normal text. In other words they run down each column and the columns run from left to right of the page.

Each photograph caption carries an alpha-numeric identity, relating it to a specific section. The letters before the caption number are simply the initial letters of key words in the relevant section heading, whilst the caption number shows the position of the particular photograph in the section's picture sequence. Thus photograph/caption 'DR22' is the 22nd photograph in the section headed "Door Repairs".

3) Figures – line illustrations follow consecutively with the photo numbering sequence.

4) All references to the left or right of the vehicle are from the point of view of somebody standing behind the car looking forwards.

5) The bodywork repair chapter of this book deals with problems particular to the Porsche 911 series. In concentrating on these aspects the depth of treatment of body repair techniques in general is necessarily limited. For more detailed information covering all aspects of body repair it is recommended that reference be made to the Haynes *The Car Bodywork Repair Manual'* also by Lindsay Porter.

6) Because this book concentrates upon restoration, regular maintenance procedures and normal mechanical repairs of all the car's components are beyond its scope. It is therefore strongly recommended that the *Haynes Porsche 911 Owners Workshop Manual* should be used as a companion volume.

7) We know it's a boring subject, especially when you really want to get on with a job – but your safety, through the use of correct workshop procedures, must ALWAYS be your foremost consideration. It is essential that you read, and UNDERSTAND, appendix 1 before undertaking any of the practical tasks detailed in this book and check with the suppliers of equipment and materials so that you have in your possesion any health and safety information relating to the work you intend carrying out. Make sure you read it!

8) Before starting any particular job it is important that you read the introduction to the relevant Chapter or Section, taking note of the 'tool box' and 'safety' notes. It is recommended that you read through the section from start to finish before getting into the job.

9) Whilst great care is taken to ensure that the information in this book is as accurate as possible, the author, editor or publisher cannot accept any liability for loss, damage or injury caused by errors in, or omissions from, the information given.

1 Heritage

"There will always be sports cars, even if the ordinary workaday car is swept away and replaced by something else, people would still be wanting sporting vehicles. You don't see many working horses today – but there are more horses than ever for sport and leisure. And so, because Porsche make only sports cars, there will always be a Porsche . . ."

"Porsche" . . . the name immediately conjures up for the aficionados and mere mortals of this world: a sleek, fast and ultimate sporting machine; a dream machine that, as the above statement by the son of Ferdinand Porsche indicates, is the result of singlemindedness, genius, vision and perhaps excusable arrogance.

In only 39 years a family name and business has become the personification in both the production car and racing fields of the supreme sports car, and this in a world market where costing and competitiveness is intense and, to stay afloat, other car manufacturers have had to severely cut their workforce; Porsche had steadily increased its numbers of employees, turnover and profits and shows no signs of stopping in the next 39 years.

The founder of this magic was, in 1893, a youth of 18 who decided to install electricity in his family home. With little formal education, the second son of a tinsmith in the small village of Maffersdorf, Austria, Ferdinand Porsche devised, built and installed an electricity system in his parents' home. This obvious manifestation of his unusual creative genius and vision (electric sevices didn't exist in his country) combined with his determination to succeed – his father was opposed to the installation of such new-fangled ideas – sowed the seeds of the "Porsche" story.

Pursuing his interest in electricity Ferdinand was invited to join Jacob Lohner, who wanted to make motor cars, but felt the future was in electric cars. The first Lohner-Porsche car was displayed at the 1900 Paris Exhibition, with the electric motors installed in the hubs of the front wheels. In later developments Porsche installed them in all four wheels; the origin of the four-wheeled drive? He was only 25!

At the age of 30 Porsche was appointed technical Director of Austro-Daimler, where he continued to develop his 'mixed' drive concept – electric current being generated by a dynamo driven by a petrol engine. In 1910 he designed his first petrol engine driven sports car, the 'Prince Henry Austro-Daimler' so called because it won the Prince Henry Trial. In addition he initiated the development of aero engines in Austria – a 1912 air-cooled four-cylinder engine being the glimmerings of the Volkswagen flat-four perhaps?

During the First World War he was Managing Director of Austro-Daimler. Amongst other military transport, specific successes were gun tractors and motorised artillery pieces. After the war he turned to small car design and 'Sascha' won its class in the Targa Florio 1922. Porsche's enthusiasm for racing was not shared by Austro-Daimler and after increasing differences of opinion Porsche accepted the job of Technical Director, with a seat on the board, at Daimler in Stuttgart, Germany.

He was responsible for designs leading to the Mercedes S and SSK supercharged cars, and experiments with diesel engines were successful but his mind kept straying back to the small car (a one litre), and ohv engines and his drawing board was developing a very advanced racing car with swing axle suspension. Daimler were content to remain in the production of safe, middle to higher price range conventional side valve cars and rejected his ideas. With increasing irritation at the restraints of being responsible to a board of directors, and a desire to return to Austria, he accepted a job with Steyr. His design for them of a

large luxury car with a 5.3 engine the 'Austria' smacks of an 'anything you can do I can do better' gesture to Daimler and it caused a satisfying sensation at the 1929 Paris Motor Show. However with production hardly underway the project's bank collapsed and the new bank was allied to Austro-Daimler!

At the age of 55 Porsche was redundant. With total belief in himself and his designs he decided that now was the time to set up on his own. Returning to Stuttgart he formed the "Dr. Ing. h. c. Ferdinand Porsche GmbH, Konstruktionsbüro für Motoren-Fahrzeug, Luftfahrzeug und Wasserfahrzeugbau" – in other words a design studio ready to try its hand at any form of transport, air, land or sea.

Ferdinand laid the groundwork for "Porsche's" future success by collecting together a group of highly skilled and innovative people including Karl Rabe as chief engineeer who had worked with Porsche as early as 1913, Mickl, an aerodynamicist and calculator, Komenda, a body designer, Porsche's son Ferdinand, known as Ferry, aged 21 and his partners, Dr Anton Piëch, his son-in-law and Adolf Rosenberger, their first commercial manager.

Their first project, No 7 – what self-respecting newly fledged company would use the number 1 for their first project number – was a car for Wanderer, a six-cylinder passenger car using Porsche's swing axle rear suspension design. An eight-cylinder version, which Ferdinand drove for a number of years, was produced only as a single prototype. A contract for development of a 'people's car' got Porsche's 'small car' out of the cupboard again: Type 12 'Volksauto' was a rear-engined five-cylinder with independent suspension all round; three prototypes were built, two with streamlined Reutter built bodies scaled down from Komenda's

design for the Wanderer eight-cylinder and pointing towards the eventual VW design. Porsche now patented his torsion bar independent front suspension with trailing arms and transverse torsion bars enclosed in a tube.

In 1932 in the constant search for new contracts and commisions Ferdinand was invited by Soviet Russia as a guest of state to inspect all their engineering and manufacturing facilities. The upshot of the visit was that he was offered the position of State Designer. Porsche was sorely tempted but felt that his ambition to build a world-beating racing car would not be encouraged by the Soviets so he declined. This ambition was given a great boost with an approach from Auto Union (a merger of Wanderer, Audi, DKW and Horch) who benefited from large sums of money from the new 'Nazi' Government. The aim was to add to the glory of the German Nation by becoming all-conquering in racing and speed cars – alongside all the other 'all-conquering' intended. The Porsche team happily produced their rear engined racing machine with its supercharged V16 engine located behind the driver and using a tubular chassis frame while those torsion bars came off the drawing board and transverse leaf spring at the rear. Ferry Porsche carried out the early test work and Grand Prix success was achieved in 1934, continuing spectacularly until 1939; good for 'new Germany's' international prestige.

Hitler, another ambitious Austro-German, then decided that the 'people' should have a car too – a 'Volkswagen' – and discussed his ideas with Porsche, his most startling being that the car should retail at the present day equivalent of £90! Porsche, undeterred, submitted a document in January 1934 entitled "Exposé relating to the construction of a German Volkswagen" and the VW was born, amidst the hostility of the

rest of the German motor industry. It was based on an air-cooled rear engine and all independent torsion bar suspension. The lengthy process of trial and error progressed until Reimspeiss (one of the original Porsche group) designed the four-cylinder air-cooled boxer engine that continued to power 25 million Volkswagens over the next 27 years. Hitler wanted it to look like a Beetle and in 1938 it was shown to the public.

Porsche became a director of Volkswagenwerke GmbH and was assigned, in 1936, to design and construct a factory in Wolfsburg where the cars were to be made. The first production car was seen at the Berlin Motor Show but only a few were made – it almost seems as if some imp were determined that Porsche-designed cars should remain on the drawing board – as Hitler's money had to be side-tracked to subsidize the war!

One more concrete step was taken during this period towards the ultimate Porsche machine; despite initial reluctance, Porsche was given the go ahead by the German Government to start producing a 'people's' sports car based on the VW, for the Berlin-Rome road race being arranged to celebrate the Axis partnership between Hitler and Mussolini. Type 114, a super-charged 1.5 litre V-engine mounted between the driver's seat and rear wheels with two overhead camshafts per bank, and Type 64, with VW engine enlarged to 1.5 litres and an aluminium body, were the designs later to be moulded into the 356 Porsche. One of these three Type 64s survived and was raced until 1951.

The War declared, the race cancelled, the VW production halted, Porsche yet again turned to the production of military vehicles. Based on the VW, the Kübelwagen became the standard 'jeep' for Germany's forces, followed by an amphibious version, the 'Schwimmenwagen'.

Porsche was made an honorary professor in 1940 and later, under the title of Reich Armaments Councillor in tandem with Albert Speer, he was responsible for the production of various tanks including the Tiger, the Ferdinand (!) and the Maus, all using hub mounted electric motors! As the War came to an end Porsche was ordered to evacuate his works and staff from Stuttgart to Gmünd in Austria. The Allied powers interned him in 1945 as he had undoubtedly benefited from Hitler's régime and the personal favour of the Führer himself – he had been allowed to visit the USA twice in 1937 to study the American motor industry when severe curtailment of travel was the order of the day. However – even Albert Speer commented that it was stupid to arrest Porsche as he had never had anything to do with politics. Obviously the Allies thought so too and Porsche was released and allowed to return to Austria. Life was as confused for the Porsche family as anyone else in occupied Germany, the family estate being in the American zone and Gmünd in the British. The Americans also occupied the Porsche factory at Stuttgart-Zuffenhausen for use as a motor pool. Porsche's daughter Louise had in the meantime taken the Gmünd works – an old sawmill – in hand while Porsche was interned, and obviously sharing Ferdinand's determination, started to re-establish its working. They initially worked mainly on repairing the remaining Kübelwagens, virtually the only cars available in Germany after the war, and repairing, modifying and servicing vehicles of all sorts from tractors to water cylinders. She reassembled the design team and kept the drawing boards working on future dreams, symptomatic Porsche vision. Porsche's freedom was short-lived: the French approached him with an idea to re-establish the Volkswagenwerke

in France and Ferdinand, Ferry and Anton Piëch were arrested at the initial meeting in the French zone. Ferry was released within a few months and returned to Gmünd, but Ferdinand and Piëch were transferred to France while the French obsessively tried to collect evidence that would put them on trial as war criminals.

Louise Piëch, aided by Ferry, by now Professor Dr. and the reassembled design team including Karl Rabe, Erwin Komenda and Haus Kern were hunting for someone willing to convert the design concepts into prototypes. The new firm of 'Porsche Konstruktionen GmbH' was approached by an Italian industrialist, Piero Dusio, who had decided to have a new Italian Grand Prix car designed and contracted Porsche about that and other projects including the ubiquitous tractor. Leaving the designers to get on with it and using the fees from Dusio, Louise Piëch entered into negotiations with the French authorities and in 1947 Ferdinand and Anton were released. Porsche returned a physically much weakened and elderly man of 72, still interested and full of ideas but having to accept that the younger generation had respectfully but firmly taken over.

The company's Type 360, 'Cisitalia' Grand Prix car, the first four-wheel-drive racing car, was not being used by Dusio because he was having an enormous success with his Fiat-based Cistitalia coupes and cabriolets; with hand-built tubular space frames, they were very expensive, considering that the engine was only an 1100. The excitement of realising that there was a market for such expensive sports cars, and with the total conviction that they could produce a faster better car, spurred Ferry Porsche and Karl Rabe into turning into reality Ferdinand Porsche's long-held dream of a Porsche-designed, Porsche-built sports car for the masses. Type 356, an amalgam of the 64, 001 and 114, was based

on Volkswagen components, Ferry's theory being that it should be a production car. The design office in Gmund became a car factory and despite their doubts about the expense of tubular frames in terms of mass production the first Porsche was an open two-seater roadster with a 1131cc VW engine reversed so that its cylinder blocks lay ahead of the rear axle, – 'mid-engined' – VW gear box, torsion bar suspension, steering and brakes, all held together by a hand-made space frame (a series a small tubes creating a frame made more of space and air than metal) and covered with a hand-built Komenda designed aluminium body, each hinged panel being hand-filled and leaded to fit its own opening. This prototype was driven to Switzerland in July 1948 and road-tested by various journalists foregathered to cover the Swiss Grand Prix at Bern. Driven by Herbert Kaes, a Porsche nephew, it won the 'round the houses' race in Innsbruck, Austria. It had taken 362 days to produce from start of design to road worthiness certificate!

The purchaser of this car placed an order for further cars and the 356/2 was set into motion, to become the actual production car, cabriolets and coupes. The mid-engine was abandoned in favour of more interior room for luggage space and the tubular space frame became a pressed steel platform chassis with integral scuttle, door pillars and inner wings. 46 of these were hand-built in Gmünd, although progress was slow because of the hand-built body construction, and the highly skilled craftsman in charge of this was inclined to enjoy his drink to the detriment of his production. Three in 1948, twenty-five in 1949 and eighteen in 1950.

This progress was obviously not satisfactory but in the meantime Ferry, becoming aware that it was essential to guarantee supplies of VW components,

entered into negotiations with the highly successful reborn Volkswagen company – see Lindsay Porter's book *Guide to purchase and DIY restoration of the VW Beetle and Transporter*. The 1949 signed agreement between Porsche and Volkswagen set the bedrock for Porsche's ability to continue the development of the 'Porsche' car; apart from now receiving royalties on every VW produced to the Porsche design, the supply of parts was guaranteed, as well as the facility to sell and service the cars through VW's growing dealer network. Porsche was not allowed to design a ''Volkswagen'' competitor for any other company and their engineers were to act as consultants to VW who in return were allowed to use Porsche patents free of charge. This was a hard but eminently constructive bargain between two tough but visionary men and it lasted until 1973! VW also ordered thirty seven cars.

Ferry now felt that work space expansion was necessary and as the company was rather hankering to return to Stuttgart (their existing premises still being in the hands of the Americans) they rented 5,000 square feet in Reutter's of Stuttgart, the bodybuilders, workshops for the final assembly of the cars. Reutter was given a contract for the first 500 German Porsche bodies, panelled instead to make production easier. An additional 1,000 sq. ft was purchased and turned into an office and design studio. The move took place gradually during 1950 but the main event was the celebration of Ferdinand's 75th birthday; a gathering of passionate Porsche owners toasted him and he was presented with one of the new 356 coupes nicknamed 'Ferdinand', which can be seen today in the Porsche museum. In October of that year Porsche attended the Paris Motor Show where 50 years of Porsche-designed cars were represented

by the electric Lohner-Porsche and the first appearance of the German 356; what a proud moment for the son of a tin-miner! Twenty years from the start of his own business and his name now stood for a world renowned car and obviously another twenty years of success was likely. The first public appearance of the Stuttgart 356 was the last of Ferdinand Porsche; he suffered a stroke and died at the beginning of 1951.

The ownership of the company was now shared between Ferry and his sister Louise and over the years they produced eight children between them, all contributing their individual strengths and ideas to the family company.

With four of the original hand-built Gmünd cars having been retained by Porsche for competitive work, plans for space-framed race and rally cars continued. The production 356 engine capacity was increased to 1500cc with the aid of a roller bearing crankshaft, but it became apparent that a new engine would have to be developed to keep the marque at the forefront of racing and rallying, especially in the US where sports cars were becoming the sales boom of the decade. Dr Ernest Fuhrmann, youngest member of the design team, was put to work on a radical new power unit with four overhead camshafts, but retaining a flat four-cylinder layout. Ferry and Karl Rabe kept an eye on him but when the engine was installed, mid-engined, in an ultra light rubular frame with a minimal open body it became the 'Spyder', after an Italian name for a lightweight open sports car, and was to become Porsche's top competition car throughout the 1950s.

These 'Spyders', Type 550s, were also produced in coupe form when the superior aerodynamics of a closed car became more suitable for fast circuits. Unlike the original Gmünd 356s, where the

hand-filled and leaded parts were made to fit the individual openings on each car and serial numbered to that particular body, making interchangeability almost impossible, all the components of the Stuttgart 356s and 550s were interchangeable, making it possible to build cars to any specification or to suit any event.

In 1952, following a suggestion from the United States, a new model was developed, based on the drophead coupe; an exclusive batch of fifteen was made and fourteen of these went to the States where they became known as the Speedster. Initially the 'American Roadster' whose two-piece Vee windshield became a fully curved elegant, one-piece windshield in the Speedster – later adopted by all the Porsche cars late in 1955 when the 356A was born.

Responding to the demand of their fanatical admirers Ferry Porsche had begun to work on a Porsche emblem; until then the simple logo 'Porsche' sited on the front of the bonnet, had been sufficient recognition. In 1953 the additional symbol, a heraldic-based design incorporating the name Porsche with the arms of Württemberg and Stuttgart, in recognition of those towns' importance in the Porsche story, appeared on the steel wheel hubs of the 356.

The essence of Porsche success in both production and racing was in the interweaving of developments along parallel and interchangeable lines. Throughout Porsche's being, successes in the fields of racing were based on the intense enthusiasm and pride in the marque of private owners; between 1954 and '56, for instance, 400 international successes were achieved!

1956 saw the Silver Jubilee celebration of ''Dr. Ing.hc F.Porsche'' company, the 10,000th car, a 356A, was unveiled and driven from the final assembly hall by the youngest

Porsche, Wolfgang, and as a special present, though perhaps not deliberate, the Americans released the Zuffenhausen factory back into their hands and it became the heart of Porsche's activities, a design office, experimental area and finance department.

The 356 was, naturally for Porsche, continuously being refined as a production car. The 356A was first exhibited at the Paris Salon of 1958, the year Ferry, travelling to New York, received the Elmer A. Sperry Prize for 'achievement of particular merit in the sphere of transport', presented in recognition of Ferdinand's contribution in this field; 356B and C being the next major model changes. In 1962 Porsche-designed disc brakes were offered for the first time as an option on Carrera models.

Work having started in 1956 in an attempt to meet the new marketing demands of a bigger car, a flat-six rear-engined 2000cc car was finally marketed in 1964; retaining the steel floorpan, the great 911 came into being. Having started life as Type 901, the alteration in number was due to Peugeot laying prior claim to the sole rights to all three digit numbers with an '0' in the middle. As this only applied to road cars Porsche hastily laid claim to the numbers 904 and 906 for racing models. The original design was by Ing. ('Ingenieur': German for 'engineer') Hans Tomala, but family took over in the person of Ferdinand Piëch, whose philosophy was "the lighter you make the car, the less weight there is to brake for a corner, to take round the corner, and to accelerate from the corner". He continued the subsequent development of the 911s and thereby as head of research was ultimately responsible for the racing cars. The family was also responsible for the shape of the 911, Ferdinand Alexander 'Butzi' Porsche being in charge of the styling studio.

Porsche took what in marketing terms would seem to be rather a rash course; the 356 was well established and responsible for the company's success, in fact it was *the* Porsche car, but instead of merely developing the 911 and adding it to the range, they decided to put their all into it and firmly to discontinue the 356. A gamble that paid off, the 911 was definitely a very expensive 'up-market' car. However Porsche managed it again and the legend of the 911 was born. What panache, what style, what absolute faith in one's decisions!

A slight unease must have rippled through this confidence however because in 1965 the Type 912 was introduced, basically a cheaper version of the 911 to cater for the market of existing Porsche lovers who no longer had the 356 to buy, but could not afford the 911. Production was limited and stopped at the end of 1968, the 914, replacing it at the same price. The 912E arose briefly like a phoenix in 1975 as an overseas export model, but died again a year later.

The next 'first' worldwide model by Porsche was the 'Targa' – for the lover of wind in the hair but with the emphasis on safety, its distinctive substantial rollover bar behind the doors strikes a visual chord among the least knowledgeable of us. The middle section of the roof was removeable like a table leaf – the original version of this leaf was a zipping-up soft section, very leaky and noisy, and it was soon replaced by a wrap-around hard plastic piece that can be stored in the boot. At the same time, with their eye on the American market (which does after all absorb 50% of Porsche's production) the first automatic version, the 'Sportomatic', was marketed; after a lengthy but extremely lukewarm response from that self-same market it was phased out in 1979.

Continuing to worry about

becoming too 'upmarket' and remembering Ferdinand's desire to produce a racing car "for the people", VW and Porsche, in the persons of Heinz Nordoff and Ferry, decided to collaborate in an attempt to produce a cheaper sports car. Returning to a mid-engined theme and based on the new VW 411 engine, thereby not needing too much additional development, it was named the 914. The project was beset by problems; a lot of discussion and agreement had been informal and when Nordoff suffered a heart attack, his successor accepted only written agreements. The car was a hybrid in production and distribution – marketed in the States as a Porsche and in the rest of the world as a VW-Porsche. All this kept its price too high and despite Porsche's flamboyant advertising "If there's one thing we've learned from racing it's where to put the engine – we think it's time you shared these advantages so we've built a couple of mid-engined cars for the street" – but without its distinctive Porsche crest, a policy decision, it was viewed by the snob as a 'Volkswagen' and therefore a 'lower' vehicle. Its production life was squeezed out over seven years but its competitive potential was eventually realised in national and international competitions.

With the success of the 911, the Porsche marque was now established with a worldwide reputation, the company a respected and accepted viable motor manufacturer not just a brief flame fed by a genius upon whose death it would die out. An astonishing achievement for a family business which has still managed to remain independent in a world where many others of that ilk had to merge or disappear. As we have seen, the initial vision, singlemindedness and engineering genius that was Ferdinand Porsche survived just as strongly in his descendants. By 1971, the head of every

department was a Porsche or a Piëch not just through nepotism but with genuine skills and worth; but the power struggles looked like the beginnings of a Greek tragedy, or to quote Ferry Porsche, "like sand in a well oiled machine".

He wisely decided to instigate major changes and persuaded the family to standback and thereby guarantee a future for the company. A supervisory board was created with Ferry and Louise at the head, 10% shares were allocated to each member of the family in exchange for the 'children' moving on to establish themselves outside Porsche – which they managed individually to do very successfully (Ferdinand Piëch for example later became the head of research and development for Audi where he produced the Audi Quattro Coupe) – but retaining their voting rights and therefore continued interest. Management was entrusted to others within and outside the company and Dr. Fuhrmann came back, as Financial Director this time.

Though Porsche as a company continued to be headed by family members throughout its continued success as a marque, the individual no longer stands out and its history becomes its cars and formidable research rather than its individuals; however the guiding principle of the 'parent' is behind all further developments as we shall see. The pioneering went on, the interweaving of the production, sports cars and racing cars a concept laid down by the founder and developed by the family, but now they were in the wings, the cars themselves became the actors in the company's continuing history.

To celebrate the 25th anniversary of the company as manufacturers, five hundred special edition 911s with individual numbers and Ferry Porsche's signature on a metal plaque were produced.

Due to increasingly restrictive exhaust emission regulations being imposed in the 'States, and looking towards replacing the 911 range, Fuhrmann decided to instigate a series of front-engined water-cooled cars. Therefore Porsche bought back from VW the rights to a small cheap 4-cylinder sports car that they had designed as VW-Porsche VG (the company formed to market the 914) and the momentous decision was made that air-cooled engines were nearing the end of their production life. With minimal changes it was marketed as the 924. It was the most 'different' Porsche in 25 years, a front mounted water-cooled engine and transaxle – yet again using the basic philosophy of constantly available production parts, i.e. a VW water-cooled unit. This was also the first Porsche that didn't use their patented synchromesh system. Incidentally it was manufactured at an Audi factory that was under threat of closure, thereby saving a number of jobs.

At the same time they were developing a far more advanced front-engined V8 luxury Grand Tourer (GT) car: the 928. All this in the middle of an oil embargo by OPEC, a time of crisis for the world's motor manufacturers. The 928 was a thirsty car in comparison to other Porsche production cars. It was in fact the largest Porsche ever built and its production was intended to last into the 21st century. With the 356 having lasted for fifteen years and the 911 for twelve so far this didn't seem too great an ambition. So, gambling again, Porsche launched it at the Geneva Show in 1977, and it was voted car of the year!

This was the first "all Porsche" car, transmission and differential combined in a rear transaxle: with all-independent suspension, the 'Weissach axle' rear suspension came into being and it was fitted with disc brakes. Drivers were to be pampered; not a noted Porsche priority up to

now! For instance, an adjustable steering wheel taking the instrument cluster with it when raised or lowered satisfied both the dwarf and giant driver.

To give you some insight into the intensive testing any Porsche car is subjected to let alone a 'special', a 924 (in recognition of the fact that rain is an inevitable hazard in a twenty four hour race and taking advantage of torrential rain conditions), was driven around and around the Weissach circuit as close behind a 928S as possible. Naturally, this produced deluges of water, drowning the 924. It was then left overnight in the continuing torrents with its bonnet off. Not only was it expected to start but it did start, instantly, the following morning.

In 1976, cruise control was offered for the first time in all production cars.

After four years' conception the 944 was launched in 1981, again at the Frankfurt Show. This followed a pattern set after 1950, when the first 356 was shown to the public at the Geneva show; new models and major modifications were unveiled at the September biennial Frankfurt show traditionally held in 'odd' years. Again an 'all Porsche' it was a development of the 924 engine which was designed to fit into the 944 engine space. It used balance shafts that had been developed as far back as 1911! The existing patent was held by Mitsubishi and Porsche tried to circumnavigate paying a patent fee by attempting to further develop the shafts. However such work proved very time-consuming and the decision was made that it would be cheaper in the long run to pay the additional cost per vehicle to use the existing design. As a production car it proved to have better handling than the 924.

Dr. Fuhrmann planned to quietly run down the production of the 911, and to terminate it with the introduction of the 944

Turbo in 1984. Ferry was very concerned about this decision. He felt strongly that the 911 should continue and actively attempted to defer the decision. Thereby, relationships became very strained between the two men. Understandably, perhaps, Fuhrmann had not felt that he had to involve the Supervisory Board fully in all the nuts and bolts of developments, especially of the 928. Eventually Fuhrmann resigned at the end of 1980 and Peter Schutz, an American, succeeded him, another breaking of the family hold, as he was given a 5% stock holding. Schutz reversed Fuhrman's the policy and announced that the 911 was to continue as a production line.

The production range was now the 911 (by this time 200,000 had been manufactured), 924 and 928 and with the addition of the 944, a medium powered car, in 1981, Porsche cars spanned all marketing needs of the sports car enthusiast. However, in the summer of 1982 production of the 924 Turbo ceased in terms of export.

Odd models turn up from time to time that may have been intended for production and were certainly planned for competition, such as the 1967 911R. Roughly twenty of these were built. Of the 1969 916, of which eleven prototypes were made: five kept by the family, five sold quietly to faithful supporters and one shipped to the States. These oddities are not shown in the 'official' list and their numbers were always very limited. However in a company where nothing is ever the absolute, there are always running changes to be made, not merely as appears to be the case in production cars of today, to tart it up as fashion dictates or to appeal visually to a trendy 'up marketing', but to the refining of the Type due to continuous research, investigation of customer complaints, and the correcting of engineering defects

as a result of using the Type in competitive work, by both private owners and official works entries. Constant modifications therefore take place if it seems 'right' to do so. The principle set by Ferdinand was design it, then continue with ideas on how to improve its performance, then before launching it as a production car, tune it and trial it by entering it into competitions for which it is suitable, then start it off on its production line role. Competition cars are therefore the forerunners of production models. It is not the intention of this Heritage chapter to go into minute detail on every mechanical and body shape alteration. A 'Production Changes' section at the end of the book will point the individual in the specific direction they wish to go.

It must not be ignored that behind all this splendid and sensational car manufacturing is a bedrock of research and development with engineering as the base and background. Starting in 1950, the company bought 1,000 square foot of space in Stuttgart. They later purchased a large parcel of land in the countryside at Weissach – hence the 'Weissach' axle – and began constructing a proving ground and test track. Over the years, they continued its expansion into a self contained research and development centre that stands in many spacious acres of its own. This has meant that apart from benefiting Porsche cars directly, it is now a centre for consultation by governments, administrations and private companies. Always having to take into account any possible future environmental legislation that various countries might impose, their work ranges from design, emission control, metrology, the effect of vibration, light metal processing and plastics, to welding and bonding techniques, naming but a few. Their techniques and progress are sold to customers in the fields of touring and commercial vehicles,

aviation and armaments with the thread, as ever, going back to Ferdinand's initial interests. Individual Porsche designs used in the outside world include baulking synchromesh found in many other gearboxes, while Porsche engines have been modified and used in marine, aircraft and in industrial projects.

One must not ignore the company's constant drive towards self-betterment, and not just in the areas of performance and engineering in the cars: in 1970 a completely new paint shop was opened and customers responded to the claims that Porsche could match anything the customer required from material to nail varnishes! As from 1976, a unique anti-corrosion guarantee was offered on all models.

Despite all these scientific advances, there have been examples of non-technological answers to problems or at least answers in the 'alternative technology' field. The 911, for example, has always been prone to understeering and Porsche's corrective for this at first was to have the car back and quietly place 11 kilo lead weights behind each end of the front bumpers! The Weissach Centre has approached the problem more scientifically now.

In 1984 the Stock Exchange flotation of Porsche was launched and a third of the capital put into public hands. The appellation AG (Aktliengesellschaft – joint stock company) was added to the name.

By 1985, the family-owned sports car company's workforce increased from 5000 to 6000; turnover and profits have increased steadily year by year and, to put the Weissach Centre into perspective in terms of importance to Porsche, it employs a quarter of the total workforce. Production now exceeds 45,000 cars annually from the Zuffenhausen Works II Industrial Centre, Stuttgart.

Racing

Ferdinand Porsche's passion for racing has meant that the production of the racing car has been, as noted, integral with that of the production car; with such successful bread and butter on offer it was possible, on the whole, to afford to continue with the scones and cream.

The accident ratio frequency of Porsches has always been comparatively low, though any accident worried Ferdinand excessively and he was always trialing his own products rather than expecting others only to take the rap.

The first accident was a Stuttgart 356, which, although wrecked in a high-speed motor accident, left the racing driver Rolf Wutherich unhurt. This gentleman led a charmed life! Later as passenger in the film star James Dean's Porsche Spyder they crashed and James Dean died. For those who have seen photographs of the crumpled Porsche, the miracle is that Rolf Wutherich survived.

An interesting but strictly 'private' venture was started by a Walter Glockler in 1949. He built an open two-seater racing car based on Porsche mechanical units with a 1086cc VW-Porsche engine running on methanol and surrounded by a well proportioned aluminium light tubular frame. In this 'Special' Walter won the 1100cc class of the Sports Car Championship in 1950, following this success with two other titles and then building himself another car based on the 1500cc Porsche engine the 'Glockler-Porsche' as it became known, won the German Championship with a maximum speed of 210kph (133mph). This vehicle was sold to America where it continued along the same lines. However this level of one-man private enterprise could not hold its own against the big production boys so the factory

took over at the end of 1952 and produced a mid-engined car based on the 'Glockler' but with the new Fuhrmann designed four-camshaft engine which was to make Porsche history, as Porsche 'Spyders'.

In 1951 Porsche works entered their first official entry in a motor sport event, the Le Mans 24 hour race in France. It won its class. A Gmünd 356 with aluminium body, the car was nicknamed the 'Aluminium box' by the mechanics. Yet another aluminium coupe was fitted with a prototype 1500cc engine and won its class and third overall. As ever, private owners (often helped by the works or driving specific works-produced series) were the back-bone of such successes in all sorts of races from rallies to dirt track. A unique modification once produced in one of the 356 'aluminium boxes' was a right-hand drive for the one-armed driver Otto Mathe for dirt track racing. Another 'achieving' 356 spent 72 hours at an average of 94.66mph, clocking up all of 6,815 miles!

The true Type-550 Spyder which had grown out of an amalgam of the 'Glockler-Porsche' and the 1953 'Le Mans' coupe made its official entrance as the 1500 RS in 1954. The factory used it until the end of the 1957 season, but private owners extended its life until the beginning of the '60s. The introduction of the greatly improved Type 550A in 1956 won for the factory the Targa Florio that year with an overall victory – and they had only made the decision to race it eleven days before that! As you can imagine work came to a halt on the production line when it came home again.

The revised version of the 550A was launched into a German racing scene that was suddenly devoid of East German competition, that country having withdrawn, presumably for economic reasons. Porsche immediately signed up the two

drivers, Barth being one of them. This car had developed two small fins and was a 1500RS-K (Type 718) known as 'K' because of the shape of the reinforcement bars visible inside the frame. Porsche was placed second in the 'World Championship of Makes' 1958.

Porsche decided to provide ardent private owners with specially-built competitive cars and the appropriately named 'Carrera' (Spanish for 'race') 356A 1500 GS model was the first, in 1955, of a continuing policy. With a Fuhrmann designed engine, it achieved successes in various long distance sports car races such as the Carrera Panamericana.

The Porsche, named after the race the 'Carrera de Luxe', that followed it was for those who liked to *look* as if they raced but had no intention of committing their beautiful machines to such destructive activities. However, the 1600 GS 'Carrera GT' with a Reutter-built body *was* ready trimmed for racing and rallying with the engine developing 115 bhp; forty of these were built.

In 1959 Porsche ordered twenty lightweight bodies with better aerodynamics, making them faster than the Reutter bodies, from Carlo Abarth in Italy. Porsche supplied all the mechanical parts, floor pans and running gear. The 'Abarth-Carrera' is a highly prized rarity despite its poor body workmanship and the first built won its 1300cc class in the Le Mans 1960. In fact, as a competitive car it had no successor for the private owner until the 911 six cylinder.

The first Porsche entry into Formula 2 was really a very marginally modified Spyder RS with the lights removed and the second one had the additional modification of centring the steering wheel: they won however and the company excitedly decided to build a real Formula 2 car. While this was happening, the racing driver Jean Behra with Porsche backing,

ordered a Formula 2 to be built to his own design. The engine, gearbox, front and rear suspensions were all Porsche. This single-seater, central engined car called the 'Behra-Porsche' finished second at Rhiems in 1959, ahead of the official Porsche entry.

The first official successes with the Formula 2 car were at Aintree, second and third places. However the overall successes that year won the factory the 'Manufacturer's Cup' (an unofficial Formula 2 Championship).

From the 356B series the 'Super 90' was added as a less costly high performance car, offering road-useable performance at a lower cost while the 2000 GS/GT ('Carrera 2') was produced in 1961 and 1963 as a 356B Type derivative, giving the owner-competitor outstanding track competitiveness.

The Formula 1 limitation to 1.5 litres in 1961 seemed ideal for Porsche, but a new engine seemed an essential as the four-cylinder had reached the limit of its development. An entirely new chassis was designed with wishbone front suspension and coiled springs, though still using drum brakes. While waiting for the new engine the chassis was raced in 1961, with the addition of Porsche-designed disc brakes. Ferrari was the 'top dog' during this period but Porsche only failed to snatch victory at Rheims by an amazing 1/10 of a second! Ultimately a low-built and very elegant car, it was proving far too expensive despite the continuing development of engines, including the creation of a new flat-eight cylinder. So, they pulled out of Formula 1 in 1962 with only one Grand Prix victory at Rouen. Incidentally, the mechanics celebrated this victory by shaving off the beards they had sworn to keep growing until the car achieved its first victory. The money spent was not wasted

however. Indeed, one might ask when any money spent by Porsche has been wasted! There always seems to be a moment in time when all the drawings, trials, expenditure and effort come up trumps with a 'winner' car, specification or component.

The '60s were financially well secured with the success of the 911 production car and a good income from sub-contracted work, but competition cars as a separate entity were costing an arm and a leg to develop so the company decided to switch to competition cars based on the 911.

The factory prepared a 2-litre 911 just months after the 911 production car was launched and this was placed sixth in the Monte Carlo Rally of 1964, having been hotly pursued and beaten by a 'private' Porsche 904 GTS placed second and driven by the aforementioned lucky Rolf Wutherich. However, the car later went from triumph to triumph, particularly in long-distance races and a number of national titles were achieved.

The next milestone was the Type 904, also known as Carrera GTS, which was the result of an entirely new design philosophy except for its power plant.

One hundred cars were made for homologation and offered at a silly low price for sale in 1964. However another twenty had to be made to cater for the interest generated; four were not completed but kept for spares. It had an attractive glass fibre body and was an immediate competitive success, starting in the 'States. Part of its appeal was its reliability. Continued development at the works left private owners on their own to increase their collecting of laurels on the track. The 'Kangeroo' was an eight-cylinder development though it had to be scrapped because of its lack of stability and was replaced by a completely new car which was rushed into the 'European Hill Climb' championship of 1965, the

decision having been made three races before the end of the season! Everybody worked literally day and night but the unions stopped the mechanics working over the weekend; with their connivance Porsche attempted to send the mechanics off on a weekend 'business' trip to a convenient garage where the work could continue, but union bosses aren't *that* daft so the ploy had to be abandoned. Naturally the car wasn't a great success in the race but it did become the basis for the 906 and 910 models.

Again Porsche underestimated the response to its next car, the 906, and the original fifty had to be added to. In a cost-saving excercise the surplus 904 suspension parts were used in the 906, also called the 'Carrera 6'. Once more this was competitively successful and ended the season with a win at the Hockenheim Ring, also taking first place in the index classification for the best overall performance in relation to the engine capacity.

1967 was the start of three champagne years: a 911S 2 litre assisted a British couple to become European Rally Champions and a Pole became the European Touring Car Champion in a 912, the "Sportomatic" automatic won the 86 hour Marathon de la Route on its first excursion.

At the end of this year 22 racing versions of the 911, the 911R – the start of the suffix R for racing Types – were built, three for the factory and the rest sold to carefully selected 'privateers' who could be expected to heighten the marque's profile with more successes. To conform to regulations they were technically prototypes but basically merely production bodies with Carrera 6 engines in them. Porsche themselves didn't seem to be very interested in this model however and though they entered one in the Targa Florio of 1969 as a

guinea pig with a four-camshaft six-cylinder engine the victorious works entry in the Tour de France was the Type's last official appearance.

The 910 was never sold to private owners and was only eligible for the prototype group and therefore never competed against privately owned 'Carerra 6s. However due to Porsche's philosophy of only running brand new cars in important races many 'one race' cars were sold off and ended up in direct competition with the factory. The 910 "Bergspyders" got lighter and lighter and were used on the hills, taking the '67 and '68 European Hill Climb titles, weighing little more than eight people!

The 907, basically a 910 with the steering column moved to the right, was added before the end of the 1967 season. Other models kept popping up, developing usually out of attempts to combat weight problems and all with interesting little nuances like the 909 with its gearbox between the engine and the differential, therefore moving the engine and the driver forward so far in fact that the pedals protruded ahead of the front wheel axis. The factory had never been happy with the aerodynamics of the 904 and 906 despite endless trials in the wind tunnels (the 910 was like Topsy, it 'just growed' without the wind tunnel facilitation) so the 907 was an attempt to lower the drag. During the 1968 season all cars were fitted with a brake pad wear warning light – found in many production cars today. Another change in FIA rules started Porsche off along the path to another milestone: the design of a new 3-litre 'flat' eight-cylinder racing engine called Type 908. It was not trouble free but to everyone's surprise won the Nürburgring 1000km race in 1968, providing a great boost to the morale of what must have been a thoroughly overworked racing department. The student

riots in May 1968 postponed Le Mans and gave them a reasonable time in which to refine the 908 for entry. It didn't win but a creditable result was achieved with second and third places. It still had stability problems however and a variety of crashes and non-qualifiers made continuous modification essential.

The '68 and '69 seasons continued to be one triumph after another: the 911Ts took first and second overall in the Monte Carlo, Porsche became the 'Rally Champion Manufacturer' and Stuttgart received from the FIA the 'International Constructors' Trophy for GT cars'. Again at the Monte Carlo, with two 911 2.0 'Monte Carlos', first and second places were achieved; victories in the Swedish Rally, the Neige et Glace, a Polish Rally, Spa 24 Hours and the Tour de France followed, to name but a few. The last 'Rally' 911 officially supported by Porsche was the 2.2 911S 'Rally' in the Tour de France of 1970. They did in fact sneak in again in 1978 because of niggling a bit at having won every major rally but the Safari. The works backed two Type 911 SC 'Safaris' but despite the good omens they only managed second and fourth places. In addition to the 911s, one must not forget that other Porsche cars were competing at the same time and often in the same place. The 914-6 was an excellent car for long distance, its lack of power being made up for by its reliability, and a sixth place overall was gained at Le Mans in 1970. At last, after twenty years of participation, a works 917 won the Le Mans for Porsche in 1970, and again patriotic Stuttgart stopped work to celebrate the homecoming. In 1971, the works then entered three factory-prepared 914-6 models for the Monte Carlo – the driver had a fully upholstered bucket seat, the poor passenger only plastic – the Targa top was screwed to the body and the pop-up lights

operated by hand – partially as an attempt to boost sales of the production car which were flagging. Sadly, it wasn't a success despite drivers who had already achieved victories in the same race with the 911s.

It was after learning that Ferrari, the arch-enemy, was planning to produce twenty five sports cars to coincide with the new FIA regulations for five-litre engines, Porsche decided to compete and the 917 was launched. At the beginning of 1969 it was realised that because the factory's production and racing cars were developed in the same department it was too much to continue to expect them to cope with the racing 908 and 917 models as well, so a partner was sought for the 917 and an English company chosen. The first victory soon came in the Austrian 1000km race of that year and in the three years before it was banned from European Racing by another change in the rules, the cars were entered in twenty four World Champinship races. The 917 won fifteen, and the 908 four.

Porsche now opted out of the 'World Championship of Makes'; three consecutive victories had been achieved and as engine capacities were again to be limited, this time to 3-litre within a minimum weight limit, 220lb less than could be achieved by Zuffenhausen, they wisely turned their energies in another direction.

The useful 'private owner' had supplied Porsche with another door to go through: the Can-Am Championship for which the 4.5 litre 917-10 'Panzer Porsches' were developed. Turbo-charged, it was not treated with great seriousness by the racing fraternity as no turbo-charged car had been successful on normal racing circuits. The challenge appealed to Porsche of course! All experiments had to be carried out on the race track due to the impossibility of creating

equivalent test bed conditions. In 1973 the 910-30 was built especially for Mark Donahue, the car's 'test pilot', who had unfortunately crashed in a 917-10 and lost a complete season. The 910-30 was the most powerful car ever to appear on a racing circuit and it won the Can-Am series twice in succession. But less successful participants grumbled that it had spoiled the fun so the rules were changed to discourage turbo charging involvement and ironically the Can-Am folded at the end of 1974. So much for sour grapes! The 5.4 litre cars carried on in private hands in Europe until they were excluded and now the only place of residence for this fabulous bird is a museum.

At the end of 1970, though continuing to offer competitive versions of production cars for private owners in small series, the company decided to concentrate on sports car and prototype racing and withdrew official works support for rallying. The last competitive 'works' version of the 911 in the old body was the 911S 2.5 but it too was finding it difficult to stay the course and so the name 'Carrera' was revived and attached to what was basically a 911S fitted with a 2.7 engine and called the 'Carrera RS'. It acquired the duck's tail spoiler that again personifies a Porsche to the layman. Though over one thousand of these were built only forty nine were rebuilt to racing specifications, yet its competitive successes were considerable and it was followed by the Carrera 3.0 RS. The 'Carrera' now took centre stage and immediately on appearance, one of two factory-prepared RSRs entered in the Daytona 24 Hours race won overall and then the works entered them at every World Championship of Makes race for the 1973 season; only one of which they failed to finish. The amalgamation of official entry wins and 'privates' won Porsche the FIA 'Cup for Grand

Touring Cars' and also the 'World Cup for Speed and Endurance' for the seventh time!

Yet again a change of rules was in the air and so expensive new prototype building was shelved and the decision was made to put a turbo-charged 911 six-cylinder engine into a standard Carrera RSR body with an outside rear wing added. The principle behind this was to continue the research and refinements started with the 917-30 Turbo, instead of concentrating on winning and thereby be ready for the 'production-derived racing car' regulations due to come in. Battling private Carrera owners dominated GT races meanwhile and with victories in the Trans-Am series and the American IMSA Championship for GT cars, the company earned the FIA 'World Cup for GT cars' in 1974. BMW brought all its big guns out in 1975 in an attempt to break the strangle-hold Porsche had achieved in the American IMSA series though they weren't successful, but Carreras were coming to an end in international racing.

However from out of their sleeves Porsche decided to bring a new explosive machine: the 934 Porsche Turbo was thrown into the arena. Based on the 930 roadcar and using the turbocharging experience gained from the RSR and 917, it swept all before it in the 1976 and 1977 GT races. The factory continuing along these lines unveiled the 935 in 1976. It pipped everybody else to the post, as Porsche was the only competitor with a car specially developed for the new Group 5 regulations. Unusually the factory had little support that year from the 'privateers' so feeling rather lonely, the prototype raced on and despite a few hiccups won the championship. In the meantime, the 936 Spyder was built for Group 6 and dominated most of the races in the 'World Championship of Sports Cars' in

1976. By 1977 the private drivers became supportive again with the fifteen factory built replicas of the 935 supplied for them; gaining points at a rate of knots the works basically left *them* to it this time. Aware that press interest was minimal in the Porsche dominated Group 5 races, the factory cheekily produced a 'Baby' 935 (in two months flat) for the under-two litre class. Its debut was unassuming; its second appearance crushed all opposition. The exercise smacked of 'anything you can do, we can do as well' – for after these two appearances, having smugly proved themselves in a field they had ignored since the days of Ferdinand, it was placed alongside the Turbo 930, in the museum! 1978 was yet another champagne year with the addition of a six-cylinder engine with four camshafts and four valves per cylinder: the 935/78 definitely the fastest Group 5 car that year, an excellent result of a five year gestation period . . . and yet again in 1979 the successes carried on mounting allowing Porsche ample justification to be very swollen headed.

In the meantime two Porsche technicians with outside sponsorship decided to develop the 924 into a Turbo version for the Monte Carlo and other long distance rallies. Its progress was exciting enough for various drivers to try, over the years, to convince the company to re-enter international rallying officially. No success was forthcoming however, though the company was sufficiently touched to offer special rally and racing versions of the Carrera 924 GT. Type 924 Carrera GTS was a limited production for Group 4 and Type 924 Carrera GTR was for serious competition work and could be obtained in rally and racing trim, when the prefix became GTR. Weissach also produced Type 924 SCCA for the American Series, specifically for chosen teams in the 'States and largely based on production parts to

keep the cost down. Continued development obtained a win in the Series and established the model. Three 924 Carrera GT 'Le Mans' were entered for Le Mans in 1980 and though they didn't win, they were themselves guinea pigs for the development of the 944, a prototype of which was entered the following year. This, however, had a completely new Porsche designed engine – a four-cylinder installed at the angle of 45 to the right.

The "INDY" project was started in Weissach in 1978 with the famous Indianapolis '500 Miles' race in mind; a 2.65 litre engine was to be developed and adapted to run on methanol, the mandatory fuel for the INDY series. Porsche publicly announced their plan to enter the 1980 race jointly in co-operation with an American team. However, the INDY was beset by its own problems and the organising body split in two, thereby creating two championships each disputing technical regulations. Work in the meantime had begun in America on the new car and when the finally agreed regulations were announced in April 1980, they made the new Porsche engine uncompetitive and Porsche decided to cancel its involvement – another car into the museum. In 1987 however the company has decided to re-enter the whole of the CART series for Indianapolis cars.

In 1981 the factory accepted a contract from McLaren to produce a turbocharged Formula 1 engine, and so, indirectly entered the Grand Prix arena again. This time the turbocharged 1.5 litre V6 "TAG Turbo" was to be raced by the experienced McLaren team, and in 1984 the Marlboro McLaren team was powered by the Porsche engine in the World Championship for Constructors.

With FISA drafting completely new regulations for the 'World Championship of Makes' to be implemented at the beginning of 1982 the 936 was ruled out of competitive work. Not downhearted, liking progression, Porsche started on a new racing car: the 956. Intended to be the *creme de la creme* in the new Group C, they started with a clean drawing board. With combined water and air cooling, a six-cylinder engine layout and an entirely new five-speed gearbox it was an immediate and sensational success. 1st, 2nd and 3rd at Le Mans in 1982 as well as the World Endurance Championship followed by the Championship in 1983, 84, 85 and 86! With three Porsche wins in the 1987 Le Mans, one could reiterate the slogan in the Stuttgart factory "Porsche – driving in its finest form".

The 911 has Heritage!

2 Buying

Part 1: Introduction

The Porsche 911 has been in production for over twenty two years and in that period has earned a place amongst the better sports cars of all time. As is typical of the Porsche marque, the model has had a glittering competition career, probably having won every major sports car race and rally at some time in its life. More amazingly, there is no sign that the 911 is near the end of its production life.

Combine such pedigree with a technical specification which, from its earliest types, is mouthwatering and there is a basis for continued sales success. What has secured the 911 a place at the top of the practical sports car league however, is an outstanding history of build quality and reliability.

The Porsche 911 is the embodiment of the totally developed and mature sports car and its solid image is a major reason why the model has survived for so long in a fiercely competitive market place.

This reliability has also benefited resale values, to the extent that the enthusiast who buys wisely can expect a very favourable depreciation rate on a car more than five years old.

The story is not all good news, however. Because the 911 is the car it is, many examples have chequered histories to a greater or lesser extent. The buyer of a used 911 should resist the temptation to buy on first impressions. There are many stories of shattered dreams, through an inexperienced buyer falling for the colour, the engine sound or just the name. Unfortunately, there are also stories of skillfully disguised former write-offs and "ringers", (cars which deliberately changed identities to catch the unwary).

What this guide sets out to do is inform; to show what to look for and where. It is down to the individual's previous experience to match his or her requirements, capabilities and resources with what is available.

It is assumed that the choice between a Coupe or a Targa is a personal one. It comes down to whether you like the wind in your hair or the security of the enclosed body. There are factors which would steer the enthusiast to choose a pre-76 Coupe rather than a pre-76 Targa, but more of that later.

Four age categories

Very roughly speaking, the 911 falls into four age categories as far as the enthusiast is concerned. The first is the new car. Enthusiasts do buy these of course, many having worked up to their dream car over many years. The comments within this book on car care apply as much to a new vehicle as the older car, so read on. The only advice to be offered on new car buying is that all the options can add a large amount to the basic price of the car (and there isn't usually any discount!).

Used car buyers tend to always think of the base model as the norm when it comes to a price guide. If one's car has a lot of expensive factory options on it, the car may not make the price expected. The only option which consistently gives a premium price to a 911 is the Sport pack fitted as an option from mid '70s 911 models.

In order to fend off the followers of detail, sport options were available on the 911 as early as 1968. One could even buy sports conversion parts for the 356 Carrera back in 1962. On current models, though, the sport pack can add a lot of money to the basic price. For later '70s 911 models expect to pay about a 10-20% premium. Generally, the many other options offered on the car at resale tend to only make it more desirable, rather then permitting a higher asking price.

The second category is the used model that is less than five

years old. These cars offer a recent spec. and reasonable mileage to the driver who will want to use the car every day without fear of breakdown or other problem, whether it's snowing or sunny. If the car is less than seven years old and has had its body looked after by an Official Porsche Centre, it will still be covered by the Longlife body warranty. This warranty has recently been extended to ten years (against rust perforation). The Longlife warranty on any 911 is only valid if the vehicle is maintained properly and any damage to the paintwork or protective coating is repaired without delay. In practice this means a yearly underbody inspection by an Official Centre. The current edition of the maintenance record for 911s recommends the annual inspection, which is recorded in a special section of the handbook every year after the first two years (the current no-mileage limit guarantee period). When considering a car in this age category, the principal items to check are crash damage and service record. This will be covered in more depth later.

The third category is the post-1976 model, which offers the buyer with limited finance the best all round value in a 911. From the 1976 model year, all 911 models were manufactured from zinc coated steel, which enabled the factory to offer the trend setting six year anti-corrosion warranty. The zinc coating greatly enhanced the life of the bodyshell and the warranty was later extended first to seven and then ten years (see above). It is still quite feasible to find an excellent condition '76 model in regular use.

The fourth category is the real enthusiast's province. 911s made before 1976 did not benefit from the fully zinc coated bodyshell. From 1970 most of the exposed areas under the car, including the wheel arches, were galvanised in an attempt to overcome rust formation. Prior to this, state of the art for corrosion protection was an electrophoretic paint base and rubberised sealing compound. It is fair to say that until the launch of the fully zinc coated models, 911s were very prone to rust. This applies even to the partially zinc coated models made after 1970. The chief cause was usually the elastomer PVC sealing compound becoming cracked, acting as a moisture trap and accelerating the formation of rust. The situation was made worse by the fact that the cracks would go undetected by the owner until telltale bubbles appeared at strategic points. We will cover later the areas where such rust traps are most regularly found. More importantly, corrosion can affect the straightness of the early Targas. Lacking the extra rigidity of the Coupe bodyshell, any corrosion in the sills/body rockers was made worse by the higher loadings taken by the undertray. Detailed inspection of the undertray is essential with these early Targas, whose resultant stress-accelerated corrosion can cause dangerous driving manners. For RHD Targas, zinc coating was introduced to the sills/body rockers from the '72 model year, considerably improving the corrosion resistance.

Suffice it to say that unless you know exactly what you are doing, the early models are now only for the owner who has good garage facilities at home and is prepared to care for the car and put some work into it.

The other side of the coin though, is that the early models are now becoming rarer and good condition models are steadily appreciating.

Spares

Spares for 911s are not a problem. Principal source of factory spares for any 911 is any Official Porsche Centre. It is often taken for granted that the level of support given to owners of older Porsches by the factory is nothing short of outstanding. The longer established Centres are usually very knowledgeable of early 911s. All parts, if not in stock, can quickly be obtained from Reading (HQ of Porsche Cars UK) or from Stuttgart. It is this type of support from the factory that fosters marque loyalty and hopefully leads one day, to extra new car sales.

The cost of official factory replacement parts is not cheap. As one might expect, prices on the high turnover parts like brake pads, etc are heavily marked up. The more obscure parts used in a restoration are freely available. In many cases, is it just satisfactory to be able to get hold of them. Factory parts are expensive relative to those of say, Ford or GM. Consider though, the smaller sales volumes and the more demanding application of the Porsche. Parts are available for the consumable items (like brake pads) from other unauthorised manufacturers. These are cheaper, but not generally recommended, as the quality is less controlled. Don't expect factory performance from non-factory parts.

Service

The first level of service for Porsche must be the Official Centre, whose facilities are amongst the best in the motor industry. They will take on any Porsche model and as one might expect, one pays for the top quality service provided there.

Easily finding a place in most enthusiasts' address books are several specialist firms who offer unique levels of service to the owners of older 911s. The pages of *Porsche Post* (the quarterly magazine of the Porsche Club Great Britain), or *Porsche Panorama* (the monthly magazine of the Porsche Club of America) have many firms offering anything from used parts to sources of tuning for competition.

More relevant might be where to find a trustworthy restoration business, perhaps offering specialist bodywork or interior refurbishment.

Be very wary of the large number of businesses that have sprung up offering Porsche servicing and general repair work. There are very few that really know their way around 911s and who don't only see the amounts of money to be made from unsuspecting owners of exotic cars. A call to the Club Office will usually establish whether a business has good references. Professional restoration is now quite an industry, but most enthusiasts will want to do most of the work themselves for cost reasons. The hourly rate for a reputable specialist restorer is very high. The best way to balance cost and getting a professional job done is to learn the time consuming jobs and contract out the high-skill jobs or those requiring expensive special tools. Doing all the work oneself will take a great deal of time, even if the restoration breaks even or makes a profit on the resale. It depends on how much satisfaction is gained from such a job, which will invariably take much longer and require more effort than at first thought. (See the Clubs & Specialists section for the names and addresses of the high quality repair and restoration specialists featured in this book).

Desirability

Once it has been decided to invest a lot of time restoring a 911, it is worth considering which model will make the best use of the money available. Certain models are more desirable on the open market than others. For example, the '73 Carrera RS saw a spectacular rise in values in the mid-eighties. Similarly, any 911S from the pre-impact bumper era is now very sought after, if it is in good condition.

The name Carrera is synonymous with the higher performance Porsche and if an RS is too expensive, the more civilised '74-'75 2.7 Carreras and the '75-'77 3.0 Carreras should be considered.

For sheer driving pleasure at much lower cost, consider pre-impact bumper 911 models that are in good general condition, or that can be restored within available capabilities. In the longer term, any pre-2.7 911 will be a good investment, if looked after.

If resources permit there is the 930 Turbo, this most classic of 911s having a unique desirability, not only because of its electrifying performance, but also due to its cult status.

The brief model histories that accompany this guide will illustrate the wide range of 911 models that are available. It is most satisfactory that the enjoyment of Porsche driving is available not only to the financially better placed but also to the enthusiast with more restricted means. The ''Porsche experience'' is there for almost all those who want it . . .

BG1. Pam Buttle's 1985 Carrera Sport is kept in pristine condition. The stone guards in front of the rear wheel arches were fitted retrospectively.

Insurance

It pays to shop around for insurance, not only in one's own locality, but also by talking to the brokers who advertise in the specialist motoring magazines and Club magazines. In the UK, the 911 falls into insurance group 9. To put this into perspective the average ''sports'' hatch (eg VW Golf GTi) falls into group 7, with most Mercedes, Jaguar, etc., falling also into group 9.

It is very important to ensure that a cherished 911 is insured for its full market value, rather than the book value as seen by many insurers. On restored or valuable cars, the market value can be considerably in excess of the book value. Most classic car insurance brokers (see 'Clubs & Specialists' section of this book) will take an authorised third party valuation as proof of value.

So, having decided that the 911 really is the car you want, there is now the enjoyable and essential experience of selecting which model suits your needs and pocket.

Photo gallery

The following photo guide may help you to identify some of the differences between the types of 911. The photographs are in no particular order.

BG2. 1977 model Targa. Compare the headlamp washers on this model to the previous type. The flush units were introduced for the 1980 model year.

BG3. Carrera Cabriolet – one needs to move quickly when it starts to rain . . .

BG4. 1974 2.7 Carrera, not to be confused with the 1973 RS model. This model has impact bumpers and is that rust coming through at the lower edge of the rear wing/fender?

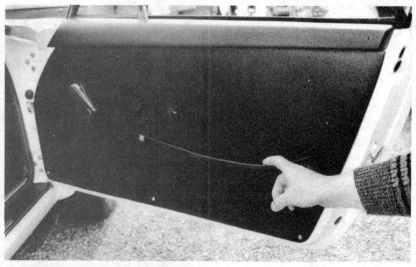

BG5. Classic five spoke forged alloy Porsche wheel. Detachable covers ahead of the rear wheels enable the torsion bars to be removed.

BG6. Lightweight door trim ▲ found on the 1973 Carrera RS. Note manual window winder.

BG7. The five circular dials on this 2.4 litre model are a 911 trade mark . . .

BG8. . . . and still remain despite many interior updates. This is a 911SC, complete with radar detector.

BG9. A Sport pack rear spoiler for the 1985 model Carrera.

BG10. The big headlamp washer nozzle made its appearance in 1976. The extended flexible lip to the front spoiler is fitted in conjunction with the large rear spoiler on this 930 Turbo. The Turbo is easily distinguished from the 911 by its flared front wheel arches.

BG11. On a well looked after 911, the door shuts and interior will be spotless. Another 911SC.

BG12. Spotlamps mounted through the horn grilles were an option on pre-impact bumper 1972 models. The lipped front air dam was original equipment from the 1972 911S and could be specified on the E or T. The chromed horn grille marks this 911 out as 1972 rather than a 1973 model (which had black horn grilles).

BG13. Engine compartment of an early 912.

BG14. An opening electric sunroof, complete with wind deflector strip, was available as a Lux option on the 911 from the late sixties.

BG15. American Bill Sargent was 1986 Porsche Club GB Overall Champion with this mint 1967 911S, which features in the following series of photographs.

BG16. Note the drain slots unique to the "O" and "A" series 911 models ('64 to July '68).

BG17. An early example of the five spoke forged alloy wheel. Original specification 165HR15 tyres mark the detail of a winning Concours car.

BG18. Elegant rear quarters impeccably correctly detailed.

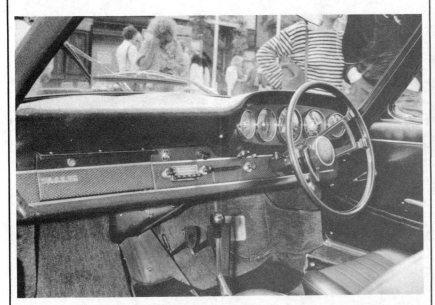

BG19. The push button door handles were found on the 911 until the 1970 model year (2.2 litre).

BG20. Functional interior of Bill's 1967 911S.

BG21. The engine compartment reveals triple choke Weber carburettors.

BG22. The fuel is supplied by a high pressure Bendix pump. Note the conventional coil ignition on this '67 car.

BG23. 1973 Carrera RS. Note the provision for a front oil cooler where the number plate is on this later series RS.

BG24. The rear end of the RS shows off the "duck-tail" rear spoiler. Note the absence of a rear wiper with this style of engine cover.

BG25. Rear three-quarter of the RS, revealing the flared rear arches unique to the RS amongst pre-impact bumper 911 models.

BG26. The RS had 210 bhp compared to the '73 911S figure of 190 bhp.

BG27. A most "collectable" white RS.

BG28. Some would say that RS models in white are more desirable than those in other colours.

BG29. Front end of '77 model Carrera 3 litre. Compare the size of the front flexible lip to that of the Turbo, shown in BG12.

BG30. At the rear it features a variation on the spoiler theme. This type was known as the "whaletail".

BG31. This 2.2 litre type has a non-standard front spoiler from the later '72 911S.

BG32. A rear shot shows it to be a 911T. Note the absence of a rear screen wiper.

BG33. A 1978 911SC. A "clean" Coupe without spoilers.

BG34.   A 1978 911SC featured a return to the 11 blade cooling fan, after an absence of two years . . .

BG35.   This 1977 model shows the five blade fan fitted to 1976 and '77 types.

BG36.   The '78 European 911SC featured a pump for exhaust manifold air injection, in anticipation of stricter emission laws. The V-belt drive to the pump from the fan pulley has been disconnected on this car . . .

BG37.	A 1973 model 911T, the last carburettor model Porsche produced.

BG38.	An '85 model Carrera Cabriolet Sport. The looks with the hood up are very reminiscent of the 356 Cabrio models.

BG39.	Another shot of the Carrera Cabrio shows off its lines. The side indicator repeaters were introduced for the 1981 model year.	►

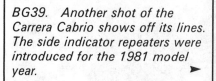

BG40.	An optional rear "nerf" bar fitted to this '72 model 911T.

BG41. A shot which shows off the aggressive mood of the 930 Turbo.

BG42. Rich man's toy. The '86 Turbo Sport.

BG43.   Cooling for the rear brakes?

BG44.   Customised interior is another feature of the Turbo Sport. The silly grin says it all about the performance.

BG45.   '72 model 911 Targa.

BG46. Wind noise and leakage around the doors can be a problem with older 911 models. It can usually be cured by replacing the flexible seal. Tape does not look too good . . .

BG47. Non-standard steering wheel on this 2.2 litre model. ▼

BG48. This car won the Custom class at the 1986 PCGB Concours. Note the turret brace . . .

BG49. . . . competition seat and four point harness.

BG50. Its owner started with a standard '73 911 and converted it to "RSR" specification . . .

BG51 . . . centre locking wheels . . .

BG52. . . .and many other details make up a unique 911.

BG53. Where the customising starts. This 911 has received new panels and paint and is ready for re-trimming . . . ►

BG54. . . . demonstrating the extent to which an early 911 can be modified.

Part 2: Take your pick

When a car is described as being a given model year, it should be understood that this may mean that it was first registered from as early as August of the previous year. So a 1970 model year 2.2 litre 911 could have been first registered in 1969. In this situation, check that the car is indeed the newer model.

2.0 litres

The 911 went into production in 1964 with only the Coupe

initially available. The first Targas followed at the end of 1965. These original cars are very hard to find now, mainly because of the corrosion problems that beset the pre-zinc coated models. Moreover, since the very early cars were LHD only, very few were imported into the UK. It is easy to identify the early 2 litre cars, since their wheelbase is 67 mm shorter than cars built after 1968. The chance of finding one in worthwhile restorable condition is remote and those that are left are usually only seen on summer days. It would be expected that Concours condition vehicles would change hands at collector's prices.

If a poor condition car is found, the full extent of the workload and the time and resources available should be carefully considered. It will only be financially worthwhile if the car is to be fully restored to Concours condition. From 1968, the wheelbase was increased to the current 2271 mm and mechanical fuel injection was introduced on the 911S and the new 911E. In 1969 the engine capacity went up to 2.2 litres, and the quality of handling and comfort were now greatly improved from the results of intense chassis and interior development programmes. These 1970 models also featured a step forward in the battle against corrosion, having a galvanised undertray, wheel arches and sills/body rockers.

Once again, the 2.2 litre 911 types have suffered with time, but they represent one of the development milestones in the car's history. As well as the capacity increase, which gave an extra 10 bhp to the 911S, the cars featured ventilated disc brakes all round and generally much improved detail.

2.4 litres

The development of performance combined with refinement

continued when, from late 1971, capacity was raised to 2.4 litres. This gave the 911S 190 bhp, up a further 10 bhp on the 2.2 litre. Such increases in capacity formed a progressive plan by the factory that steadily worked towards an engine size of 2.7 litres, which was finally achieved in a production 911 in 1973, (the Carrera RS).

The 2.4 litre types are the most sought after of the pre-impact bumper 911 models, not only because of their larger engine size, but because of the steps to improve corrosion attack. With the optional five-speed gearbox and Lux equipment, the 911 range suited all tastes of sporting driver. Even the 911T, the only 911 by now on carburettors in Europe, offered exhilarating performance with excellent road manners. Below 3000 rpm the car behaved like a small hatchback, but when the revs rose above that, greatly improved torque would make the car a delight to drive quickly. The 911S showed the first visible sign of an aerodynamic development programme with the objective of improving high speed stability. This took the form of a front air dam, which was an option for the 911E. Generally, 2.4 models are discernable from the earlier models by their black rear lettering and front intake grilles. One other difference between '72 and '73 2.4 models was the location of the oil filler. On the '72 models the oil tank was located ahead of the right rear wheel, with the filler located on the outside of the wing/fender. On subsequent models the tank was located behind the wheel, filling from inside the engine compartment (as it was before the '72 model). The 1973 911E saw the first use of the "cookie cutter" cast wheels, as opposed to the forged five spoke wheels or the base model steel wheels. For the 1973 model year the front air dam was standard on the E and T as well as the S.

As mentioned, the 2.4

models are the best target for a 911 suitable for restoration within sensible timescale and with restricted resources. Careful buying of any of these models can mean little work is necessary, save that of regular maintenance. Without exception the bodywork is the main area for attention. For reliability the T will probably have had a less frenetic life than an E or S. As for performance, a good 2.4 S will go to sixty in about six and a half seconds (the T only takes about 1.5 secs longer!). There are many enthusiasts who feel the 2.4 types were the best of the everyday 911s of the 'seventies.

Sportomatic

Before progressing further, a short note must be made about the Sportomatic. It is perhaps surprising to find a sports car with an automatic transmission option, but probably because of Porsche experience of the American market, a semi-automatic box was made available from the 1968 2 litre models. The transmission still requires the driver to move the gear stick in the conventional way, with the clutch being actuated by electric contacts at the base of the stick to detect lever movement. The clutch is not used to pull away, only for gear changing. A torque converter copes with the transmission of torque from the engine to the clutch input. It is a very simple arrangement, which permitted the driver to use the gears as in a manual box, but with the facility of no clutch pedal. The original "Sporto" box was designated the 905 and was last used on the '72T. Keeping the existing four-speed layout, the Sportomatic box was redesigned to accept the steadily rising engine outputs, the new design being seen first on the 2.4E and S. This box was designated the 925/01. In 1975 the Sportomatic was revised again (and called the

925/10) offering three speeds and further torque capacity. The use of three speeds offered less potential for enthusiastic driving than the earlier four-speed unit and was not so popular. The Sportomatic was not seen on the European 911S after 1975. The last year that the Sportomatic was available was 1979, but it was offered as a brochure option to 1980. It is now not possible to order a Sportomatic even as an option, although it would be possible to convert a used current model.

The Sportomatics offer easier driving, without compromising performance at all. It may offend the macho element amongst drivers, not being able to pedal their way through the gears, but the factory clearly believes in the further development of the automatic transmission, as shown by the use in racing of the PDK automatic transmission from 1985. For the seller of the used 911, the Sportomatic generally is not so easy to move as a manual. The plus aspect though, is that the car will probably have had a quieter life from less demanding drivers and of course, the ''Sporto'' offers 911 driving to those who are restricted to two pedal vehicles.

Carrera RS

The first 911 to feature the 2.7 engine was the Carrera RS which, due to its superb performance and limited build numbers, is now one of the most sought after 911 models. Good examples are an appreciating asset and now change hands rarely. It is wise to check the chassis and engine number for authenticity on this model, more than most 911 models. The 1973 RS must not be confused with the larger volume Carreras produced in the subsequent years, both in 2.7 and later 3.0 form. Whilst the '73 911S boasted 190 bhp, the RS offered 210 bhp. As so often with

Porsche, the car was built to satisfy homologation requirements for racing. It featured lightweight panels, rear wheel arches flared to permit 7'' wheels as well as its increase in capacity. Its main identifying mark was the ''ducktail'' rear spoiler designed into the engine cover. Only 1036 RSs were produced (including both LHD and RHD versions). The prospective buyer could choose between the RST (which offered the same level of comfort options as the 2.4S), the basic RS (which had wind up windows, no rear seats and other lightening deletions) and finally the RSR, which went all the way with the lightening exercise and was built specifically for racing customers.

2.4 litres

Building on the success of the RS, a civilised Carrera was offered as top of the range in '74, with full upholstery and comfort options. The car still featured the mechanical fuel injection engine, giving 210 bhp and was a developed version of the RST. The ducktail was not a standard fitting on the '74 Carrera but the Carrera was available for the first time as a Targa. The 911 and 911s fulfilled the roles previously played by the T and E respectively.

The most notable change in '74 was the introduction of impact bumpers to satisfy the then new 5 mph collision regulations in the 'States. The change in the bumper style in '74 in many ways was the visible sign that the 911 was becoming a mature and practical sports car. The use of the new K Jetronic fuel injection on the 911 and 911S, together with other improvements, were turning the car into a smooth and tractable vehicle, a long way removed from the early models.

The 1975 range remained unchanged, but included further improvements in comfort. For the

first time the Targa had a black roll over bar in place of the previous stainless steel finish.

Gearboxes

A few paragraphs on the development of the gearbox might be useful at this point.

On its introduction, the original 2.0 litre 911 used a then-new five-speed gearbox. This early type 901 gearbox was improved so that it was still suitable for the 2.2 911E and S. Design work went into making the 911 an easier car to drive. In the transmission area this resulted in the 2.2 litre 911T offering four speeds as standard and introduction of the previously discussed Sportomatic.

The original five-speed gearbox had been developed to transmit the 2.2 litre engine's output, but a new gearbox was designed for the 2.4 models. All 2.4 models had four speeds as standard, but with five speeds available as an option. This new transmission was known as the ''Type 915''. This gearbox was unaltered until the 1975 models when the top ratios were revised. It was not until the 911SC of 1978 that the five-speed gearbox was offered as the list specification on non-Turbo models. The five-speed box has been the standard 911 fitment since then, with of course, considerable attention to detail development.

1976 models

These models offered a major advance in quality, with the adoption of a fully zinc coated bodyshell on all models. The panels were zinc coated prior to assembly, so that rust was inhibited from forming during welding operations and later, when in service.

The elevated temperatures at weld locations on unprotected mild steel can accelerate the formation of rust in those areas,

38

so that corrosion can be effectively built into a car during manufacture. This undesirable situation can be made much less likely by using a sacrificial metal, rather than the base steel, to react with any moisture. The resultant product of the chemical reaction will form over the mild steel and maintain its protection. This applies equally to a stone chip as to a weld. A protective paint layer is still required to prevent the protective coating (zinc) from reacting with moisture until the base metal is threatened.

The cars themselves began to achieve new levels of performance and fittings, the Carrera 3.0 living up to its famous title, going from 0 to 60 mph in 6.0 secs. It featured also the appearance of the "black-look" to the window surrounds on the non-Turbo models, which further enhanced their aggressive looks. On a detail level, those huge electrically operated and heated external mirrors also appeared in this model year.

The following year saw only detail changes to the 3.0 Carrera, which must rate as one of the most desirable of the 911 family.

Only one 2.7 model was available for 1976-77, which differed only in detail to the previous 2.7 models, excepting of course, that it also received the zinc coated body.

911SC, Carrera 3.2

From 1978 the basic model was the 911SC, this being the only non-turbo 911 available. Derived from the 3.0 Carrera, the performance was further developed so that although power was reduced to 180 bhp from 200 bhp, maximum torque was improved.

The early Sports Equipment option offered forged alloy wheels, sports seats, uprated dampers and low profile tyres. Also available was the fitment of improved aerodynamic aids to improve high speed handling. The large "tea tray" rear spoiler fitted to the engine lid could be fitted only in conjunction with a deeper front air dam.

The large rear spoiler has been revised several times since the first rubber "whaletails" appeared on the 3.0 Carreras. The 911SC used a smaller Turbo style spoiler initially, with a small additional grille near the edge of the spoiler to exhaust the air conditioning heat exchanger, if fitted. In 1982 this changed again to a deeper-lipped version, with a single central cooling grille. This grille has since become colour coded. The power of the SC did not dwell long at the early figure of 180 bhp, and by 1983 was developing 204 bhp in very refined form.

In 1983 the Coupe and Targa body shapes were joined by the Cabriolet, a full soft-top version of the 911. The practicality of such a car is questionable, not only from a weather viewpoint, but also from the ease with which thieves can gain access to the interior. For "rag-top" fans though, the combination of Porsche performance and wind-in-the-hair exhilaration must be difficult to resist. In exhibitionism, it does excel, however.

From 1984 the 3.2 Carrera replaced the SC range. Yet another engine capacity increase gave the new model a power output of 231 bhp and a "time-to-sixty" of six seconds, only a couple of tenths off the equivalent time of the RS Carrera of eleven years previously. The differences between those two Carreras was substantial, however, in terms of tractability, handling, comfort and especially fuel consumption. The RS would probably consume 10 to 12 miles per gallon, when pressed; the new 3.2 Carrera would exceed 25 mpg in similar conditions and it is claimed that the 3.2 engine had 80% of its components modified from the previous 3.0 SC unit. The remarkable point being that although the power was raised by 27 bhp, the fuel consumption actually was reduced. This was to some extent due to the use of the new Bosch Motronic ignition and injection control system.

The differences between these later 911 models and the early cars are total. Unlike say, the Austin Mini, which also has been in production for many years, the 911 has virtually been redesigned several times over. Each chapter in its evolution has produced a sports car that is world class and yet retains the spirit of the early 2.0 litre cars. Resources will dictate which chapter of that evolution the prospective buyer can look at.

The selection of which car within that group will depend on the use the car is to be put to, be it daily transit, summer weekends or racing. The second factor will be whether you wish to take the car off the road for renovation or not. As stated pre-zinc coated cars must be very closely examined for corrosion because what may look like a small tidy up job can easily turn into a major rebuild. If the car is taken off the road, the job might as well be done properly. In that situation, is the work to be DIY or professional? That question is answered by realistically assessing the resale value after the work is done.

912

Porsche have always tried to offer a model which catered for the popular sports car driver. The 912 was produced in Europe from 1965 to 1968, with a 1.6 litre engine derived from that of the 356SC. In all other respects the 912 was identical to the 911 and even the Targa body was available. Its 90 bhp gave it a level of performance that drew the same comments as the 924 did some ten years later. Here was a relatively expensive, underpowered sports car, which could even be out-performed by

some saloon cars. It was no surprise that the model was discontinued in 1968, in an era of some outstanding British market competition from the likes of Lotus and Jaguar.

However, the 912 was more successful in the States and was even revived in the mid 'seventies as the 912E, fitted with the 2.0-litre 914 engine.

Today its rarity makes it desirable, although it is difficult to justify its purchase in preference to an equivalent age of 911. Like the 911, it will have suffered with time and good ones will be hard to find.

930 Turbo

The Turbo is considered as a separate category of 911, because it differs in so many ways from the other models. It was for this reason that the factory gave it a separate model number. It is probably the best recognised of all 911 models to the layman and enthusiast alike.

The 930 Turbo went onto the market as a 3.0 litre for the 1975 model year. With an engine derived from the limited edition 3.0 RS racer, the 3.0 Turbo offered excellent performance (0 to 60 mph in approx 5.4 secs) and stunning appearance. In later years, it epitomised what the man in the street regarded as the "classic" Porsche, with its flared wheel arches and large spoilers.

Early Turbos were intended to reflect the latest in vehicle technology, much as the 959 did on its introduction in 1985. The engine reflected Porsche's experience in racing with the 3.0 RS and turbocharging. This latter especially gave valuable development to the problem of "turbo lag" and the use of the Porsche's own bypass (valve) system to maintain turbo revs against a closed throttle.

A new four-speed gearbox was designed for the Turbo to transmit the new engine's 254 lbf ft torque.

Driving a 3.0 litre Turbo is a snapshot of '70s racing technology in many respects. The enthusiast will enjoy playing with the inherent delay in the acceleration as the car is powered out of a bend and the anticipation of the tremendous push in the back when the boost has its effect.

The early Turbos though, missed the racing development of ventilated and perforated brakes. These were not fitted to the Turbo until the 3.3 litre model, announced for 1978, although some may wish to retrofit the later brakes to their 3.0 litre models.

For Turbo buyers, the major factor after cost is that 1975 models were not fully zinc coated, so are corrosion prone. Careful inspection of the service record and bills will establish the car's history. This is especially important, as so often Turbos have had very chequered histories. Look for the long-term owner who looks after his turbocharger and has the oil changed regularly. Early mineral oils really were not up to the temperatures seen in a turbo and regular (3000 mile) oil changes were essential. The advent of enhanced mineral oils and synthetics has enabled longer change intervals, but careful use will make the turbo last longer. A smoky turbo means an overhaul or replacement is due soon and it will be very expensive. Aside from these detail points buying a Turbo will require the same inspection as detailed for the 911 in subsequent sections.

As might be expected used Turbo prices are high, which not only reflects a stationary depreciation rate, but also its classic status.

Part 3: Where to look

Many enthusiasts graduate to a 911 as a progression in a series

of high performance cars. The decision to look for one is usually based on a quick look in a car park or garage forecourt. This is where emotion can cloud better judgement.

If you are happier trusting the experience of a garage to sell you a car that they feel confident will give you good service, only go to those garages that deserve that trust. For newer 911 models this means an Official Porsche Centre, where the pre-owned after sales package is the best money can buy.

For older 911 models that are more than approximately five years old then, a well known Porsche specialist should be consulted. In Britain, Autofarm Ltd, of Tring, Hertfordshire have a wealth of experience from the earliest of the 911 types. They will advise on cars that have been serviced with them, even if you are not buying from them.

It is generally recommended not to buy from a small dealer who professes to be a "specialist", but who has no service facilities, or who makes his living from moving mass market cars. He has probably taken the car in part exchange, which can be a sign that the previous owner was not able to sell it. The dealer may even have given it a quick spray job to make it look pretty. A rough guideline as to reputability can be gained from a review of the adverts in magazines like *Classic Car* and *Porsche Post* (in the UK), and *Panorama* (in the States).

Buying from good specialists and using their experience obviously will put a premium on the price. Buying privately can involve a lot of travelling, looking, haggling and most importantly, risk.

In the UK, the *Exchange and Mart* is the best place to look for a used 911, closely followed, and generally for more recent models, by the *Sunday Times*. The magazines to check on a monthly basis are *Classic Cars* and *Motor Sport*. The many others do carry

Porsche adverts, but their quantities are usually inconsistent. *Porsche Post* and the *Newsletter* are published alternately to Club members by the Porsche Club of Great Britain every six-odd weeks. They both carry extensive numbers of 911 adverts, usually from members.

In the USA, *Porsche Panorama* (the monthly magazine of the Porsche Club of America) is the prime source of a good used Porsche. The magazine *Road & Track* is another national source, but often local newspapers will turn up good cars within realistic distances.

Using the checklist

This checklist is designed to show step-by-step instructions for virtually all the checks to be made on a car offered for sale. After each check, the possible fault is indicated. The "!" sign is a guide to the cost of rectifying the fault. "!" indicates that the cost is equivalent to the price of a quality 205/50VR15 high performance tyre. This assumes that all the work will be done by a professional, which would be a normal bargaining position. "!!" indicates that the work will cost equivalent to five similar tyres. "!!!" suggests the cost will be similar to fifteen such tyres and "!!!!" means the cost will exceed that of fifteen tyres.

When examining the car take a copy of this checklist with you and work through it. Ignore the efforts of some owners to rush you. Keep a note of the work you think needs to be done with these rough costings, and use it to haggle over the asking price, if this is unrealistic. A roadworthy 911 can cost a considerable sum, so use the time efficiently and if something about the car turns you off, retire politely.

It is assumed that you have read the various references and know what to expect from the specification of the car, when you first visit or ring up. Consult the

Haynes Owners Workshop Manual for the 911 before viewing, so that some knowledge of the layout of the car is gained.

Buying a car privately is a balance of several factors, so don't be afraid to use your previous experience to measure up the seller as well as the car.

Stage A of the process is the coarse filter. This stage might be possible by just a telephone call, if the car sounds unsuitable from the owner's description. Stage B assesses the car in depth. This second stage should always be performed during daylight hours, preferably when it is not raining, etc, which can obscure certain paintwork defects.

Safety

When inspecting a car don't forget safety. NEVER rely on the handbrake to hold a car that is on a slope or up on ramps. Ensure that the wheels are chocked when using jacks or ramps. Use axle stands if you have to inspect the underside of the car. Do not use a naked flame or smoke when inspecting the underside of a car.

Toolbox

Old, warm clothes (if it's cold). An old mat or board if the ground is wet. A bright torch. A screwdriver or other probe. A small magnet will seek out filler in bodywork (but know where aluminium panels are used).

For the detailed inspection, a trolley or scissors jack is required. A bottle jack may be too tall to fit under the area to be raised. Axle stands should also be taken to support the weight of the car, once raised on the jack. Take also a copy of these notes and highlight the items that might be forgotten. Take a pencil to make notes.

Stage A: First impressions

A telephone appraisal can very often save a lot of time spent travelling to look at a car.

Firstly, size up what is for sale:
1) How long has the seller owned the car and how many owners has the car had? A good reason is needed if the car is being resold a short time after purchase. Be wary if the car is being sold on behalf of someone else. A loved car will not be treated in this way!
2) What mileage is on the car? What proof is there that it's genuine (for instance in the UK, are all the MoT certificates available)? Be wary of the car that cannot offer this proof. The 911 should be good for 100,000 miles without a major mechanical rebuild, but it obviously depends on the kind of life the car has had.
3) What use has the car had in its immediate past? Is the car used daily or through the winter? It is quite normal to hear of enthusiasts using a 911 daily, irrespective of age. What needs to be established is that maintenance and care is put into the car, appropriate to its age.
4) Does the car have the fittings and options that you require? For instance does it have a leather interior, electric sunroof (can be abbreviated to "esr" in adverts), or passenger door mirror (abbreviated to "pdm"). Is it the colour you want? Generally, it must be said that as long as the colour is satisfactory, then it is the condition of the car which is important. There are certain colours, however, which may not be quite what you expect!
5) What is the condition of the car? Has the car been resprayed? If pre-'76, is the car showing rust signs or has it been restored already? Unless the car has had an almost unique life, be wary of any pre '76 911 that claims to be

rust free and has not been subject to new body panels, etc.
6) Make a decision on whether to progress, based on this initial conversation. Assess the owner for honesty, as far as is possible whilst forming an impression of the car. Be prepared for the seller who says the car is in superb condition on the telephone, but after a long journey to inspect it, the car is seen to be a wreck at first glance.

Stage B: Body inspection

The condition of the body is considered before inspection of the mechanics or interior, since it is the body that is generally most difficult for the enthusiast to rectify.
1) Look for evidence of previous accident repairs. Look along the sides and roof of the car at eye level. Are there any paint or panel irregularities? Ripples or rough paint surface indicates a cheap repair possibly covering filler and rust. Such rust will come through in six months or less in the British climate. Are there any strange curves in the roof, that might suggest a twisted bodyshell? Are the door, engine bay lid and engine lid gaps equal? Is there evidence of repainting of certain panels or the entire car? Look for overspray on difficult to remove/mask items such as the thin black neoprene strips which separate the valances and front wings/fenders from their adjacent body parts. Overspray on window surrounds and wheel arch edgings point to an economy repair. Use the magnet to look for filler on suspect areas. A heavy crash can be given away by the trimstrip beneath the rear threequarter window. It can be nicked at its front edge by the window frame of the door in an accident and is often not replaced. Proper repairs to recent cars are very expensive

(!!!!+), but to preserve the resale value (and as appropriate, the Longlife body warranty), it is essential.

Inside the car lift the carpets to reveal the undertray. If the undertray is bowed, especially behind the rear seats, this is evidence of a previous accident. Do not be confused by the strengthening ribbing that is normal in the undertray.

Look inside the front luggage bay lid, ahead of the petrol tank. The tank sits on a cross-member with an open area ahead of that. Does the open area look original? Does it look as though it has been beaten flat or are there weld marks around the stamped-in areas of the petrol tank front support? If these signs are present, leave the car.

If the undertray is bowed then the car may have odd handling, which should be checked later. It is possible the car has been repaired correctly, with rejigging if necessary. Evidence is required to satisfy the buyer.
2) For older cars, the rust situation must be established at this early stage. This will affect mainly the pre-'76 models, although badly crash-repaired later models will rust just as easily. Use the illustration to check the key areas. Are replacement front wings/fenders required (!!!) including respray, although these are bolt-on items)? Are the front inner wings/fenders and the front wing/fender support panel (in front of the door) sound? This latter can corrode and let moisture through to the sills/body rockers and undertray. (If not !!!+.) Is the petrol tank front support (inside the front luggage bay lid) sound? Similarly check the front cross-member underneath it, by looking under the car (replacement cost !!+). Is the underseal on the crossmember sound and not cracked? Is the towing eye (in the centre of the cross-member) still soundly attached to it?

3) Are rear wings/fenders rusted (!!!)? Probe also the inner wings/fenders, especially in the oil tank area. Is the under wing/fender area clogged with mud/leaves, etc? A good owner will keep these areas free of road debris. Laying in replacement sections to the inner rear wings/fenders cannot be realistically done without taking the outer wings/fenders off. The rear wings/fenders are not as easy to replace as the fronts and will demand a high degree of skill from the enthusiast.
4) Is the rear centre valance sound (behind the silencer)? (but could be expensive). This can easily be replaced and the respray is well within the average enthusiast's capabilities. Similarly, check the lower edge of the engine cover (!!).
5) Are the sills/body rockers sound? Are jack points sound? Check outer sills/body rockers and surrounding structure are sound (replacement can be !!!). More importantly check the spread of corrosion to adjacent undertray, repairs here add !!. Check drain slots from lower sills/body rockers are free of debris. On the sill/body rocker and undertray area be very wary of new or non-standard underseal. Use the probe to establish soundness of metal, especially in the areas splashed by the wheels. Targas with rotten sills/body rockers are prone to sagging in the centre section. With the Coupe the roof tends to hold the structure in shape. The door gaps will give an indication of a Targa's condition.
6) Are door supports near lower hinges rusty (adjacent to sills/body rockers, replacement !!).
7) Are doors rusted? Look at underneath of doors. Are drain slots free of debris? Is there evidence of waxed oil coming from drain slots? This can indicate care of car, but is no good if rust already established. Use a magnet along lower edges of door to search for filler. New

door is !!. After the body inspection, especially on pre-'76 cars, a decision should be made on whether the car is what you are looking for.

Body inspection – the evidence

The following series of photographs amplify the points made in the previous section. Most of these apply to pre '76 models (non-fully zinc coated). To help understanding of some of the English terms used, it may help to note that wings are fenders and sills are body rockers.

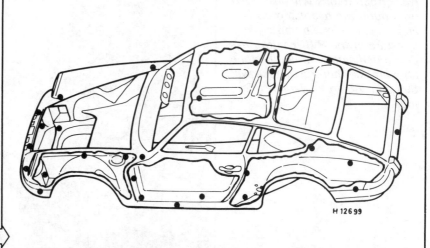

Fig. 2/1: Potential rust areas on pre-zinc coated 911 models

R1.   RS Carreras are worth a lot of money when in top condition. It is as well to appreciate the amount of time and money you will have to put into the car to get it to a collectable condition. (Courtesy, Autofarm).

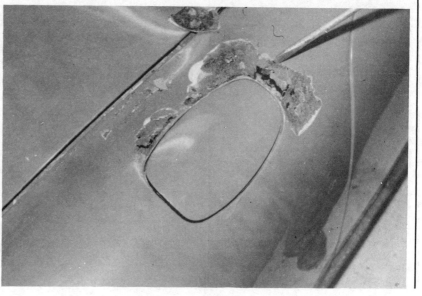

R2.   Heavy corrosion behind the fuel filler. This area will collect road debris over the years and trap moisture against a possibly damaged protective coating. The first signs would be small bubbles in the paint. Be very careful to check newly painted cars, if the history is unknown or vague. It is relatively easy to fill such rusted areas and do a quick spray job. In a Northern European climate, the rust will bubble through again inside six months. A small magnet will help to identify such repairs.

R3. Road debris will also build up around the headlamp bowl area. Again this will trap moisture. If the PVC coating has developed small fatigue or stone chip cracks, then rust attack will be rapid. Again beware of filler jobs.

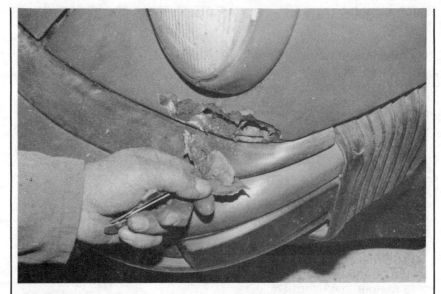

R4. Corrosion around a jacking point. Such corrosion can be initiated by fatigue cracking of the PVC coating, if the jacking point is used regularly to lift the car. Moisture will find its way into the cracks and attack the metal beneath.

R5. The next stage of corroded jacking points. The rust attack has spread to the undertray. Note also the hole in the rear wing – a result of debris build-up behind the rear sill/fender body rocker support.

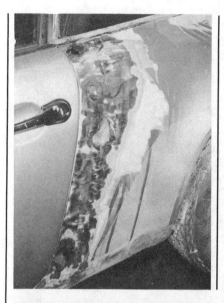

R6. With the rear wing/fender stripped, the extent of the damage can be seen. Again, beware of patch jobs.

R7. Getting at the rusted areas. The three-quarter rear panel is rusted through and the paint is concealing more internal corrosion. Note the lifted paint on the wing fender, just above the lights.

R8. The front wings/fenders have been removed from this 911. Scrape the inner panel with a screwdriver, searching for corrosion. Check especially along the top edge of the inner panel, (the area of the double curvature).

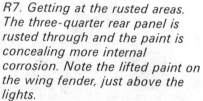

R9. This front wing/fenders support must be replaced. With a hole like this, road spray will have penetrated the sills/body rockers.

R10. A sharp probe will quickly reveal this type of corrosion in the door hinge supports. This 911 will need extensive work.

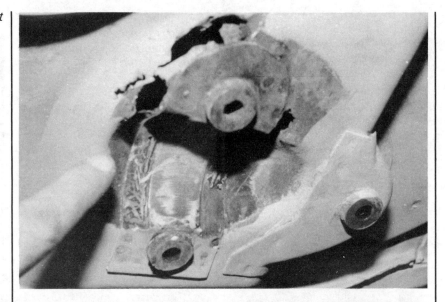

R11. Corrosion around the front torsion bar supports is accelerated by the flexing of the body reacting to the suspension loads.

R12. Doors – a quick paint job has covered filler and heavy corrosion at the bottom edges of this 911 door. Use the magnet again to seek out filler.

R13. Inside the rear wheel arch looking forward, the rear sill/body rocker support has rusted out and must be replaced. Build-up of road debris and stone chip damage would have accelerated this corrosion.

R14. Rusted out rear torsion bar support. Note the non-factory black underseal coating given to the underside, that would have concealed this serious (and potentially dangerous) corrosion.

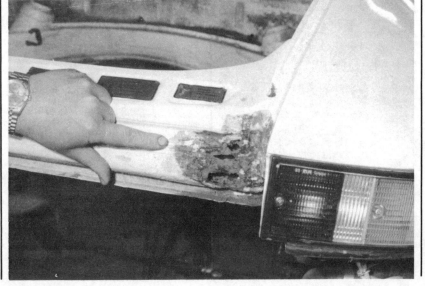

R15. This damage will have been caused by build-up of road chemicals and debris in the hot area over the silencer.

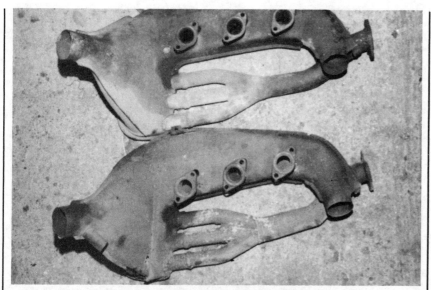

R16. Heat exchangers will last for years if looked after, making the high initial cost of stainless steel types only worth it if the car is a show model or very irregularly used. The lower exchanger in this shot shows corrosion at its lower edge, which will have resulted in poor heater performance.

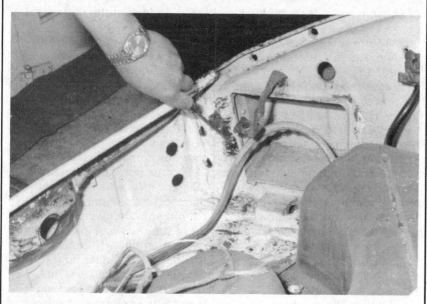

R17. The result of front inner wing/fender corrosion. Eventually, it penetrates the front compartment. Look also for corrosion around the base of the battery areas, which can have been caused by accidental acid spillage. The battery boxes themselves are attacked by stone damage and road spray from their outsides. It is quite unusual to find a pre-zinc coated car with good battery boxes!

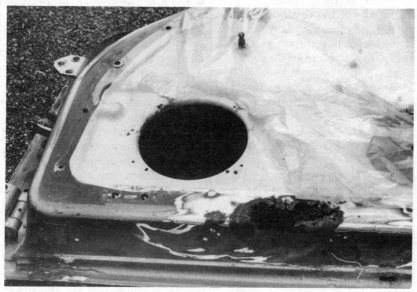

R18. This door has rusted out at its lower edge, directly under the front window guide. The water drain holes in the base of the door may have been blocked also. Note the split at the lower left edge, suggesting that there has been prolonged water build-up inside the door skin. Such corrosion has probably bubbled through the outer skin as well.

R19. Another example of heavy front wing/fender damage due to road debris build-up, etc.

R20. Worn out bushes on the rear radius arms. This would have resulted in odd handling and excessive suspension noise. (Courtesy, Autofarm).

Stage C: Mechanics inspection

This section examines all the vulnerable areas of the running gear, mechanics and interior.

Suspension, brakes and steering

1) Front suspension. Are the front wishbones sound (!! +)? Are the dampers effective and leak-free? (!! for front and rear). Is the torsion bar mounting at the front sound? (!!). Check for wear of the lower strut balljoint on pre-'71 models. On self-levelling strut models ('69 – '71 911E), check that the suspension has not settled.
2) Steering. Are the steering rack gaiters sound? Hold the front wheel and rock it; assess free movement before steering wheel moves. There should be none. New track rod ends, (!) or new steering rack, (!!) may be necessary.
3) Front brakes. Are the brake pipes corroded? Are there signs of cheap repairs, (or even thick coating of grease smeared on pipes)? Are there signs of fluid leakage. Are the front discs scored? (!!).
4) Rear suspension. There is no quick way of telling whether the transverse tube which carries the torsion bars is about to fail. Inspect for heavy rust with a small probe at the bottom of the torsion bar and its mountings to the body. Look also for corrosion around the inner wings/fenders, near the torsion bar mounts. It does happen, due to fatigue and the result is bottomed out suspension (to repair might cost !!!). It is really only likely on early cars.

Look at the gearbox mountings at the torsion bar and the engine mountings on the rear of the body. Leave the car if heavy rust is found in these areas.
5) Rear brakes. Check as fronts. Check also operation of handbrake.

Engine and gearbox

It will facilitate engine/gearbox inspection if the car is put on the axle stands at this point, if this is possible. Only do this if you think the car is a good one and the owner agrees. It may not be possible to put the car on stands. In this situation, a mirror may be useful to look at the undersides of the car.

Ask the owner to start the engine. Let the engine idle for several minutes to allow it to warm up. Whilst the engine is warming, carry out the following checks.
1) Is the engine difficult to start from cold? Warm up regulator may need attention, (!).
2) Do the revs fluctuate when idling or miss when the throttle is blipped? Is there popping/banging on the overrun? Any of these suggests fuel injection needs attention, (!!! potentially). It could be a random bug(s) in the fuel or electrical system, which sometimes take a long time for the enthusiast to track down. Best to ask for the car to be set up on a rolling road before sale, if this is all that is wrong, (!!!) if not.
3) Is there oil leakage from the engine, either from the rocker cover gaskets or the camshaft housing return pipes, (the approx. one inch diameter pipes that run from the heads to the crankcase)? Leakage from the rocker covers may be caused by a poor fitting gasket. To stop the seals on the tubes leaking may mean replacement of the O-rings or even the tube in total. Either way this is a head off job, (!!!).
4) Visually inspect the crankcase from below. Is there excessive oil

leakage from the crankcase or too much engine sealant around the joints? Suggests a poorly reassembled engine and maybe cheap rebuild. Oil around the ends of the crankcase suggests worn oil seals, (!!). There should be no paint or heavy grease obscuring the open areas of the crankcase. If there is, probe behind the covering to search for cheap repairs to the crankcase, either with epoxy glue or aluminium welds, (this has been known after major engine blow ups!). If such a repair is found, say thank you to the owner and good-bye!

5) Ask the owner to hold the engine revs at about 1200. From the rear of the car is there a clattering noise from either timing chain case? This tends to be lost in other noises as the revs are slowly increased to about 2000. If there is such a noise, then one or both tensioners need replacing, (!!). If the owner says these have been replaced recently and there is still a poor quality clatter from the central rear area of the engine, it is possibly caused by a worn intermediate gear, (possible on 2.7 and 3.0 Carreras). Replacement of gear means engine strip down, plus expensive parts, (!!!!+). From the 1984 Carreras, oil-fed tensioners were introduced which can be fitted to all post-'68 911 models. These "ultimate" tensioners can be identified by oil feed lines entering each chain case cover at the rear of the engine. Consider it a bonus if the car under consideration has these tensioners fitted. The best of the pre-'84 tensioners should give a reliable 30,000 miles or more, depending on use.

6) Now that the engine has warmed, does the exhaust blow smoke when the throttle is blipped? Possible worn valve guides may also be detected by a "bag of nails" sound from engine (cylinder head rebuild, !!!!). If bills show recent (last twenty thousand miles) rebuild by recognised specialist then the

piston rings may be worn out (engine rebuild with possibly new pistons and barrels, !!!!). Engine may now be switched off.

7) Heat exchangers. With a torch look up at the heater control boxes and their cable operation. Is there evidence of heavy corrosion around the flaps? (Replacement boxes are ! each). Are heat exchangers heavily corroded or split? (Replacement !! each). Fitting new heat exchangers is not an easy job, especially if the stud nuts are corroded. Similarly inspect the silencer for splits or corrosion (!!). New exchangers should last 2 to 3 years in normal service.

8) Gearbox. Is it damaged from bottoming or is there welding on the casing? If the gearbox number has been removed, double-check the car chassis number with the registration document. If there is any doubt on authenticity, leave the car. Is there leakage from front end of gearbox? Worn selector shaft oil seal is !!. Even worse is a worn input shaft oil seal, which will need a total box rebuild (leaks from clutch bellhousing, !!!).

9) Whilst under the car check that the rubber gaiters around drive shaft couplings (where appropriate) are in good condition (replacement Lobro joints, !!!).

10) Oil tank, oil cooler and fittings. Check all oil plumbing for leaks. Is oil cooler leaking (!!)? Is oil tank corroded (!!)?

Front compartment

The ideal here is an original interior, once the carpets and spare wheel are lifted.

1) Remove all carpets. Are these in good condition (!!)? These can be quite easily replaced by the enthusiast by making new items.

2) Remove the spare wheel. Is the wheel and tyre in good condition? Check for dented rims (!!). If Space Saver tyre, inspect the tyre for evidence of wear or cracking. Check inflation

compressor present and works (!).

3) Inspect car tools and jack. A well looked-after car will have a good condition full tool kit.

4) Battery(ies). Is the battery (or two batteries where fitted) new? Are the terminals corroded or is there evidence of acid spillage onto battery box or tank support? To check corrosion of the battery boxes on an older car pull out the battery (ies) and probe the box structure (repair of battery box,!!). If acid has been spilt onto the tank support, is the structure sound?

5) Brake fluid reservoir. Is there evidence of fluid spillage onto the inner wing/fender or internal structure? Probe areas for corrosion (repair can be !!).

6) Front luggage bay latch panel. Is the panel corroded in the corners? Are the front wing/fender attachment bolts accessible at the sides? Heavy corrosion here means a replacement panel and possible rebuild of the inner wing/fender attachment points (!!).

7) Check the chassis number against references to ensure the car is a genuine model. Clearly, if it looks as if there are weld marks around the chassis number, leave the car.

Interior

1) Examine the seats, including the seat backs, for damage and wear. Rips in seats are difficult to repair well on visible areas. Check that the rear seat backs can be clipped in the upright position. Do both front seats operate as they should? Is the suspension in each seat sound? Used seats from a specialist can replace broken or damaged items (! each).

2) Check the condition of the headlining. Is headlining discoloured from tobacco smoke, or ripped? New headlining means glass out (!!!). Cars that have not been smoked in will generally be in better condition inside.

3) Assess the condition of the floor carpets. Are the carpets wet

or damp? This might suggest a leak from the door or window rubbers. Inspect the chassis metalwork adjacent to damp carpets for corrosion.

4) Door panels. Are the panels ripped or damaged? (!).

5) Inspect all glass for cracks or chips. Replacement glass may be obtained new or as a used item from a specialist (!!).

6) Inspect the area under the dash. Is the wiring professionally tidy? Untidy wiring suggests previous problems with electrics. Are these shown on bills?

7) It is important to establish whether a 911 is a conversion from LHD to RHD. Whilst it is possible to do the conversion with factory parts, it is very expensive (!!!!+) to do it properly. Several businesses offer cheap conversions, which involve potentially unsafe modifications to the steering and brake pedal area. A LHD car will always sell for less than a RHD car in Britain. A 911 cheaply converted to RHD should sell for less than the value of a LHD car. In investment terms, if a 911 is thought to be a conversion, leave it.

The front bulkhead, between the front luggage area and the passenger compartment, are quite different from LHD to RHD. Easiest way to check that a car has not been cheaply converted is to look inside the front luggage area, with the carpets removed. There is an inspection hatch for the steering linkage, located to the rear of the fuel tank. The black protective cover to the rear of the hatch should point towards the steering wheel. Look for well spaced welds in the top of the bulkhead, with the hatch open, that might show that originally the steering column went to the left side of the car rather than the right. Inside the car, check the lower side of the steering column ducting. Does this look factory finished? Check also that the brake/clutch pedals show no signs of poor welding. A look in the UK registration document will also show up any

breaks in the car's history. For instance, you may find a car made in 1975, but first registered in the UK in say, 1980. Clearly, an explanation would be required.

8) Whilst seated in the driver's position, check the speedometer for signs of tampering. Is the glass smeared or spotlessly clean when compared with the other instruments, suggesting the speedometer has been worked on recently? Grip the instrument by the outer bezel using both hands and by twisting pull it outwards from the dash panel as far as possible (maximum three inches). Does the instrument come out very easily? Are there signs of tampering around the back of the bezel where that part attaches to the rear of the speedo? Is the plastic clip that holds the cable to the speedo broken? All these checks investigate whether the vehicle's recorded mileage has been interfered with. The only real way of feeling secure about the mileage displayed is a watertight service history (plus, in the UK, all MoT test certificates). Replace the speedometer.

9) Start the engine. Is the engine easy to start when warm? If not see earlier. Is oil level indicator at the top of the instrument? Low oil level indicates poor maintenance. It should be said that many enthusiasts claim oil consumption is reduced by running with the level indicator at half full. This is satisfactory if the car has not had a lot of town use (and hence would run most of the time at a hotter than recommended temperature, resulting in excessive wear). The engine oil performs a major cooling function on the 911, so running with less than the recommended amount requires careful consideration. Check all other instruments are functioning correctly.

10) Operate all lights, indicators, fog lights, brake and reversing lights. Investigate any malfunction to assess whether problem is easily solved or

whether it covers something more major. For instance, a non-operative brake light could be due to heavy corrosion in light cluster.

11) Operate all accessories, especially the electric windows, roof (if fitted), wipers, etc. Check the electric mirrors (if fitted) for movement and heating (feel the glass after a minute). Dampness and contact failure often mean that window motors or other electrical accessories have stopped working. Assess time to repair electrics and assume nothing is straightforward. Use these details to haggle over a good car in other respects.

Wheels and tyres

Clean wheels and tyres have an immense psychological effect on a buyer. Look closely at all the wheels, including the spare. New wheels are very expensive (!! each).

1) Are the wheel rims bent or distorted in any way, as a result of kerb bumping or accident? Bent rims are dangerous, since tyres can deflate at speed.

2) Are the tyres worn or damaged? Tread depth less than 1 mm across the tread width and around the complete circumference is illegal in Britain, but this amount of tread depth should be considered completely unsafe, especially on a 911. Check also for bulges on the inner and outer walls, perishing of the rubber on older cars, or uneven wear. This latter suggests possible camber or tracking misalignment, possible even due to bent suspension.

3) Are the tyres right for the model? Check the *Haynes Owners Workshop Manual* for correct fitment for earlier models. All post-'75 models should be on VR rated tyres, not HR. Remoulds/retreads should not be fitted to any Porsche. Low profile tyres may be fitted to the vehicle, as a retrofit; the speedometer reading may be in error as a result.

Road test

A prospective buyer should always drive the car prior to a decision. Adequate insurance will be necessary for this. If you have not driven a 911 before, be ready for a heavy long-travel brake pedal on pre-'77 models without servo. Be ready for the feel of the clutch. More importantly, if the weather is wet for your test, take care! It takes quite a while to adapt to the handling characteristics of the 911, especially the early ones.

At all times take careful note of road conditions when carrying out a road test.

1) Start up should be satisfactory on a warmed up engine. If not, the engine will require diagnosis of fuel or electrical system.
2) Depress the clutch. Is the clutch release bearing or engagement of clutch audible? Clutch replacement is !!!.
3) Drive off. Have you been alerted to possible timing chain tensioner problems earlier? Are these clattering noises still present at low revs (less than 2000 rpm)? Oil pressure should be strong when the engine is under load (about 50-60 psi when accelerating). Oil pressure can drop to 20 psi at idle when hot.
4) Do all gears engage freely? Worn synchromesh will mean a gearbox rebuild (!!!). It is not unusual for second gear synchromesh to wear first.
5) Does the car steer in a straight line with your hands off? Make allowances for road camber. If car steers continuously off course, there is possible undetected crash damage to a suspension member or, worse still, a twisted chassis. The problem may only be sticking brake pad, worn track rod or heavily scoured disc. Have this problem checked by a specialist if you are unsure about the car. Otherwise assume the worst.
6) Brake the car in a straight line. Does the car pull to one side? Again problem could be any of those in 5).

7) Drive at 50 mph, take out of gear and allow to coast. Is there a whine from gearbox or wheel bearings? It must be expected that older, unrestored cars will have gearbox whine to some extent. It does not generally signify a problem by itself and a rebuild would normally only be contemplated if there was difficulty engaging a gear or an oil seal was badly leaking. A gearbox rebuild would be !!!.
8) In normal driving at 50 – 70 mph, is there a vibration from the front or rear of the car? Could be damaged wheel or tyre, or simply a lost balance weight.
9) Are there any unexpected impact noises or vibrations during driving? Investigate any sources to assess importance. Annoying rattles or wind noise can be simply an old door surround seal or indicate badly fitting parts following accident repair.
10) The previous checks should have been carried out both in a straight line and in fast and slow bends.

Buying: in conclusion

If the full inspection of the car has been completed, it now remains to balance the faults that one has found and the condition of the car with the proposed sale price. Previous research will have given a fairly good idea of the price range for equivalent models of the same year and type.

Isolate the potentially big problems, if any have been found. Consider first, the time and funds that are available to rectify problems, before negotiating with the owner. The car may already be priced to reflect a known problem.

Consider also, that with further effort a better car could be found or a similar condition model at a lower price.

In conclusion, it is body condition that will set the value of pre-'76 911 models. With the later models, corrosion was not so much a problem, but look out for crash damage. Generally speaking, there is nothing that impresses as much as a full service history, with all services, bills, (and MoT certificates if appropriate) and previous owners listed. Even accepting a few problems, the history establishes as far as possible that what one is looking at is genuine. It may be worthwhile to ring up a garage to discuss a bill, or ask if they remember the car and likewise a previous owner.

Finally, don't ignore the first impressions. The key factors are the type of person selling the car and the cost of bringing the car to the standard you want. Don't get hooked on the sound of the engine alone or a gleaming set of wheels!

This checklist may seem as if a good 911 can be impossible to find. That is not true. It is a common factor across all well looked after 911s, young and old, that they have excellent reliability to go with the performance. The buyer who carefully sorts the good from the bad will be very happy with the eventual purchase. Be patient in the search!

3 Bodywork

Part 1: Examination and stripdown

Before any work can commence on body restoration, the full extent of the work to be performed must be assessed. Much of what is about to be said is common sense and a little thought at this earliest of stages can save a lot of time when the rebuild is started.

The bodywork section of this book will cover all the repairs and replacements that might be performed by the competent enthusiast. It must be stated that if the car is being repaired after accident damage or there is the possibility that the structure is distorted for another reason (eg corrosion), then the bodyshell should be checked out on a chassis jig.

A requirement of any stripdown is ample storage space to store all the pieces. The parts should be labelled and stored in boxes with the smaller trim items

BSM1. Repairs to suspension mountings also should be performed with the body on such a jig. This puts the job in the hands of an Official Porsche Centre or a good specialist. (Courtesy, Autoform)

being placed in small labelled plastic bags. Often, stray nuts and washers are best stored by fitting them temporarily back on the component from which they came.

At time of taking the pieces off, it may seem obvious how the parts reassemble and one could not possibly forget how they all go back together again. It will not look like that in a few days' or weeks' time! Tag all electrical wires with masking tape and label their location.

Care is necessary when storing the interior components, if these are removed. Items like carpets, seats, etc, should be covered and not be susceptible to accidental passing damage or paint overspray. Flammable items, like fuel tanks and lines, upholstery, etc, should be out of range of welding sparks. If the car is to be repainted store any glass under cover and mask off any glass that is left, including instrument glasses. This also applies to dash trim, etc, that is left in the car.

Tool Box

Axle stands or ramps, a thin bladed screwdriver, eye protection, paint stripper, rubber gloves and a narrow bladed

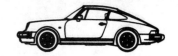

scraper. Suitable storage bags or boxes should also be available. Releasing fluid and a standard range of spanners, sockets, screwdrivers, together with pen and notepad will be required.

Safety

Take note of information in the text on safety hazards. NEVER drain petrol over a pit nor anywhere where a spark could ignite the vapour, eg. near a central heater boiler – outdoors is best. For obvious reasons, attempting to weld a fuel tank can be lethal and should be left to a specialist. Never use a flame near the fuel tank or lines. Drain fuel only into suitable containers. Do not use plastic containers which are attacked by petrol.

Battery(s) should be taken out prior to fuel tank

removal, to prevent accidental shorting in the presence of fuel vapour. When storing battery(s), take care to ensure that no object will fall unnoticed across the terminals and potentially cause a fire.

Paint stripper is damaging to the skin and eyes – read instructions before use and wear gloves, goggles and protective overalls. Ensure that the car is firmly supported when lifted off the ground – a jack is NOT safe enough. Wear goggles when probing beneath the car and beware of rusty, jagged edges.

Never work beneath a car supported on a jack: use axle stands, ramps or a roll-over cage (see Suppliers section) and, in the former case, securely chock the wheels that remain on the ground.

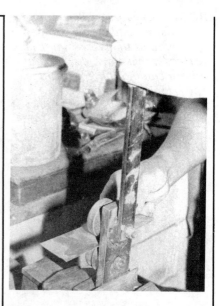

BOD2. This Sykes-Pickavant tool is ideal for letting patches into the bodywork. It allows you to join two flat pieces of metal with all the smoothness of a butt joint but with the strength and ease of welding of a lap joint. The two rollers form a shoulder along the edge of the steel.

BOD1. This cutting tool, made by Sykes-Pickavant, consists of a pair of cutting wheels which pull the steel between themselves as they cut. It works really well and takes up far less room than a guillotine.

BOD3. Although a little more expensive the Sykes-Pickavant sheet metal folder enables you to create perfectly formed folds and box sections in sheet steel.

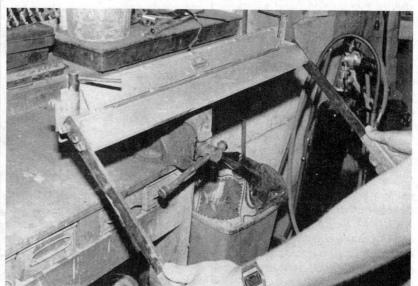

BOD4. An electric drill is one of the most versatile tools you can have around the workshop. Black & Decker make a wide range of drills including the 'Professional' and 'Home mechanic' rechargeable drills and the plug in drills shown here. At the front is a Black & Decker Workmate which, as a do-anything workbench, is a must for any workshop.

BOD5. While on the subject of power tools, it's worth pointing out that there is Black & Decker equipment for just about every purpose. This shot shows (from left to right) a sanding tool, ideal for preparing for paint, a 'Proline' heavy duty angle grinder and polisher which will help to bring up a mirror like finish on paint without hours of elbow grease, a random orbit sander which sands filler, primer and paint without leaving any scratch marks, a small angle grinder used for cutting and grinding steel before and after welding operations, and a general purpose palm-grip sander. In the foreground is the revolutionary Power-file which shapes metal, wood and plastic with remarkable ease.

BOD6. For temporary repairs with fibre glass or permanent finishing where a fine and flexible filler is required, Plastic Padding make a wide range of high quality materials. Also in this shot are Plastic Padding's aerosol cans of 'Stonechip' sill and underbody protector to give a tough, professional finish beneath or on top of paintwork.

BOD7.   Having invested a fortune in restoring the bodywork it would be the height of stupidity not to protect it. Corroless produce corrosion inhibitors in aerosol cans which have excellent 'creep' qualities and contain additives which stop any rust which may have already formed. Corroless body filler, primer, touch up paint and underbody paint also contains the same inhibitor. Surely a unique combination!

BOD8.   On the left of this picture is the Air Products Weldpak which can be purchased for home use from any Air Product centre (see telephone directories in the UK), while the 911 in the picture is tipped over on a wonderfully useful roll over cage which may still be available from Classic Car Restorations (see address in the back of this book).

Examination

E1.   The first task in a restoration of any size is to inspect the car from top to bottom methodically. Resist the urge to wade straight into a problem area and strip off parts at this stage.

A useful aid will be to use sketch views of the car (see fig 2.1), on which can be marked areas or points that need attention. It is after this close inspection, making notes on what needs to be done, that life can be very depressing! The attitude to take is that at least now it is clear what work needs to be done. The best policy is to assess what work should be performed by a professional (either because of skill level or need for specialist tools), and then make a sequential list of the major steps that will make up the total restoration work. If the restoration a big task, plan the job out logically setting goals to be achieved during the work.

Restoration to a high quality is a painstaking task and should not be rushed. Timescales should be set for achieving the goals, but it is the quality of work by which the car will be measured later that matters, not how quickly the job has been done. Never try and compare the speed at which a professional can do an equivalent task; he will be trained and have extensive experience in his work. His speed comes from practice; the enthusiast will probably be learning all the way.

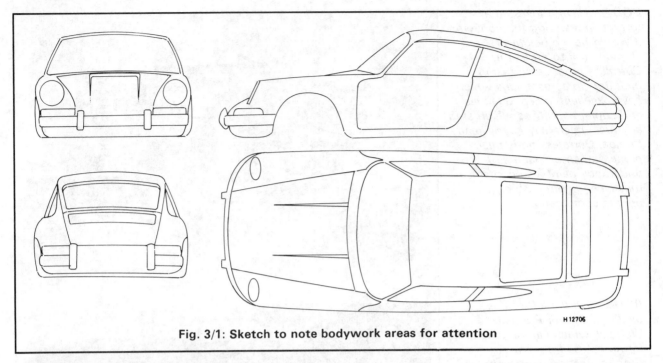

Fig. 3/1: Sketch to note bodywork areas for attention

E2. Every project has that stage when it looks as though no progress is being made and the end is nowhere in sight.

E3. It can be of enormous help to have the professionals assist at these points, perhaps doing some complex operation or fabrication and it will also help boost confidence (Courtesy, Peter Monk).

Stripdown of front section

It is not suggested that all the following items must be removed for any attention to the front end of the car. The individual must decide whether the task is made easier by removing certain items. For a total restoration, it is assumed all detachable parts will be removed.

Battery removal

On most models the battery is located in the front luggage compartment on the left-hand side. The front compartment carpeting must be lifted to get at the battery. From 1969 to 1973, the 911 used two batteries connected in parallel and located on the right-hand as well as the left-hand side of the front compartment.

Note that the 911 uses a negative earth electrical system.

B1. To remove a battery, disconnect the earth lead first,

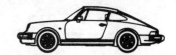

followed by the positive lead. ➤ Only then unclip the battery location strap. This procedure prevents accidental shorting of a lead against the body when removing the battery. The battery can then be lifted out.

If only one of two batteries is being removed, do not allow the two disconnected leads to touch each other, or the positive lead to touch an earth/ground.

When refitting the battery, clean up the terminals and leads. A smear of one of the copper 'lube' pastes will deter terminal corrosion. Make sure you have a good electrical contact between the terminals, leads and earth/ground points as relevant.

Fuel tank removal

The tank must be drained before removal. It will be necessary later to inspect it for internal and external corrosion. **NEVER drain a tank indoors or anywhere near a naked flame or spark.**

FTR1. Depending on the model, a drain plug may be provided, otherwise carefully loosen the fuel feed line at the lower rear of the tank to allow the fuel to drain. This tank is being lifted from above.

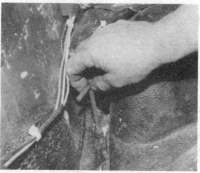

FTR2. The fuel tank is located by three clamps at its front and sides. The clamps are secured using socket head bolts into the chassis, and are reached from within the luggage compartment.

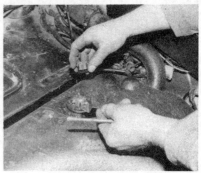

FTR3. Remove the fuel sender connector, vent pipe and fuel filler tube ...

FTR4. ... prior to lifting out the tank.

The tank may not easily lift out even though the socket-head bolts are removed, since the foam gasket which the tank seats on can become hard and forms an effective glued joint between the tank and the chassis. In this situation place a stout piece of wood beneath the tank and apply a jacking force to the tank, which should then ease out. Do not jack the tank directly as it may be damaged. The wood spreads the load and protects the protective coating on the tank. White spirit may also help to soften the gasket.

Place the tank in a safe place, noting any repairs that it needs (cracked coating, etc). Ensure that all the openings in the tank are plugged with tape or rags, to prevent moisture from collecting inside the tank during storage and to prevent a spark entering the tank. Have the tank steam-cleaned prior to storage to remove the risk of petrol fume explosion. Refitting of the tank is the reverse procedure. If the foam seal around the body aperture was damaged on removal, this will need replacing. It may ease refitting of the fuel pipes if this is done before the tank is located fully into position. Check flexible fuel pipes at the tank for damage or perishing. Replace if necessary.

Front valance (or air dam) removal

It is not strictly necessary to remove the front valance to repair the cross-member, but doing so eases access.

1) Pre-Impact bumper models

It is likely that the bumper mounting bolts will be heavily corroded. In this situation it may be necessary to drill out the bolts or use a saw to cut the nuts from the bolts. A liberal application of releasing fluid beforehand may render this action unnecessary, though.

Unscrew the bolts at each side of the bumper that attach it to the front wings/fenders. It may be easier to remove the bolts that attach the bracket to the battery box or inner wing/fender, if the single bolt holding the bracket to the bumper is corroded.

Unscrew the two bolts on the left- and right-hand side immediately behind the front wall. On pre '69 models these bolts are removed from inside the wheel arch, whilst on remaining pre-impact cars, the bolts are removed from within the front compartment.

The bumper can now be pulled forward and away from the car. Detach the sealing strip, noting whether a new one is required for the rebuild.

When reassembling the bumper, fit the sealing strip to the

IB1. Remove the bolts which locate the bumper side skirts to the front wings, inside each wheel arch. This shot shows a skirt removed from the bumper – note the screws attaching it to the flexible section. Graham Bason of Porsche-approved body shop Autotech of Belbroughton commences the bumper strip-down.

main frame with flexible adhesive. Starting with the four main bolts that attach to the inner wheel arch, fit all the bolts that locate the bumper to finger tightness. Push the bumper upwards against the seal to seat the bumper firmly and evenly against the seal. The end of the bumper must blend with the curve of the wheel arch. It is important also that there is no contact between the valance and the front dividing wall that might damage the valance or cause an irritating vibration. When satisfied, tighten all the bolts, whilst maintaining the even pressure on the seal. When refitting the electrical connections in the wheel arches apply a small amount of body sealer to the completed connectors to seal out moisture.

2) Impact bumper models

IB2. Another shot with the skirt removed shows the bolt holes in the front skirt.

IB3. Prise off the rubbing strip from the bumper to reveal the mounting nuts.

IB4.   Undo the nuts holding the bumper to the energy-absorbing struts (be they deformation tubes or hydraulic devices).

IB5.   Pull the bumper a short distance away from the front skirt and disconnect the electrical connections and headlamp washer pipes from the bumper. Lift the bumper away from the car.

IB6.   Undo the bolts holding the front skirt at its sides . . .

IB7.   . . . and the two at the front. Note the headlamp washer plumbing pointed out by Graham.

IB8.   The front skirt can now be removed. The presence of the side skirts here shows there is more than one way to do this job!

IB9.   From inside the luggage compartment, use a screwdriver to remove the self-tapping screws that hold the front sealing strip to the front bulkhead.

IB10. The energy-absorbing struts will now be fully accessible. These ones may need replacing.

IB11. The struts can be removed by undoing the rear nut and loosening the clamp bracket at the side of the strut.

IB12. Looking inside the removed bumper. The left finger is pointing out the strut mounting holes, which are elongated to give some lateral adjustment in position. The right-hand is pointing out the connector holes for the electrical (top) and headlamp washers.

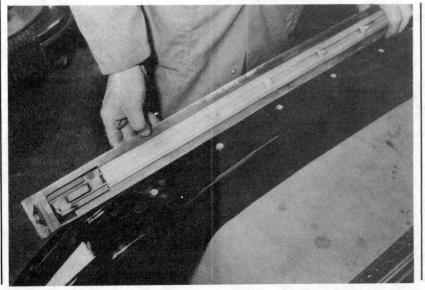

IB13. A new rubbing strip can make a big difference to the look of the front of the car. Note the closely spaced mounting screws.

IB14. When fitting the strip, make sure it is seated correctly, by using the palm of the hand.

IB15. When the front mounting nuts have been fitted, position the self-tapping screws at each side of the strip.

IB16. Certain models will have an extension lip fitted to the front skirt. This is most easily removed when the skirt has been removed, but the mounting nuts can be reached with a bit of dexterity, whilst the skirt is still on the car.

IB17. The rear impact bumpers are easier to remove. Remove the rear side skirts and flexible sections first, in the same way as described for the front bumper. Prise off the small black caps in the rubbing strips to their mounting screws and remove the screws and the strips.
◄ The bumper can now be removed from the rear deformable struts.

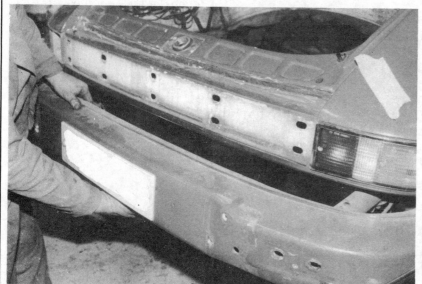

IB18. The over-riders are attached by two nuts, which can be removed whilst the bumper is still on the car. Access to these nuts may be difficult if there is a lot of road debris behind the bumper area.

IB19. A general view of the dismantled bumper area. Note that this 911 has been resprayed in a different colour from the original . . . ◄

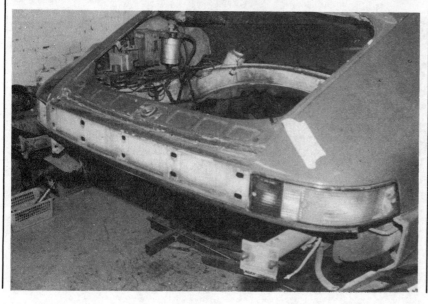

Refitting is the reverse procedure.

Removing the front wings/fenders

The use of bolt-on front wings/fenders theoretically means that replacement is so much easier than if they were welded. The ravages of time and corrosion can make the wing/fender stripdown on pre-impact bumper cars as difficult as if they were welded on.

Removing the front wings/fenders will be necessary in order to properly inspect the inner panels and wing/fender flange supports (in front of the door supports). With the front wings/fenders removed it is also easier to work on the front of the car.

FWR2. Make a note of the electrical connections in the front wheel arch areas, especially those to the horns and auxiliary lighting.

FWR3. The electrical harness should be unplugged from the connection in the inner wing/fender and detached from the car (as a unit with each light box, if pre-impact bumper). Be careful not to damage the plastic fittings of the light boxes (and horn grilles if appropriate) when removing them from heavily corroded panels. Drill the screws out if necessary.

FWR1. If the intention is to ► replace the front wings/fenders as part of the restoration then the headlamps, light boxes, horn grilles (as fitted to pre '74 models) and other trim should be removed before removing them.

FWR4. The wing/fender removal task can be described as straightforward: unscrew the attachment bolts along the inner wing/fender (reached from the luggage compartment), the wing/fender support flange (accessible from the wheel arch) and the windshield pillar (accessible with the doors open). Paul Rosenthal, partner at Autoprep of Worcester demonstrates.

FWR5. In practice, the front bolts near the front dividing wall and bumper tend to corrode heavily on earlier models. A similar situation occurs with the wing/fender support flange mountings, even if the wing/fender is still sound.

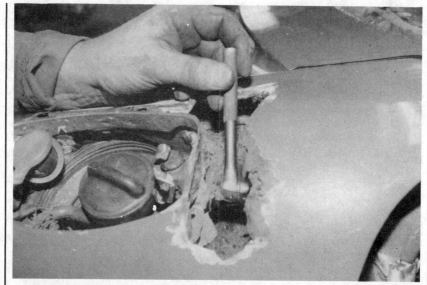

FWR6. Access to the innermost bolt on the windshield pillar is difficult and is best done with a 0.25 inch square drive socket, fitted with a universal joint. It is only necessary to back this bolt out a few turns as the wing/fender is slotted for easier (!) removal here.

FWR8. On the left-hand wing/fender, from inside the wheel arch, pull off the rubber gaiter around the fuel filler cap housing. (Viewed from beneath wing/fender.)

FWR10. The washer bottle assembly can be removed from the wing/fender afterwards.

FWR7. Unscrew the attachment bolts between each wing/fender and the bumper (located beneath the headlamp bowls), if these have not already been removed. The right-hand wing/fender may now be detached.

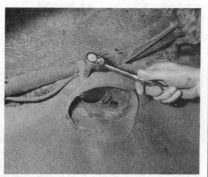

FWR9. Again, from beneath, unscrew the washer bottle filler tube from its inner wing/fender mountings.

FWR11. Disconnect the cable that opens the filler flap ...

FWR12.   ... and at the same time disconnect the overflow tube and earth tag, (if fitted), from the fuel filler neck.

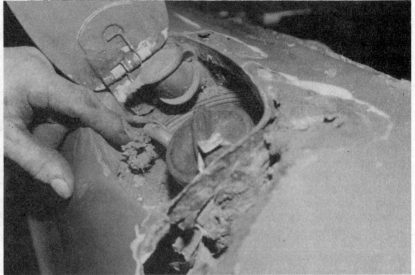

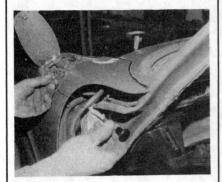

FWR13.   Withdraw the flap operating cable from inside the car.

FWR14.   The left wing/fender may now be removed.   ►

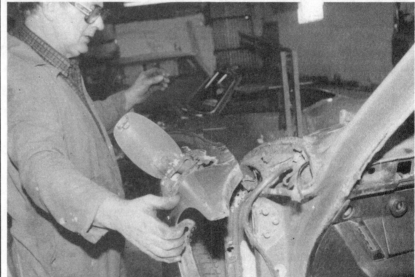

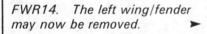

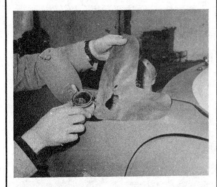

FWR15.   Don't forget the sealing sheet around the filler neck.

FWR16.   If the filler pipe is difficult to remove from the wing/fender, disconnect it at the tank end, remembering to seal off all tank openings for safety's sake ...

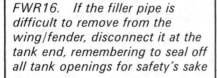

FWR17. ... and manoeuvre the pipe through the inner panel as the wing/fender is removed.

(This section was photographed at Classic Car Restoration and Autoprep, both near Worcester, England).

Door stripdown and removal

To remove the doors a special tool (P290) is used by main dealers to drive out the hinge pins. Everyone else removes the screws, as shown! Handling of the door is made easier if the trim, window lifting mechanism and glass are taken out before the door is removed from the car. It should be realised that fitting a new door involves resetting the door gaps. The dimensions for the gap gauge is given here (fig 3.2). The enthusiast is advised to avoid removing the doors, if at all possible, since refitting and achieving an even door gap is a difficult task.

The door trim assembly was simplified for the 1974 model year. Prior to that removing the trim was a fiddly business, involving elastic cords etc., but should not present any real difficulty to the enthusiast. The post '74 procedure is given here first, followed by step-by-step notes and captions on the pre '74 arrangement.

Procedure for removing post '74 door trim.

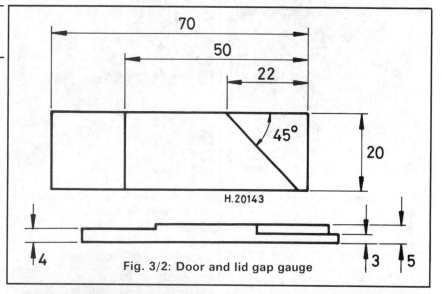

Fig. 3/2: Door and lid gap gauge

H.20143

DR1. Remove the internal door lock button, by unscrewing it.

DR2. Unscrew the screws retaining the top trim panel at its front.

DR3. Remove those at its rear ...

DR6. ... and underside ...

DR9. Unscrew the socket-head bolts holding the door pull in place top and bottom, and remove the door pull.

DR4. ... and remove the trim panel.

DR7. ... and where it attaches to the armrest. Remove the compartment.

DR10. Remove the screws attaching the hingeing compartment lid to the door frame.

DR5. Remove the six sheet metal screws from the main storage compartment at its ends ...

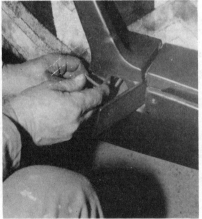

DR8. Detach the latch connecting rod from the handle.

DR11. Remove the remaining trim panel retaining screw ...

DR12.   ... and carefully remove
the door trim panel. Detach door
trim panel carefully from door
shell, taking care not to break the
plastic fasteners. Carefully peel
back the plastic protection sheet
and remove.

Procedure for removing pre '74 door trim

Unscrew the top trim strip and remove the door lock button, if this is located in the trim strip. If appropriate, remove the plastic cover from the hand window winder and unscrew the handle.

Unclip the lower rear storage box from its spring clip and disconnects the elastic cord retainer. The box should now open right out.

Remove the screws retaining the base of the storage box and remove the box.

Pull away the plastic sheeting from the door frame and find the retaining nut for the front storage box, from inside the door structure. Remove the front attachment screw of this box and let the box hinge out.

Remove the screws retaining the base of the forward box and the box will come away.

Using a socket type key unscrew the three retaining screws for the arm rest. Unclip the door handle location peg behind the arm rest before withdrawing it. If the arm rest has a door pull, this will need unscrewing from its location just below the window.

Separate the door panel from the door frame by carefully prising off the plastic clips around the edge of the panel. Remove the plastic sheet.

Pull off the exterior window seal on the top of the door and the sealing strip along the top of the inside of the door.

Unscrew the socket-head screws that locate the window frame.

Lift the window frame upwards and out of the door, leaving the glass still in place.

Coupes only: push the glass forwards and feel for when the two rollers on the base of the window glass frame find the clearance holes in the lift runners. The glass can now be lifted out of the lifting mechanism and free of the door.

Targas only: detach the

window lift retaining screws and then proceed as wth Coupe glass removal.

To remove the outside door handle, find the two nuts from inside the door frame with a small (0.25 inch drive) socket.

Unscrew the door lock mechanism, disconnecting the remote operation of the interior opening handle and lock. Lift out the lock mechanism.

DSR1.   Unscrew the
connections for the electric
window lift at the connector
panel in the door, noting the
positions of the various wires.

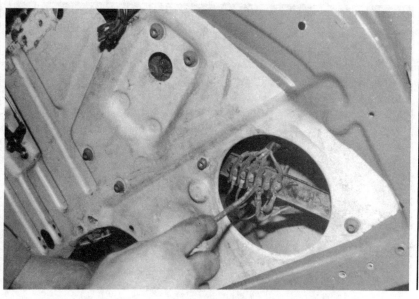

DSR2. *Unclip the connections to the electric window switches, if appropriate, noting the position of each lead on the numbered tags of the switches. Remove the switches. Unscrew the retaining screws for the window lift mechanism and lift it out through the larger aperture in the door interior side. Unscrew the exterior mirror mounting screws.*

Depending on model type, location of the door mirror varies. Disconnect the electrical connections on electrically-operated mirrors.

DSR3. *Remove the door stay clevis pin retaining clip and tap the clevis pin up and out.*

DSR4. *After pulling the door stay clear, replace the pin and clip for safe keeping.*

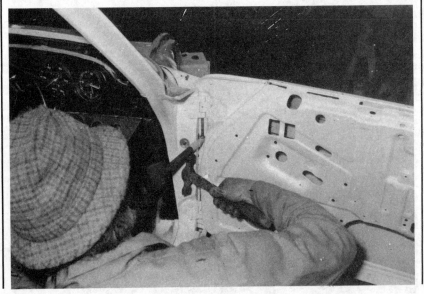

DSR5. *Drive out the hinge pins with the special tool P290, or with a suitable drift using a 1 Kg hammer.*

DSR6. If the latter method is used, ensure that the pin is drawn out of the hinge by blows evenly placed around the circumference of the pin head.

DSR7. The door may now be removed, taking care not to damage the wiring harness.

DSR8. Bear in mind that it may be far simpler to remove the hex-Allen bolts and take the hinges off the hinge pillar complete.

Renovation of doors

Before assembling the the various components into the door, the door gaps with the surrounding body should be checked. If the hinge pins have been driven out to remove the old door and a new door is being fitted, the hinge brackets may need adjustment. If the old door is refitted, the gaps may not change, but it is worth checking them.

RD1. It is not considered necessary to dwell on the

renovation of the doors, since patching will be extensively covered in the sections on general renovation to the front end of the car. Major corrosion areas will be found next to the top exterior trim strip, the base of the door and the lock panel. When letting in a patch to the door outer skin, consider the final appearance. Recess the weld line and fill the area afterwards. The vertical door sides are not the places to learn the art of body leading, either! Consider also that it may be more sensible to acquire a good used door shell from one of the specialists or to have a genuinely skilled welder

patch the door for you: the welding of flat surfaces such as these is extremely difficult to carry out without causing severe distortion.

Reassembly should be the reverse of the stripdown procedure, after checking the gaps. The door internal components, including the window lifts and motors (if appropriate), should also be inspected for correct function.

Door gap adjustment

If the old door is being refitted by replacing the hinge pin (i.e. if the screws have not been removed, holding the hinges in place), check gaps without adjusting the positions of the hinges. If the gap is incorrect, further adjustment will be necessary as described below.
    Screw the door shell onto the hinges, but only finger tighten.
    Set door height and gap. Aim to line up the outside surface of the door with the sill/body rocker surface. Use the palm of the hand to make small changes

in position inwards or outwards. When satisfied pinch up the hinge bracket bolts. The door gap should be 3-4 mm all round. The gap at the windshield pillar should be no more than 4 mm.

Adjustment in the forward direction can be made using a hardwood drift against the hinges. To move the door backwards, place equal thickness packing pieces behind the hinges. It is important the packing pieces are of equal thickness, so that the door hangs squarely in the aperture. If the door is out of square with the aperture, careful adjustment with the hardwood drift will be required.

Adjust the door catch striker plate (on the rear of the door aperture), to the set position of the door. A packing piece may be necessary to bring the striker plate to the correct position.

Fig 3.2. This sketch shows a simple gap gauge that can be used when checking door position.

Renovation of door components

If electric lifts are used, check the operation of the motors by removing them from the frame and running on a battery or battery charger in both directions.

If the motor does not run, open the casing and inspect the bearings at each end of the armature for corrosion. The sintered metal bearings can dry out and the armature corrode. Clean up the corrosion and reassemble with general purpose grease in the bearings.

Whilst the armature is out, clean up the commutator using a pin and methylated spirit to scrape between the segments. Check there are no shorts between the poles. Check also the brushes for wear and contact spring force. If there are any problems with the motors, a replacement will be necessary.

Before fitting the glass, fit the external weatherstrip to the outer side of the window aperture.

When refitting the window glass, lower the lifting mechanism to half travel. It is easier to fit the rollers onto the raiser bar at this position.

When the window frame has been refitted, pack body sealer strip around the edges of the door window aperture to prevent water getting into the door shell.

Part 2: Restoration of front section

This section covers repairs or replacement of the front cross-member, front tank support, patching the front inner wings/fenders and other front section renovation.

Tool Box

Sharp, thin bladed chisel; air chisel or similar mini grinder; goggles; electric drill and bits; tinsnips; variety of welder's clamps; MIG or oxy-acetylene welding equipment, (but see notes on zinc coated metal which follow); 2 or 3 "mole" type welding or "G" clamps; butane lamp to remove old leading; approx. 2-pound engineer's hammer; basic spanners, sockets, screwdrivers, etc; releasing fluid; zinc or zinc rich primers (but ensure that any primers you use are compatible with any finish paint you may use later).

Welding zinc coated metal

From 1970, the vehicle undercarriage was made from galvanised steel and for the 1976 model year, the entire vehicle was protected in this way. When welding zinc coated panels, the

Safety

**Beware of sparks from the grinder and hot metal when cutting away. Wear goggles and thick industrial type gloves. Ensure that the car is securely raised off the ground in such a way that:
a) it cannot topple onto anyone underneath it, bearing in mind the amount of force that will be applied to it and
b) it will not twist or distort as old panels are cut out.**

NEVER rely on the handbrake to hold a car that is on a slope or on ramps. Ensure that the wheels are chocked when using jacks or ramps. Use axle stands when working under the car, NOT the jack.

Take all the usual precautions when welding. See the appendix at the end of this book and contact your supplier for specific safety information. You should seek training in welding skills before tackling oxy-acetylene welding. Follow the maker's safety instructions carefully before carrying out electric arc welding of any kind. Wear goggles when working beneath the car. Remember that all Porsches are high performance vehicles and that sub-standard workmanship can be dangerous. NEVER attempt work for which you are not qualified. Have a qualified specialist check over each stage of your work before you proceed. If in any doubt whatsoever, have important work such as panel and component alignment and welding carried out for you by a qualified specialist.

factory recommends using either a spot welder or an inert gas arc welder (for instance, MIG) on clean, grease-free surfaces. These joining methods melt away the zinc layers and the mild steel forms a weld in an area of intense heat. The inert gas will blow away the zinc oxide formed in the arc, if the equipment is used correctly.

These methods are preferable to gas welding, which spreads heat over a wide area. Gas welding can also destroy a large area of the zinc coating and distort the panels being welded.

After completing a section of welding, the weld area should be wire brushed and treated with a rust inhibitor, such as Jenolite, prior to priming with a zinc based paint.

MIG (Metal Inert Gas) welding is therefore a factory approved welding method. The enthusiast will find that after a little practice, satisfactory welds can be made with the equipment mentioned at the start of this chapter, using carbon dioxide as the inert gas, although argon carbon dioxide mixed will give a much smoother looking weld with less "spatter". It will be assumed from now on that the welding kit available is a MIG system and that a spot welder is

not available. However, one could be hired for the few occasions when its use would be preferred.

Always clean as much as possible of the area to be welded, prior to starting. Ensure that the current is set correctly. This comes at first by experiment and later, by experience. The maker's instructions will give enough information to start the novice welder off. The mating pieces should also be approximately the same thickness.

PVC undercoating

The curse of the pre-galvanised 1970s 911! From 1970, all 911 models were PVC undercoated. Before any renovation work is started on the underside of a 911 which has this coating, it should be given a close inspection.

PVC1. Look for cracks, chips, etc., expecially around seams. Check also for areas where the PVC has come away from the base metal and so formed an air pocket. This shot shows the rear torsion bar tube where it joins the inner wing. Cut away damaged areas or loose sections.

If the PVC is cracked around weld seams in the undertray, it will almost certainly have led to seam corrosion. The rotted metal should be cut out and all surface rust probed, wire brushed and treated prior to priming. Repairs to the undercoating should be made with a proprietary PVC undercoating, for instance Wurth Body Seal or Stoneguard compounds. Mask off water drains and suspension prior to re-covering with body sealer.

If undertaking a full scale renovation, you might find a bead blaster (using fine grit) useful although you must first strip away the PVC undercoating manually. Care is required not to completely blast away base metal where it may have been weakened by corrosion. Don't grit or bead-blast in an area where mechanical components remain in place, since the spent grit is very penetrative and highly abrasive. Bead blasters are available from better equipped tool hire shops.

Replacement of front cross-member and tank support

The work in this section was carried out by bodywork specialist Dave Felton in Staffordshire, England.

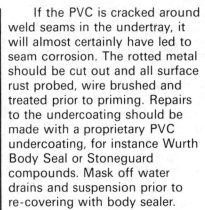

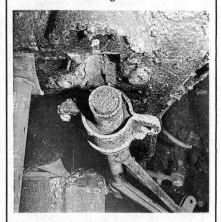

FCM1. The initial inspection may have revealed heavy corrosion in the front

cross-member. This usually is initiated by stress cracking of the underseal in the vicinity of the torsion bar front mountings. It can also be as the result of an excursion over a kerb or gate centre post stripping away the underseal on the lower area of the cross-member.

FCM2.   It is also quite possible that only the front tank support needs replacing (shown here ➤ about to be removed). This can become corroded due to acid spillage from the battery(s). The first task is to strip out the battery(s), wash bottle and wiring, together with the petrol tank, from the front luggage compartment. (See earlier sections.)

The working area should be clear of unnecessary fittings. It will also be necessary to unbolt the front torsion bar mountings from where they attach to the cross-member.

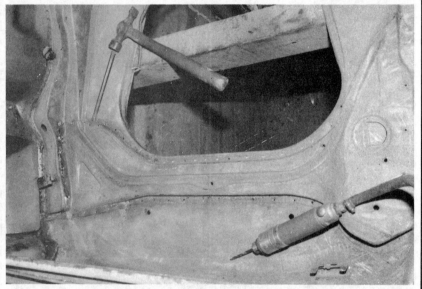

FCM3.   In order to expose the ➤ top area of the cross-member, it is necessary to remove the front tank support. This should be stripped of its body sealer in the vicinity of the spot welds, carefully using a blowlamp and a scraper. Following this, drill out the spot welds – just the top half, if possible. A chisel can be used to ease off the old panel. Refer to the bodywork introduction section for notes regarding welding onto zinc coated metal, if this is appropriate to your car.

FCM4.   With the tank support removed, the full extent of the work required on the cross-member can be seen.

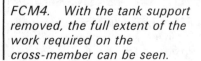

FCM5. Close examination of this 911 shows that new front bar mountings are required. A complete cross-member replacement is not necessary. Mark the area to be cut out.

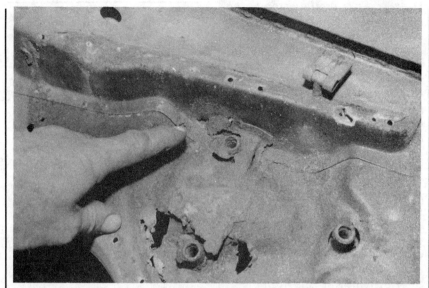

FCM6. Cut out the corroded area using an air chisel, mini-grinder or electric drill and hacksaw. Be sure to cut so that the new panel can be easily fitted and that no corroded metal remains.

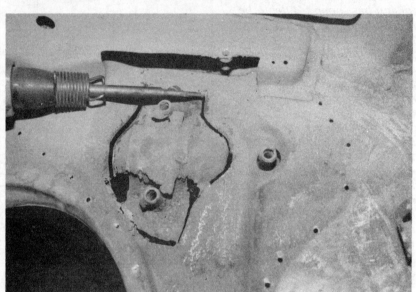

FCM7. Dave Felton made his own repair patch but you could cut the necessary section from a new item. It may be possible to obtain a used panel from a specialist such as that shown here, but ensure that it is rust and damage free.

FCM8. Offer up the patch to the trimmed structure. It will be absolutely essential to ensure correct positioning of the front bar mountings. The front suspension can be used for this. **It is essential that a recognised specialist carries out this part of the work so as to ensure perfect suspension alignment when the job is complete.**

In the absence of a chassis jig, the procedure is to patch one side at a time. Use the holes of the remaining mounting to determine the position of the new mounting. The dimensions required are given in Fig. 2/3. Start by removing one front torsion bar support. Attach the free mounting to the patch and tack weld into place when positioned correctly for height and spacing as measured from the other mounting. Use the reference measurements given in the illustration.

If the complete cross-member is being replaced, both torsion bars should be detached from the cross-member, to allow the latter to be cut away. The new cross-member should be clamped in place and the bars bolted back in position. This will give the approximately correct location, which can be checked against the dimensions given.

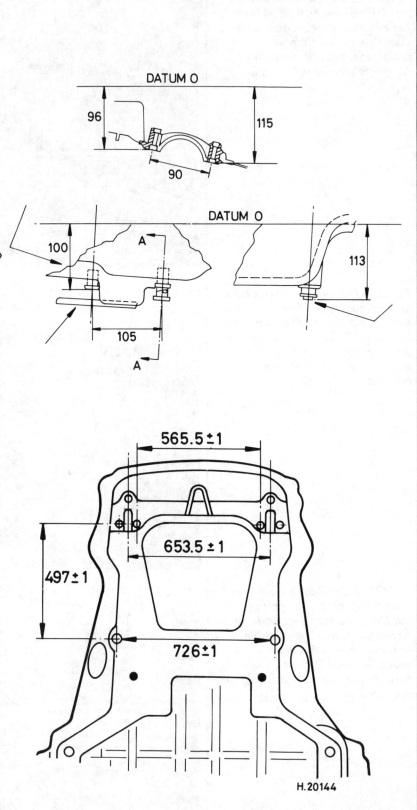

Fig. 3/3: Views of front undertray area, showing torsion bar front mountings

FCM9. When satisfied with the location of the patch or cross-member in all planes, it should be tacked firmly in place. Tap down the rim of the remaining unwelded areas and re-check the critical dimensions. Complete the welding operation. The accuracy obtained with this method is dependent on careful checking of location, which takes time and patience. It is a job which the specialist does quickly and accurately on a chassis jig.

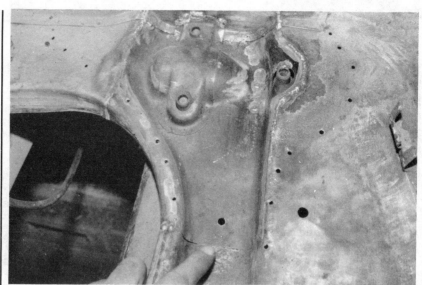

FCM10. Note here that to complete the structure a small extra piece of metal has been shaped and tacked in by Dave Felton, to fill a gap between the cross-member patch and the main structure. The original metal was heavily corroded, but was not part of the cross-member. After work with the tinsnips, the small replacement patch was welded into place after the cross-member was positioned satisfactorily. Remove the setting jig if one was used and attach the torsion bars to the mountings and check their positions again, just to be sure. Clean up the interior of the cross-member and treat it with a rust inhibitor and when clean, give it a coat of zinc based paint.

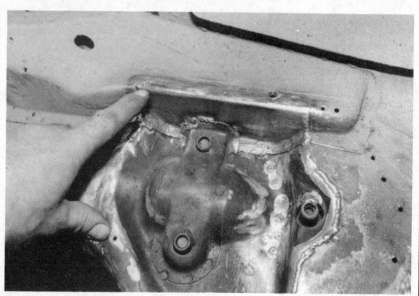

FCM11A. The interior of the replacement tank support panel should also be painted with zinc primer at this stage, prior to offering it to the structure.

FCM11B. The panel should be clamped in position as shown. Its position will be governed by the position of the existing structure.

FCM13. Weld the tank support in position then sand the welds off smooth with the angle grinder.

FCM14. The towing eye will have to be replaced if the eye mounting was corroded and the area has had to be patched. This bracket was recovered from a used cross-member. ▼

FCM12. Tap down the edges of the tank support, so that it forms a weldable seam with the adjacent metal, especially in the areas around the front corners. Note that the seams have been pre-drilled for MIG welding through the panel beneath. ▲

FCM15. Note the guide slots in the cross-member, to assist positioning. If this area of the cross-member has been patched, use the torsion bar mountings to find the centre position for the bracket.

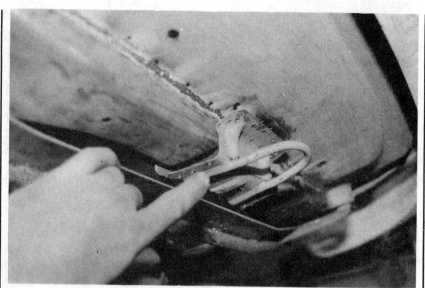

FCM16. The finished ▲ metalwork: the left torsion bar mounting and the towing eye have been replaced and a new tank support positioned on top. The external metal should now be wire brushed, rust inhibited and zinc primed.

FCM17. A complete 'floorpan' area is available for the luggage bay area. You could use it for (expensive!) repair patches or better still, have it fitted by ► specialists. (Courtesy, Autofarm.)

Removing the front compartment cover

FLM1. The cover is removed by unscrewing four mounting bolts at the hinges. Before removing the cover unclip the connection to the front compartment light at the lower end of the lead (out of sight in this picture). The cover is quite heavy and awkward to lift without help. Protect the paintwork ahead of the windshield during cover removal, with a blanket or equivalent.

FLM2. The gas struts on older cars commonly lose their ability to support the weight of the cover. They can be removed with the cover in place or as here, afterwards. Pull the spring clip from the dowel pins and then pull the dowel pin out from the hinge bracket. The strut can now be separated from the hinge. Repeat the removal of the dowel pin at the other end of the strut and the strut can be lifted out. If the struts are removed with the cover in place, open the cover fully and support its weight to remove the load from the struts. After the struts are removed, the cover should be closed to prevent accidental damage.

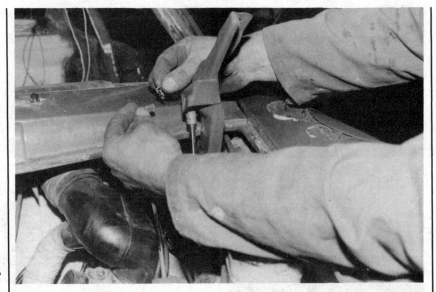

Front dividing wall and battery boxes

FP1. Typical corrosion to the front dividing wall on an H series 911 (August '74 – July '75). The rim carrying the sealing strip can be removed by drilling the spot welds or chiselling off. The rim can be replaced by fabricating a new section or using a replacement part.

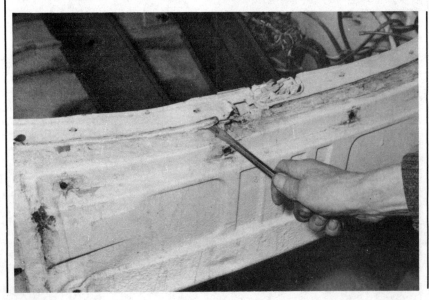

FP2. More serious long-term corrosion on an early model. This is a job for the specialist or the experienced and qualified enthusiast only. The front dividing wall needs replacement.

FP3. The replacement panel gives a guide to the cutting work which needs to be performed. Mark reference positions on the sound inner wing/fender areas adjacent to the dividing wall, to accurately position the new panel.

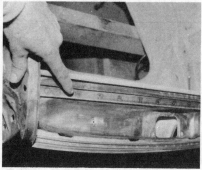

FP4. When the front wall is tacked in place, the inner wing/fender front flanges should be tacked on. Before fully welding the replacement sections check the fit of the front outer wings/fenders and alignment of the mounting holes..

FP5. It may not be necessary to go as far as replacing the whole front dividing wall. Replacement sections are available for the luggage bay lid sealing strip guide, front wing/fender flanges and ...

FP6. ... front bumper sealing rim. Note the drain slots that should be kept clear of debris.

FP7. Battery boxes are subjected not only to wheel spray, but accidental acid spillage. It is quite unusual to find an older 911 with good battery boxes!

FP8. Cut away the rusted metal
and make up patches to fill in.
Since the boxes are out of sight,
appearance does not matter as
much as achieving a good weld
on the thicker section metal. The
boxes are thus good places to
polish up welding skills at the
start of a big job.

FP9. Where new top sections
butt against the inner
wings/fenders, sealer should be
used to prevent moisture getting
at the seam.

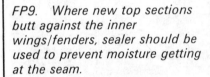

As noted earlier, the welded
areas should be wire brushed,
treated with rust inhibitor and
then zinc primed. Do not leave
areas untreated after completing
the welding.

Heater ventilating case and wiper motor removal

The heater ventilating case and
windshield wiper motor assembly
are located in the rear section of
the front luggage compartment.

H1. Remove the four screws
which locate the cover over the
heater/ventilation assembly.

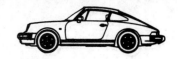

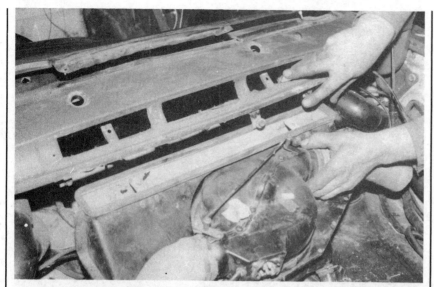

H2.   Remove the large hose clips that hold the ducts to the ventilator body. Remove the brace which connects the panel under the windshield to the floor of the front compartment. Ease the ventilator assembly out, taking care to unclip the drain hose at the base of the unit and not to kink the operating cables, if these are not to be disconnected. This shot shows the drain pipe at the lower right of the unit.

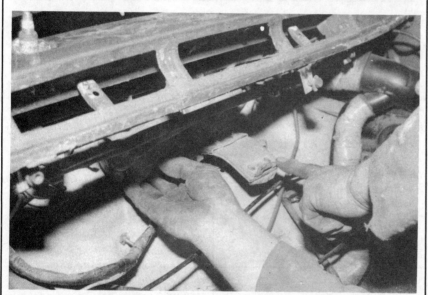

H3.   The wiper motor and linkage should be removed as one. Firstly, remove the nuts which hold the wiper blades to the spindles on the panel beneath the windshield. Take off the wiper blades.

Lift off the plastic protectors and unscrew the nuts which locate the spindles to the panel under the windshield. Before removing the wiper motor assembly, make a note of the connections to it (or tag the leads with masking tape and mark the connection position). Pull off the five leads from the motor and remove the motor from its mounting.

H4.   The wiper motor assembly will now pull out from within the luggage compartment.

H5. The ventilation grille should be removed prior to painting or for cleaning, by taking out the four self-tapping screws.

Washer components

H6. This shot shows removal of the headlamp washer pipework after the front skirt and bumper have been removed.

H7. A view of the washer bottle after the left front wing has been removed. With the wing in place, the left front wheel should be taken off to give access to the bottle.

    This shot shows the clamping strap tie bolt fitted in such a way as to make it difficult to loosen with the wing/fender in position. A better position for the tie bolt is at the base of the bottle.

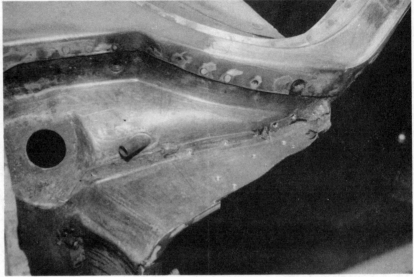

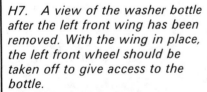

Renovation of door pillars

DP1. The tops of the door ▲ pillars are prone to rust, generally after the wing/fender support flanges have corroded through. The door pillars and sills/body rockers are then exposed to the spray from the front wheels.

DP2. Proximity to the heater ducting at the bottoms of the doors can result in heavy corrosion there also on pre-galvanised 911 models. This shot suggests that the sills/body rockers will also have to be replaced. ◄

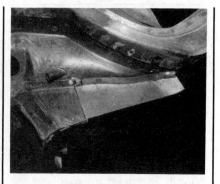

DP3.   The top guttering can be fabricated from an off-cut of mild steel 1 mm thick and formed to the final shape. It is important to cut away all the rusted metal prior to fitting the new patch, as Dave Felton has done here.

DP4.   The new section is clamped prior to tacking in place.

DP5.   When tacked, a small hammer can be used to form the new section to the mating area. Notice that the patch overlaps the old metal to permit water to run off.

DP6.   When satisfied with the shape the welding is then completed.

DP7.   Complete pillars are available for specialist fitting. Correct alignment is essential and is beyond the scope of the DIY-er.

A similar patching procedure can be used for the lower areas, after the new sill/body rocker panels have been tacked in place. Replacement of the sills/body rockers is dealt with in a subsequent section.

Renovation of front inner wings/fenders

Whilst it is considered beyond the scope of the average enthusiast to replace the front inner wings/fenders, renovation of the old ones is feasible, if the strut supports and outer wing/fender mountings are sound. The need for specialist help also applies to the wing/fender support flanges.

FIW1. The simplest way of patching elegantly is to acquire a new (or good used) replacement panel. This especially applies if the area contains complex curves or brackets (as with the inner wings/fenders).

For simpler patches, it will be cheaper to make up sections from flat mild steel sheet. This can be purchased in small quantities from a light engineering stockholder or a small jobbing workshop. Thicknesses should go from 1 mm for a non-structural part, to 2.5 mm for stressed sections. Only weld together pieces of metal of approximately equal thickness. If the current or heat is measured to produce a good weld on the lighter material, the join to the thicker gauge will be weak. Similarly, if the current or heat is measured to the thick section, holes will be blown in the lighter metal.

In order to patch repair this area first cut away the corroded metal and clear away the PVC underbody protection from at least 100 mm all round the work area.

Cut a patch to cover the hole, with an overlap of about 25 mm. Roughly form the patch to the surface shape of the area to be covered.

Tack the new patch in place.

Smooth the patch down to the surface of the base metal using a panel beater's hammer.

When satisfied, complete the welding. Treat the exposed metal after welding, as mentioned earlier.

Rebuilding the front body area

Before commencing the front end rebuild, go around all the exposed structure and clean out any traces of seam or surface rust. Look again for signs of cracked or lifted PVC seal. Chip this away and treat all exposed surfaces with rust proofer. When happy with this stage, touch up all the bare metal with a zinc primer. If the car is being prepared for Concours competition, it will be necessary to spend much time during the rebuild cleaning each part before assembly, as well as bead blasting the underside.

Where blasting is not used, it is assumed a hose pipe or, better still, a pressure washer will have been used to clean off the majority of debris, before the strip-down began in earnest. At this stage, with the car on stands in the workshop, a bristle scrubbing brush with hot soapy water will remove remaining dirt.

The repaired areas of the underbody should be re-covered with a body sealing compound rather than a bitumastic sealer, since the former can easily be painted over when cured.

Refitting the major components is largely a reverse of the stripdown procedure. All the components should be inspected and repaired/replaced as necessary, before refitting. Front wing/fender refitting is covered in detail here.

Fitting the front wings/fenders

Fitting of the front wings/fenders is not difficult. It is time consuming because it is important to get the panel positioned in the right place. This also means checking the gaps between the adjacent doors. The front wings/fenders should not be fitted before painting, if this is required, although the underside and concealed flanges should be painted first. The work here was carried out largely by Dave Felton.

FW1. When satisfied with the paintwork, the inner wing/fender cavities should be sprayed with a rust preventive fluid (see Supplier's section). Access at this stage is easy through the fuel

filler opening. Coating the exposed areas behind the filler neck, on the inner wing/fender and wing/fender support flange is also easier to do now than when the whole wing/fender assembly is in place.

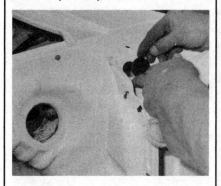

FW2. Plug in the door electrical harnesses, if these have been removed during the renovation (for instance to protect them from overspray if the doors were not removed). Reposition drainage tubes to the wing/fender support flanges, if these are fitted and replace grommets.

FW4. Position the deformation tubes with the clamps as shown.

FW5. Use a thread tap to clear any new paint or other blockage from the tapped holes in the inner wings/fenders.

Corrosion protection confidence can be improved by squirting corrosion inhibitor into the cavity below the windshield.
Note that where the wing/fender attaches here, adjacent to the windshield base, the mounting point on the wing/fender is slotted. This is to facilitate fitting. Hand turn the

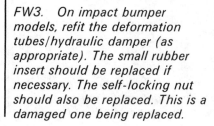

FW3. On impact bumper models, refit the deformation tubes/hydraulic damper (as appropriate). The small rubber insert should be replaced if necessary. The self-locking nut should also be replaced. This is a damaged one being replaced.

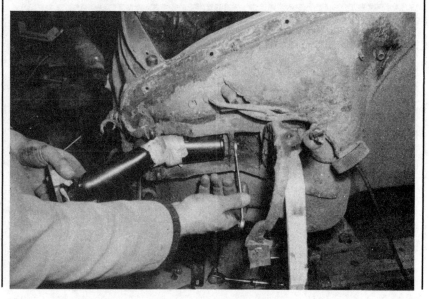

bolts at these two points before mounting the wing/fender. The wing/fender is then hung on the bolts and they will only need tightening. Fitting these bolts after the wing/fender is in position could be described politely as fiddly.

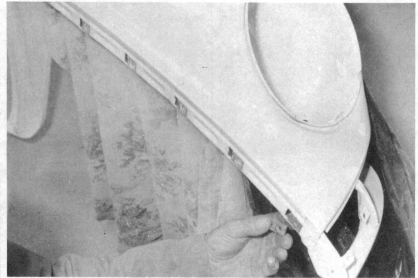

FW6.   Ensure that all the attachment clips are in place on the wings/fenders, before offering the wing/fender to the structure.   ▶

FW7.   De-grease those parts of the body structure where the wing/fender will touch so that you can ...

FW8.   ... apply body sealer strip along the mating surfaces of the wing/fender structure.

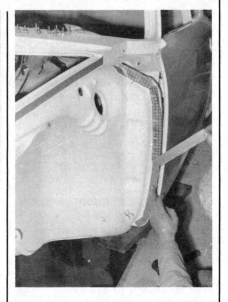

FW9.   Dave Felton, in this shot, ▲ *applies the tape to the wing/fender support flanges also.*

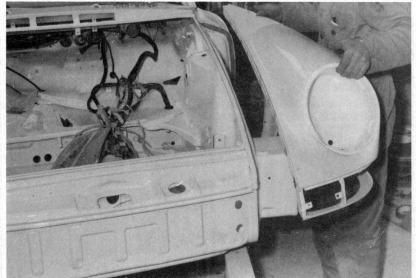

FW10.   Offer up the wing/fender to the structure, taking care not to chip any paint whilst handling.

FW11. Locate the wing/fender over the previously fitted windshield base bolts and push it into alignment with the remaining mounting holes. On early models, the dowel pins fitted to the inner wing/fender panels will help this process.

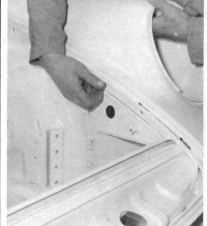

FW12. Hand fit all the mounting bolts, tightening to the extent that the wing/fender can just be moved about.

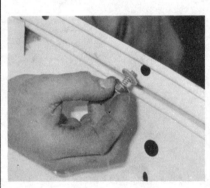

FW13. Each bolt (or hex-headed spiral screw) should be fitted first with a plain washer and a fibre washer. Purchase the correct bits from your specialist supplier.

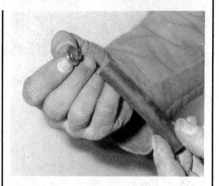

FW14. Insert hard-to-reach bolts by adding a piece of rubber tube over the end to reach in and start off.

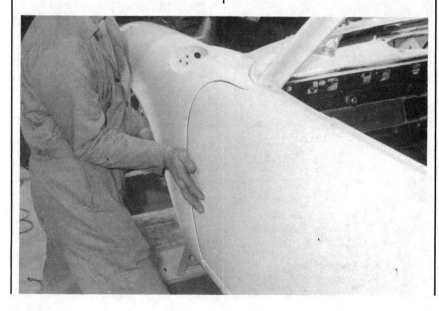

FW15. Align the wing/fender so that the door gap is a uniform 4 mm and the panel heights are to within 1 mm in the area of the windshield.

FW16.   Position a new trim strip between the wing/fender windshield base. This is also a good point to refit the plastic pipe that carries the fuel flap cable. Again, this next job is best described as fiddly: the tube should be pushed onto the wing/fender flange and then manipulated back on to the outlet in the body.

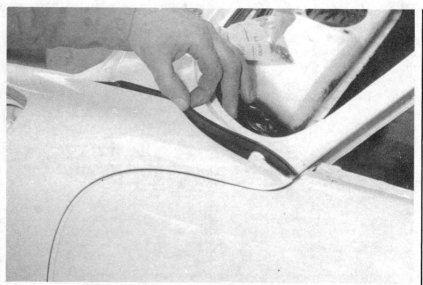

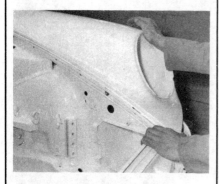

FW17.   Push the whole panel back tight onto the trim strip.

FW18.   Tighten the mounting bolts, using a mini-socket set (0.25 inch drive) with a universal fitting to get in at the ones at the base of the windshield. It's worth checking the door gaps again to ensure correct positioning after several (well distanced apart) location bolts have been tightened. The remainder can then be fitted. ▼

FW19.   Locate the rubber gaiter between the inner wing/fender fuel filler opening and the outer wing/fender. It is retained in the outer wing/fender by a wire clip.

FW20.   Feed in the fuel filler neck from outside the wing/fender. When positioned correctly connect the earth lead from the neck to the outer wing/fender.

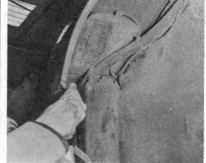

FW21.   Re-attach electrical or ▲ other lines fitted within the wheel arch. Since there are so many variations of plumbing in this area, no specific procedure is relevant to all models. Ensure all pipework and leads are clipped clear of moving parts, using the

brackets provided or plastic hose clips as appropriate. Do not use tape: it will peel off and in any case looks tatty anyway.

FW22.   Refit the bolts that support the wing/fender through the headlamp bowl to the inner wing/fender. Refit the drainage grommet and pull through the electrical connections to the headlamps, ensuring a good fit of the cable grommet in the headlamp bowl. Use a blank grommet to seal any other machined holes in the bowl. Spray the inner bowl area with waxed oil. This is a shot of an old wing for illustration purposes.

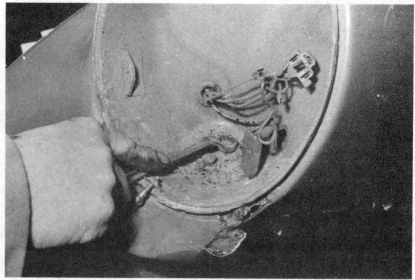

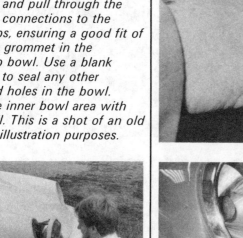

FW23.   Refit the headlamp assemblies, assuming these are clean and corrosion-free.

FW25.   Fasten in position with the single screw at the base of the trim. Be careful not to cross thread the screw or have the screwdriver slip off onto the paintwork. (In this shot the headlamps lens is not fitted.)

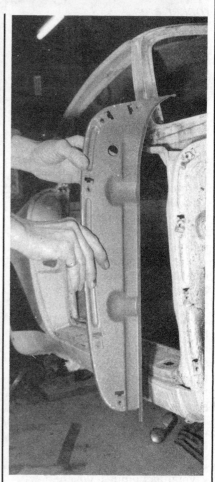

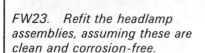

FW24.   Re-connect the electrical plugs at the rear.

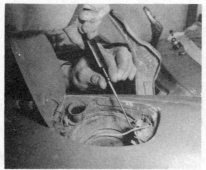

FW26.   Finally, push through the fuel flap opening cable from inside the car. This may need a degree of twisting to feed it around the connector tube and into the wing/fender. A little lubrication of the cable will help.

FW27.   New front wing/fender support flanges are available should the old ones have corroded.

FW28. Take great care to remove the old one in such a way that the new one sits sweetly on the inner wing surface. Tack weld it in place after meticulously measuring its position and only seam weld after the wing/fender has been fitted to ensure the correct positioning of the new panel.

Part 3: Restoration of sill/body rocker and rear sections

Inspection – sill/body rocker area

It is assumed that during the initial inspection the sills/body rockers have been noted as areas for further attention. If the work necessary on the front end has now been completed to satisfaction, then renovation of the sills/body rockers should be undertaken before fitting the front wings/fenders. If the front end has not been renovated, it is recommended that the front wings/fenders are removed prior to major work on the sills/body rockers.

It will also have become clear whether extensive work will be required on the rear inner and outer wings/fenders. If the rear wings/fenders are to be replaced, it will make things easier to remove these before starting the sill/body rocker work. To remove the rear wings/fenders the three-quarter side glass and rear screen should be removed first. These operations are covered in the Trim Chapter.

Replacement of the rear wings/fenders involves the use of several techniques, which demand skill and a high quality of work, such as metal forming and leading. Consider these paragraphs before starting to rip off the rear wings and assess whether it really is a job that would be better done by a specialist. This will be the case if you do not possess a high level of welding skills. You should also have considerable experience in body repair and weld-on panel alignment.

It is essential that the car is supported beneath the floorpan with baulks of timber running front-to-rear in such a way that the bodyshell cannot sag or twist when the old sills/body rockers are removed. Use the door as a template to aid sill/body rocker alignment. After tack-welding the sills/body rockers strongly in place, **HAVE THE CAR CHECKED BY A SPECIALIST WITH A BODY JIG** before fully welding the sill/body rockers onto the car. This is doubly important if the car is a Targa model.

The work shown here was carried out largely by Dave Felton in Staffordshire and at Classic Car Restoration, Worcestershire, England. (See 'Clubs and Specialists' section at the back of this book.)

RWS1. Rear wing/fender corrosion revealed. Before the paint was cleared away this area appeared sound, save for a few bubbles. The front corner of the rear wing/fender is a superb trap for road debris. Small stones or fatigue have probably cracked the PVC undercoating (if present), then moisture trapped in the debris has been able to attack the base metal.

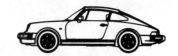

RWS2. The area behind the door latch support is very prone to corrosion on pre-galvansised models. If the outer wing/fender has bubbled through, then probe in here to assess the extent of the damage. ►

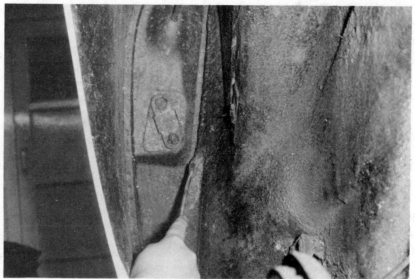

RSW3. Replacement rear ▲ sill/body rocker support offered to cleaned-up inner wing/fender.

RWS4. When the sill/body rocker support is in place, the outer sill/body rocker can be mated to it and checked for position. ►

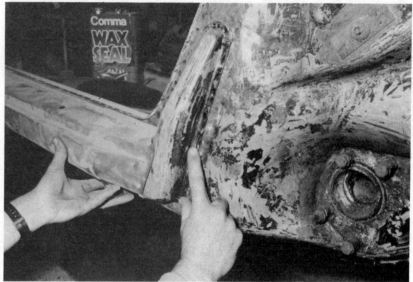

RWS5. This picture shows a ▲ replacement door support/'B' post, which could be used as a complete piece where corrosion is heavy, or trimmed and used to repair a corroded section adjacent to a sill/body rocker.

RWS6. This area can be patched after replacement of the sill/body rocker. It is assumed here that the door hinge supports are basically sound. It is suggested that replacement of the door support panels should not be attempted by the enthusiast, since the positioning is critical for door gaps. It is not necessary to remove the doors to replace the sills/body rockers, although access is improved if the doors are off. ◄

So, having shown the extent of a work that may be required, it will now be covered in more detail. Firstly the rear wings/fenders must be removed.

Removal and refitting of engine cover components

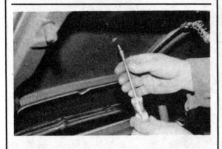

EL1.   If a "tea tray" type spoiler is fitted, this can be taken off by removing the screw in the engine cover . . .

EL2. . . . don't forget the one in the centre rib of the cover. Note the prop to support the cover, if the strut has been already removed.

EL3.   When all the screws are removed the spoiler can be lifted off.

EL4.   Remove the four mounting bolts at the hinges.

EL5.   Lift off the engine cover. The gas strut is removed in the same way as described in the front compartment cover section.

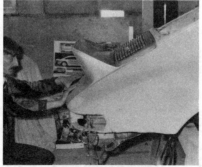

EL6.   When refitting the engine cover, here on a different 911, hand fit the mounting bolts and then carefully position the cover to obtain the correct gaps . . .

EL7. . . . and align the lower edge with the rear wings. When satisfactory, tighten the mounting bolts.

EL8.   Loosen the bolts mounting the latch and . . .

EL9. . . . position the latch so that it aligns with the catch plate. Tighten the bolts.

Removing the reflector plate

RRP1. This shot shows how, after removing the retaining nuts and washers from inside the luggage bay, the reflector plate comes off on impact bumper models. This could be where you discover your pride and joy has had a respray.

Rear wing/fender removal

The rear bumpers must be taken off first. In the case of pre-impact bumper 911 models, the rear centre valance must be removed before the quarters. Firstly, remove the plastic plugs covering the over-rider socket-head screws and then undo the screws. Remove the over-riders.

Undo the two lower screws attaching the centre valance to the quarters. Remove the valence.

RW1. For impact bumper models, the outrigger is attached to the edge of the quarter at the wheel arch. Undo this bolt and ...

The quarters are attached to the chassis at three points. The front attachment is to an outrigger tube from the chassis rail, with the two rear mountings bolted directly into the chassis member. The quarter will come away when these are removed.

RW2. ... then remove the sheet metal screws that attach the quarter to the outer wing/fender.

RW3. Remove the rubbing strip from each bumper.

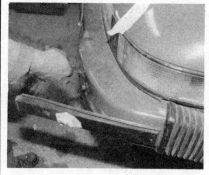

RW4. Undo the bolts supporting the deformation tube/hydraulic damper and lift away the bumper assembly.

RW5. Unplug rear lights cable from connectors.

RW6. Remove lens cover from rear light box.

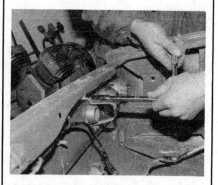

RW7. Undo screws attaching light box to rear wing/fender and pull assembly out.

RW8. Remove trim strips from around the wheel arches, if these are fitted. This also applies to the tread plate on the sill/body rocker. The pop rivets retaining these can be drilled out with a 3 mm bit. Pull off the door seal surround. Remove the side and rear windows as described in the Trim Chapter and unscrew the handle that opens the engine cover. Remove the cable from the car.

RW9. If the headlining is not to be replaced, carefully pull it away from the seams around the side and rear windows, safely bagging the clips for later re-assembly. Ensure that the loose headlining cannot be damaged during welding, etc., later on. Pull back any other trim, carpet, etc., that may be accidentally damaged during the work.

RW10. Chisel off or cut off with oxy-acetylene the rear wing/fender seam with the door lock pillar, to the top edge (adjacent with the side window). Use the chisel and blowlamp again to remove the leading around the sill/body rocker joint and break this joint. A nibbler or even an electric drill can be used to cut off the unwanted sections. Use the latter to make a series of pilot holes and then use tin snips or a hacksaw to cut from hole to hole.

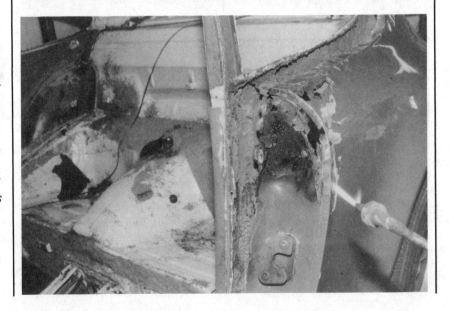

RW11. With the chisel break the spot welds around the side window seams. Similarly, remove the leading and break the joint along the engine cover recess.

RW12. Alternatively, cut a little away from the joint ...

RW13. ... and trim back later

RW14. With the rest of the outer wing/fender free, use tin snips to cut up to the guttering and then break the seam at the guttering. The wing/fender should now be free to lift away. Clean up any remaining ragged edges and with a blow lamp, remove any remaining leading from around the areas to be renovated. The inner wing/fender is now clear for inspection and renovation. This will be discussed after the removal of the sill/body rocker sections.

RW15. It may be that, as in this case, the door latch pillar will also have corroded badly and will have to be removed at the same time. If so, free the brazed-in guide tube end where it fits into the pillar.

Sill/bodyrocker replacement

SR1. Corrosion ahead of the sill itself is common on pre-galvanised models and can be patched separately, using scrap sections or a trimmed original panel.

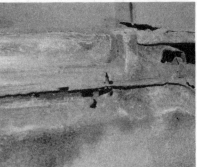

SR2. Further corrosion at the rear and in the adjacent floor pan, also requiring patching.

SR3. Full or half floorpans are available, but fitting one is a specialist task, needing a chassis jig.

SR4. Cut away the corroded metal here, at the rear of the sill/body rocker, to assess the extent of the repair. ◄

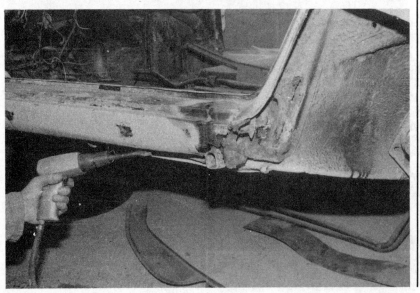

SR5. Drill through the spot welds and use an air chisel or tin snips to remove the outer sill/body rocker. (Wear heavy duty gloves!)

SR6. With the outer sill/body rocker removed assess the condition of the outer side member. Probe the metal surrounding the jacking point. This picture shows a new outer side member being offered to the old structure. This determines the amount of metal to be cut out. Note that rear outer sill/body rocker support and the jacking flange have been removed.

SR7. If the outer side member is in poor condition remove this also ...

SR8. ... to reveal the heater ducting. (Courtesy, Autofarm).

SR9. This shot shows the rearmost extent of cutting away and simple repairs to the base of the door pillar. (Courtesy, Autofarm).

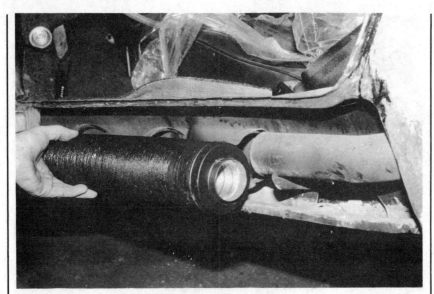

SR10. Fit a new ducting and silencer, ensuring that it cannot rattle. (Courtesy, Autofarm).

SR11. Ensure that the curvature and fit are good and that all surfaces to be welded have been sanded back to bright metal.

SR12. New jacking point supports are fitted after the inner panel but behind the outer sill/body rocker. The jacking tube itself is fitted with reference to the outer sill/body rocker.

SR13. The side member should ideally be spot welded to its mating inner member at the top edge, but careful MIG welds produce a satisfactory result, and they can be ground to a better finish if required. If the jacking point is to be replaced, drill out its spot welds and use these as the position indicator to locate the new item. Again, careful MIG welding can replace the spot weld. Wire brush, rust proof and then zinc prime the outer member at this point.

SR14. Cut off the corroded rear sill/body rocker support with reference to the new one.

SR15. Offer up the rear sill/body rocker support and determine its position by using the spot weld drillings from the previous item. If the inner wing/fender has been patched in this area, then clamp the new sill/body rocker in the correct position (see next paragraph), and tack the support to the inner wing/fender. When satisfied remove the outer sill/body rocker and finish welding the support to the inner wing/fender.

SR16. The door bottom gap is determined by the sill/body rocker position. Use clamps to hold it in place and move the sill/body rocker around until the correct position is found. The front joint face of the sill/body rocker with the front wing/fender should be 2 mm in front of the door edge. There should be a 4 mm gap between the sill/body rocker and the lower edge of the door. The sill/body rocker should form a uniform contour with the door when viewed from above. When satisfied with the position tap down the proud edges of the panel to the surrounding structure. Weld the sill/body rocker to the hinge pillar, using additional patching in this area as necessary. Do not weld onto rusty metal. ►

SR17. Additionally, weld the front of the sill/body rocker to the front wing/fender support flange, the undertray seam, the rear sill/body rocker support and the jacking point flange. ►

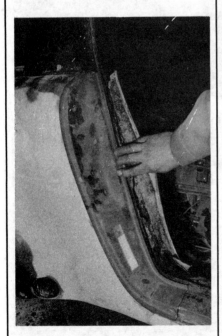

SR18. Replacement of the door ▲ latch panel requires careful positioning, not only for the door latch itself, but also because it

locates the rear outer wing/fender at its front. The panel should be tacked on and the rear wing/fender offered up, to ensure that the correct 4 mm door gap can be achieved. When satisfied with the position of the panel, the rear wing/fender is removed and the welding completed. Use of a MIG welder will require careful work and grinding-off of excess weld before further finishing, such as leading.

SR19. This picture shows the door lock panel ready for welding. The rear wings/fenders are sound and have been left in place in this instance. ►

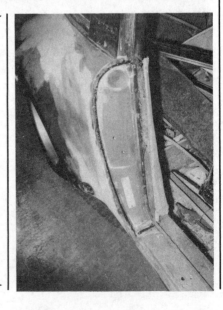

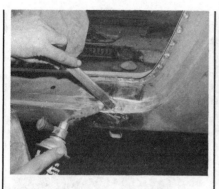

SR20. In order to thoroughly seal this joint, you could well lead load it. (See later section for details).

SR21. File the lead so that the contour ...

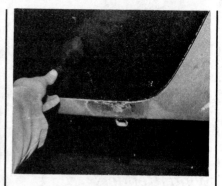

SR22. ... fits that of the door. Whilst fitting the new sill/body rocker, be sure to temporarily re-hang the door **before** welding the new panels in place, as a sure check that the position is absolutely correct.

Rear inner wing renovation

Before the rear wings/fenders are fitted, it is prudent to inspect the inner wings/fenders, especially in the areas that have caught road spray and debris. Look also around the "hot" areas like the oil filter body mounting and near oil lines or tank, patching as required.

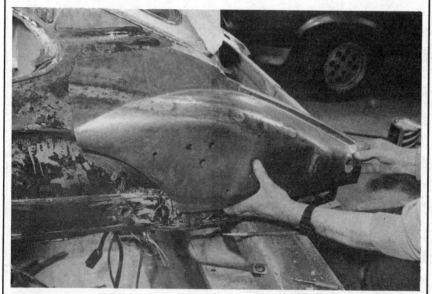

RIW1. Although replacement of the entire inner wing/fender is considered to be beyond the scope of the enthusiast, sections such as this can be laid in. This panel has been hand made by Dave Felton (see 'Clubs & Specialists') but could be cut from a replacement inner wing/fender.

RIW2. This inner wing/fender has been tidied up, patched as necessary and primed.

RIW3. You may have to remove oil pipes before repairing this area.

Replacing the rear wings/fenders

RWF1. Dave Felton offers the new wing/fender panel to the body. Using the old wing/fender position as a guide, trim the flange where it attaches to the ▼

door latch pillar. Insert the rear engine cover cable guide tube (removed from the old wing/fender), along the left-hand wing/fender. ◄

RWF2. Where you can't spot ▲ *weld, pre-drill for MIG welding.*

RWF3. Clean off any primer before welding.

RWF4. Position the wing/fender in the correct position by closing the doors and checking the gaps (4 mm).

RWF6 ... and constantly checking the gap and the faces of the door and wing/fender.

RWF8. Match the surface of the wing/fender adjacent to the base of the rear window and tack in place.

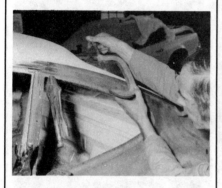

RWF5. Clamp the wing/fender in position and spot weld or carefully MIG the wing/fender to the door latch flange as a lap joint, working towards the bottom ...

RWF7. Using a dolly, David taps over the gutter flange, starting at the top and working towards the light box. Tack the guttering at its top edge.

RWF9. Check the position of the wing/fender using the engine cover. The gap should be a constant 4 mm.

RWF10. Clamp the lower part of the rear section in place and tack weld. ◀

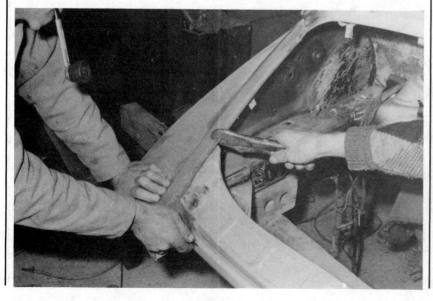

RWF11. Using the dolly, again tap the window flange to butt against the inner wing/fender seam.

RWF12. Use a spot welder where you can 'get at it'. Tack the wing/fender to the sill/body rocker, jack flange and rear cross-member. Before fully welding up seams, check position of the new wing/fender again by measuring the gaps with the door and engine lid. Finally, weld the cable guide for the engine cover latch in position on the door pillar. ▶

After completing the welding, grind off excess weld and lightly tap down the seams to be leaded (to recess them). These are the joints between the sill/body rocker, the rear guttering and in the region of the rear cross-member.

On completion of the welding, wire brush, rustproof and prime the exposed areas of metal.

It may not be necessary to replace the entire rear wing/fender, in which case, careful thought should be given at this stage as to how much of the old wing/fender is to be removed.

Rear wing/fender repair section

RWP1. It had been decided to only replace the front part of this Turbo wing/fender by Autotech, Porsche approved body repairers in Belbroughton, Worcestershire, England. A complete rear wing/fender assembly is shown being offered up. It is important to cut out all the corroded/damaged metal and be satisfied that what is left is sound and provides a suitable means of attaching the new section. Only then should you mark out the new panel, allowing an extra 50 mm overlap. This minimises the chance that a wrong cut will be made in the new panel. ▼

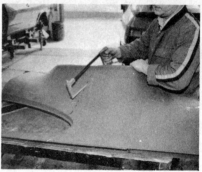

RWP2. Cut the panel along the scribed line. The door pillar section will also be cut off here.

RWP3. Offer up the new section.

RWP4. Use the door to position the panel correctly, setting the gap to a uniform 4 mm. Clamp the wing/fender section in position when satisfied.

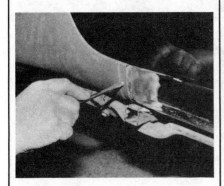

RWP5. Scribe the small sections to be trimmed in order to achieve a good joint. Here the sill/body rocker is marked.

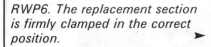

RWP6. The replacement section is firmly clamped in the correct position. ►

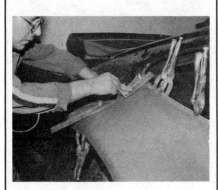

RWP7. Mark the small section to be trimmed off the main joint, leaving sufficient for a lap joint of about 10 mm width, unless you have sufficient skill to carry out the butt-joint being carried out here. (Lap joints are a lot more prone to starting fresh corrosion in future).

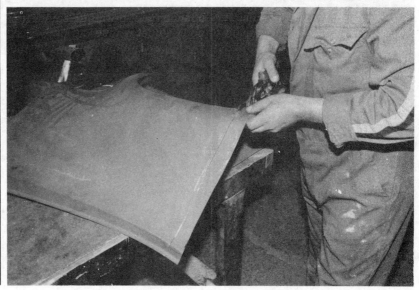

RWP8. Remove the section again and trim with tin snips.

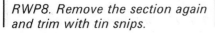

RWP9. When satisfied with the joint, clean up the metal with a small grinding attachment fitted to an electric drill. This operation should also be performed on the other mating surfaces. When the cleaning up is completed, clamp up the new section ready for welding.

RWP10. As noted at the start of the bodywork section, gas welding is not the best method for joining sheet metal. Distortion effects are minimised here with the aid of outside assistance.

Tacking the seam initially at several well spaced apart points is the best method, before running the weld all around the section.

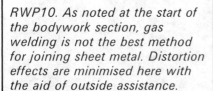

RWP11. After tacking, lightly beat the joint down below the general surface level.

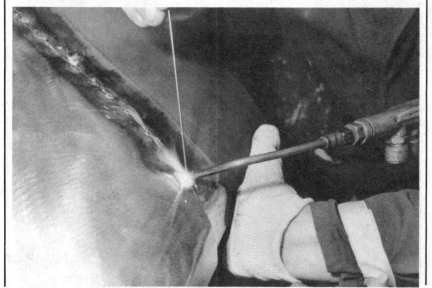

RWP12. Finish the seam weld.

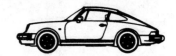

RWP13. When complete, beat
down any proud points, using a
dolly with the metal worker's
hammer to tidy the seam, if it has
been gas welded. If the seam has
been MIG welded finish off with
a 40-grit disc on a rubber
backing pad, fitted to an electric
drill. This is because the harder
MIG weld beads can damage the
sheet metal worker's hammer
face. Take care not to heat/distort
the panel whilst grinding the
excess welds.

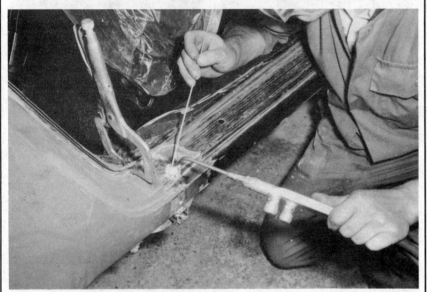

RWP14. Complete the welding.
Here the section is attached to
the sill/body rocker using a
recessed lap joint. Although a
spot welder is ideal for the joints
with the door post and top of the
inner wing/fender, a MIG or gas
unit can be carefully used to
produce satisfactory results.

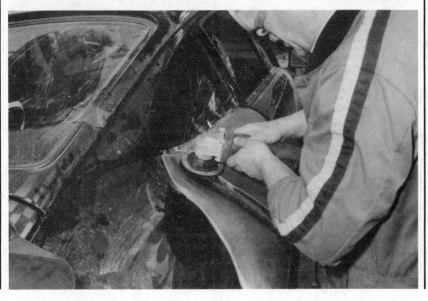

RWP15. After the welding is
complete, finish the seam with
the hand grinder to remove
remaining proud areas of weld,
etc. The joint is now ready for
lead filling, which will be fully
described after the next section.

RWP16. Where appropriate, the stone resistant covering is stuck down onto the panel and a spreader used to ease out any air bubbles.

Roof replacement

Removal and replacement of the Coupe roof section is considered to be beyond the scope of the average enthusiast, since templates for the window and door openings are required. The job should only be attempted by a specialist with the correct tools. *The following photographs are for illustrative purposes only. They are not a complete step-by-step section.*

RR1. Ken Wright of Classic Car Restorations has cut off the left side with reference to the new left side roof side-member.

RR2. Then he trims back and makes the side-member ready to fit.

RR3. Ken braze welds the panel in place. This is a good principle for parts that may later have to be moved – braze re-softens easily. Further steel welding is necessary later, of course. For that reason, the braze should only cover a small area – steel won't 'take' on top of it easily.

RR4. With both side-members in place, Ken clamps in the front cross-member.

RR5. Ken uses the door to check alignment.

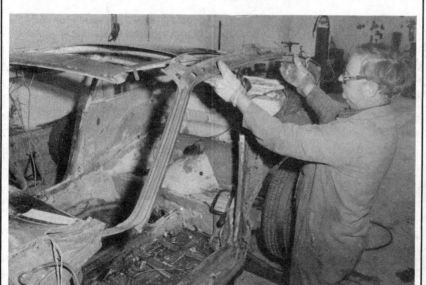

RR6. Before the roof panel is fitted, the drain tube is reconnected.

RR7. Ken offers up and fits the new roof panel.
Remember – this is a job for specialists only!

Engine bay patch repair

EBP1. On this car, Dave Felton found a small area of corroded, thin metal in the engine bay.

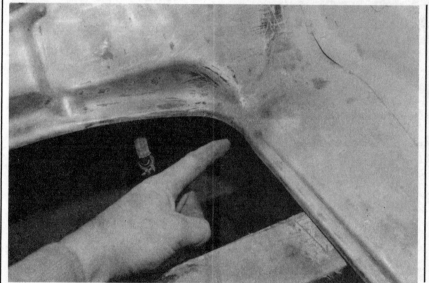

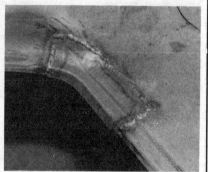

EBP4. The new piece was butt-welded in. When the welds were sanded off, the repair was almost invisible!

EBP2. He carefully formed a patch repair, placed it over the corroded area, scribed around it ...

EBP3. ... then cut away the corroded stuff.

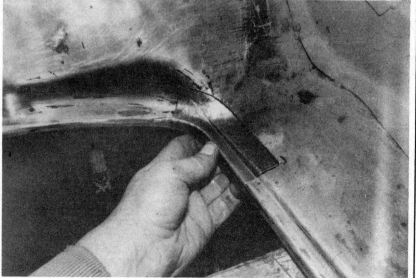

Bulkhead/firewall top panel replacement

BFR1. Once again, a new panel is available for replacing a rusty one, but its replacment is beyond the scope of the home restorer. Your specialist will have to ensure that surrounding panels are correctly located.

BFR2. He will be able to spot weld along the top seam but in other areas, MIG 'spot welds' will have to be made then ground smooth.

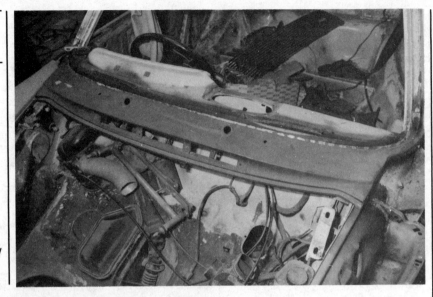

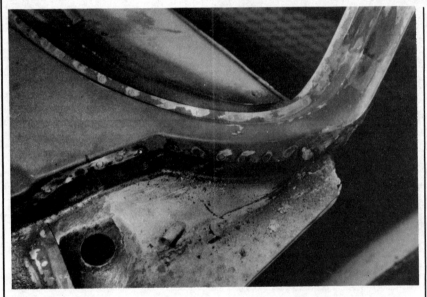

Three stages

There are three distinct stages to body soldering. The first involves thoroughly cleaning the seam or area to be filled. The area must be perfectly clean for the solder to key onto.

The second stage is to tin the surface to be filled. The solder used for this is called tinman's solder and is 60% lead, 40% tin. The lower proportion of lead makes it easier to key onto clean steel surfaces. Unfortunately, it is more difficult to work than body solder (going from solid to liquid phase within a small temperature range).

The task of tinning has been made much easier by tinning paints, which have been used here. These are a mix of flux and powdered solder. They are easier to use, when the art is mastered, than a stick of solder and a can of flux. It should be said that in the early experiences the latter may be more productive as one learns the heating skills, especially with a drip tray under the work area, for recyling wasted solder.

The third and final stage is the body filling. The solder used has a higher lead content (about 70% lead, 30% tin) than tinman's solder. Body solder has a good

Body soldering or leading

In itself, body soldering is not the solution to all problems of body filling. It certainly demands the most skill and patience from the restorer. On a correctly prepared surface, it does not matter whether a plastic type filler or body solder is used; the results will probably be the same. There is no less likelihood of rust forming on a leaded joint than a plastic filled joint. Shrinkage with the latter needs to be understood (see Suppliers section for details of "shrink free" epoxy based

fillers) and sufficient time should be allowed for the plastic filler to cure. For the enthusiast restorer though, there can be an old fashioned desire to try out the craft of the tradesman and produce "properly" filled seams and joints. It is certainly true that leaded joints match the elasticity of the base metal more closely and, as a result, are less prone to cracking.

There are two reasons why body soldering may give poor results. The first is unsatisfactory surface preparation. The second is not appreciating that two types of solder are needed, namely tinman's solder and bodysolder.

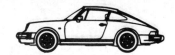

working temperature range between softening and going liquid, which makes it easier to form to the surface contours.

The following leading suggestions are not aimed at any particular part of the 911's structure and although the photos show a rear wing/fender repair, the technique is the same for all areas. It will help the novice to make the first attempts on a horizontal seam (like a sill/body rocker) rather than a vertical infill. The 911 makes much use of filled joints, especially around the roof guttering and rear wings/fenders.

Tool Box

Electric drill with rotary wire brush attachment; sanding disc with coarse grade emery sheets; soft *clean* lint free cloth; methylated spirit; hand held butane blow lamp and spare gas cartridges; supply of tinman's solder in stick or paint form, tinman's flux; body solder in stick form and body solder flux; wooden spatula (to work body solder); drip tray to catch wasted solder, if learning. Materials can be purchased from your local body shop supplier.

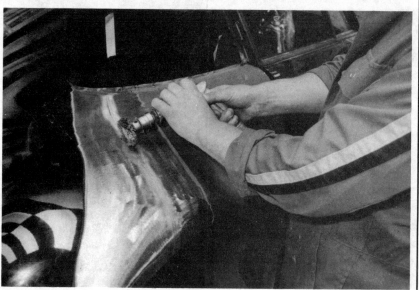

Safety

Methylated spirit is highly flammable. Use in a well ventilated area and do not expose to naked flame. Fully complete the cleaning operation, close storage container securely and allow spirit to evaporate off before lighting up the leading torch. Mop up any spillages on floor or surrounding area before commencing soldering. Wear protective glasses whilst soldering as flux can spit in certain circumstances. Do not use power tools to sand solder, as the lead dust produced is poisonous. Wash hands thoroughly after using any lead-based products; do not eat, drink or smoke and keep lead away from small children.

Procedure

L1. Here the surface is being cleaned with a rotary wire brush, to remove all traces of paint, rust, etc., on the surface to be tinned. A sanding disc should also be used to finish off the abrasive cleaning. In a warm, dry environment, rinse the surface off with methylated spirits. Do not touch the surface as the natural

greases in the skin will set off rust formation.

L2. The prepared surface is painted with tinman's paint; a mixture of solder and flux.

L3. The entire exposed area is covered to ensure an even fill.

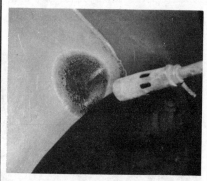

L4. It will be a question of experience before the right amount of heat is known to melt the tinning solder just enough, without it running off. Adjust the torch to give a fan rather than a concentrated flame and "brush" the flame along the surface rather than concentrating it too heavily in one area.

L5. As each small area is warmed use a cloth to wipe the solder into the area to be filled. The cloth should be constantly dipped in flux to prevent the solder sticking to it. It will be necessary to keep warming the work area with the torch at intervals. If you're concerned about 'brushing' the flame onto your hand (not recommended!), wear an industrial weight protective glove.

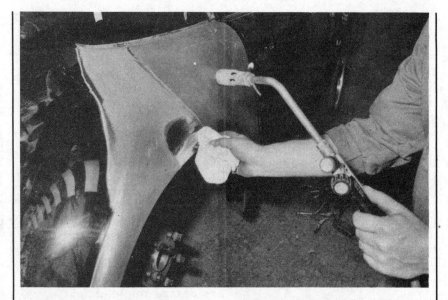

L6. Work outwards from a convenient starting point, aiming for a thin bright layer of solder over the entire area to be filled.

L7. With tinning completed, the body solder is ready to be applied. First put body solder flux on the area and warm the panel directly, without the tinning running off.

L8. The objective is to put lumps of the solder on the body. As with conventional soldering, heat the metal initially, not the solder itself.

L9. The solder will become workable fairly progressively. When it sticks to the metal, play the flame up the stick to separate off a lump. Don't let the solder get too runny.

L10. The first lump is placed on the work area.

L11. With a wooden spatula coated in flux, work the softened lump down to the profile required. There are a variety of different shapes available for spatulas, to suit the type of area being filled. If too much solder has been applied work the excess towards an edge and part it off.

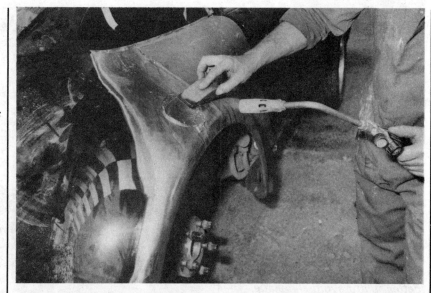

L12. Careful heating of the panel and solder should keep the solder soft and workable but not runny. Remember to keep dabbing the spatula in the flux to prevent the solder sticking to it.

L14. The wooden spatula can be used to work the soft solder into difficult spaces.

L16. The residue can be melted down in a "vee" of board or metal, both smeared with flux, to make new sticks. This craftsman at Autotech uses tallow in a tray to prevent the solder sticking to his spatula.

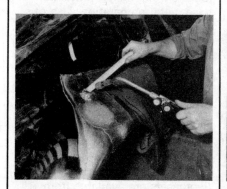

L13. Further lumps of solder can be applied if insufficient has been laid on initially.

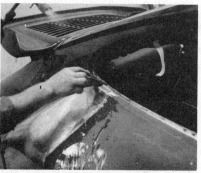

L15. This picture shows the spillage that can occur. It is worth having a drip tray under the work area, but don't mix up the solder types.

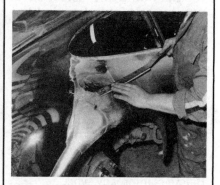

L17. It is very difficult to get a blemish-free finish so expect to use a Surform file or body file ...

L18. ... followed by a coarse sanding block, to finish off the work. A resin or epoxy filler can now be used to touch up any small imperfections. Before applying the filler ensure that all traces of flux, etc., have been removed, using hot soapy water in copious quantities. Methylated spirit can be used later to ensure that all traces of oil have been removed, but allow this to completely evaporate off in a well ventilated atmosphere.

Apply a light coat of primer compatible with the finish coats and then fill any imperfections with the correct stopper (for instance cellulose stopper or, better still to avoid shrinkage, 2-pack stopper).

Part 4: Paintwork and protection

Safety

Paintwork stripping and application are the most dangerous stages of car restoration. It is important to wear goggles and gloves when using paint stripper or sanding. Cellulose paint is the only suitable paint type for the home enthusiast to use, but is highly flammable and can cause giddiness and headaches when used in a confined area. When spraying cellulose, use a charcoal filter mask; a simple cotton layer type is not suitable.

Preparation

Before starting any work in preparation for painting, sweep the work area comprehensively. Whilst bearing in mind that the need for safe ventilation is paramount, it is desirable to work in an environment where draughts into the work area are

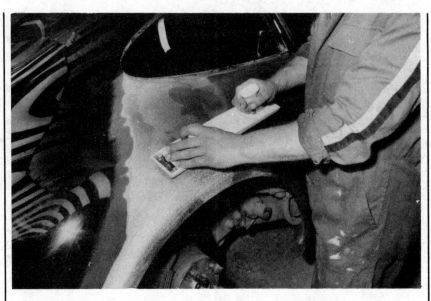

minimal. An extractor system should be used for ventilation, if possible. Shortly before spraying, wet the floor area to keep dust down. Use a tack cloth to go over the surfaces prior to painting, to remove any last dust deposits.

It is not proposed to go into detail on the preparation and application of paint. *Haynes' Car Bodywork Repair Manual* by Lindsay Porter looks at every imaginable aspect of car bodywork preparation and painting, including all the paint types and how to apply them. The following notes may help the understanding of the techniques used.

For a proper restoration a back-to-metal paint strip is really the only way to be sure of a well levelled and properly prepared surface. This will mean a long time spent with paint stripper and sanding disc. An orbital sander will do the job of a sanding disc, but is much less likely to scratch the surface of the metal in the way a disc can. To do the job properly, it is also recommended to virtually strip everything off the car that can be removed. This is especially so if the colour is different from the original.

Small depressions and sanding scratches should be levelled and filled with resin filler or knifing stopper. Do not use a

cheap filler, as these contain extra amounts of chalk and can break up. Another important factor is flexibility of the filler, to cope with bodywork expansion/ contraction and also to enable easier sanding. This stage of sanding should be finished off with about 200 grit paper.

Once the surfaces have been taken down to the metal and all paint and flaking rust removed, the entire panel(s) should be further treated with a rust dissolver.

There are many opinions on the best preparation for mild steel panels, to deter future corrosion. Without exception the key to long term corrosion protection is base metal preparation. Use of phosphoric acid based rust dissolvers can eliminate last traces of rust and etch the surface to be primed.

A "professional" degreasing fluid, one which is specially formulated to remove silicones, should be used to clean the entire surface before priming. This is especially true if rust dissolvers have been used. Such degreasers are available from trade paint factors or suppliers.

Do not leave the surface after the final clean before applying the first primer coat.

Primers

The traditional method is to use

red oxide primer as a base coat onto the clean metal. Probably tougher are red oxide primers (such as Bondaprimer). Developments have seen paints like Hammerite and epoxy coatings, and these offer very good scratch and chip protection, but be certain that the primer you choose does not react with the finish paint. The proven state-of-the-art method is a zinc coating next to the base metal. Ideally the zinc is applied as a hot dip to the panels, before welding together (using a spot or MIG welder). It is quite easy to find a metal treatment firm who will hot dip separate panels, although it is wise to check on the maximum size that is possible. Cold zinc paints are highly recommended for repairs to factory zinc coated panels on the 911. The cold zinc sprays by the German firm Wurth are the standard, but these are expensive if large areas are to be covered. paint primer available and the differences should be understood. Etch primer is a normal primer with a small percentage of phosphoric acid. It is essential to use this if painting onto new metal or aluminium. Ordinary primer will not fill scratches and should not be flatted down, only use fine wet and dry (800 or 1000 grit), prior to top coating. Filler primer is more robust and will fill small scratches, etc. It is applied more thickly than ordinary primer. It can be flatted down to a smooth finish, using say, 400 or 600 wet and dry. A good method of checking the standard of finish of a primed and filled body is to give it a light coat of a dark colour. Go over the area with fine wet and dry, which will reveal any pits or scratches as dark marks.

Thinners

For cellulose painting, the normal thinner to use is "fast" or "top coat" thinner. There are others that can be used in hot weather, such as "slow", or high humidity

("non bloom"). These should be used if conditions warrant it. Do not mix different thinners together. Normal mix for paint/thinners is 50:50 whether using primer or top coat, but these proportions can be altered to suit the temperature or finish required. Such variation in quantities should not be attempted by the novice.

Sanding

An idea of what grit carborundum (dry), or silica paper (for wet and dry), can be used when preparing the body has already been given. Once the final coat of primer is applied, a last flatting with 800 grit will prepare the surface for the first top coat. For flatting the top coats, 1200 grit should be used. Change the water regularly, to prevent scratching.

Masking

If the body has been stripped this is not such a difficult task. Remember to use masking tape to cover screw threads, etc. and other items not to be painted. If the glass is still in place, mask the rubber surrounds well. Nothing looks more unprofessional than overspray on these. Also remember to remove the front wing/fender sealing strips, near the base of the windshield. These can be replaced easily after painting with new ones.

Top coats

Mix the paint well both before and after addition of thinners. This applies especially to metallic paints. Ensure the right colour primer has been used for the top coat. See the car handbook for the correct colour code. This will also be shown on a chassis plate on the car, either on the passenger door pillar or on the main chassis plate, inside the front luggage compartment.

Spray onto a test surface to

get the right pressure and technique. Always spray from side to side with a parallel motion, not in an arc. The gun should be about 200 mm from the surface and pointed always at right angles to it. If runs occur then the gun is probably being held too close. If a dry, sandpaper surface is formed, the gun is too far away. Overlap spray motions by about 50% and plan the spray pattern around the car in a set order. Spray door shuts, seams and recesses first, then main panels after.

Leave the final coat for as long as possible before final flatting with 1200 wet and dry (if this is required). Certainly leave at least a week in the case of cellulose paint. Clear lacquer applied over a base coat can also be flatted with 1200, if the surface is not smooth enough after the final coats.

The surface can then be polished using a lambswool attachment in an electric drill set at slow speed. Be careful not to use too much pressure whilst doing this as it is possible to burn the surface. Alternatively, an electric polisher can be purchased which operates at lower speed and is less likely to result in a burned surface, if too much pressure is used.

This brief discussion is not meant to be an exhaustive presentation of the painting process, but only an introduction. As mentioned at the start, the reader is strongly advised to go through a standard text on this specialised subject.

Bodywork preservation

Once the final coats have dried out, it is recommended that a rust inhibitor is sprayed into every crevice, to deter corrosion caused by moisture.

Before this is explained, it should be said that applying most such fluids is pointless to an

older car where rust is established. It will not stop the corrosion. In fact, poorly applied it can actually accelerate it by providing small pockets for trapped, moist air next to the metal. The trapped moisture will dissolve enough of the base metal to form an electrolyte (the anode of the electrochemical reaction that forms rust) and imperfections in the "protective" layer will set up a cathodic reaction with free oxygen in the air.

Inhibitors are now available which contain "rust killers" as well as improved additives to prevent the penetration of moisture (see Clubs & Specialists section).

That said, the following indicates some of the areas that the preservative fluid can be injected into. If spraying, a good pressure (approx. 3 bar or about 45 psi) will be needed unless you are using an aerosol based fluid. The thicker types of oil can be made more liquid by warming for some time before application. Standing the can next to a radiator or on the domestic boiler will help, but do not heat the oil directly. White spirit can be used to thin the oil.

Tool Box

Preservation fluid sufficient for needs (see Clubs & Specialists section). Five litres is average for a complete car application. Spray equipment; small paint brush (to aid application); clean cloth and newspapers to collect drips; old clothes (it is a very messy business!).

Safety

Rust inhibitor fluids are flammable, do not apply near naked flame. Always keep away from eyes and use goggles if working above eye level.

Application of body preservation fluids

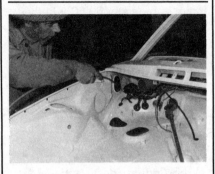

WOA1. Starting with the body cavities, inject in the inner front wing/fender cavity near the door pillar ...

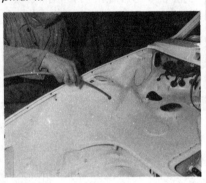

WOA2. ... around the wheel arch ...

WOA3. ... and into the cavity at each end of the front tank support.

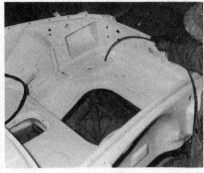

WOA4. The front tank support should be coated. Drill small (5 mm) holes in the centre section to coat in this area. Fill holes using rubber grommets from a motor accessory shop.

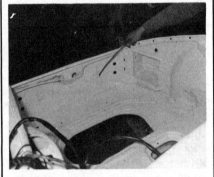

WOA5. Coat the front dividing wall cavity and other concealed corners that might collect moisture or debris. Be careful not to block drainage slots.

WOA6. If the front wings/fenders are off, inject into the socket hole for the door electrics.

WOA7. Apply the fluid to the inside of the sills/body rockers. With the treadplates etc. removed there are sufficient injection points to coat the inside. Again take care not to clog the drain slots on the underside of the sills/body rockers.

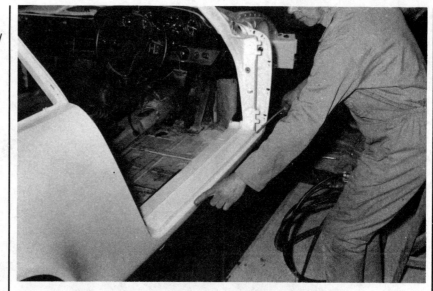

WOA8. Don't forget inside the rear of the inner side members.

WOA10. ... and the rear.

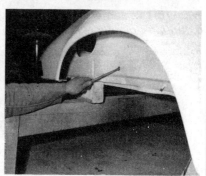

WOA12. Coat the inside of the rear structure box sections.

WOA9. If the headlining is out, inject into the roof seams at the front ...

WOA11. Inject into the forward area of the rear wheel cavity, and into the sill/body rocker rear support.

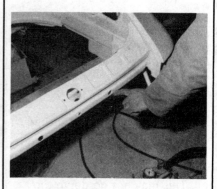

WOA13. Apply to the rear cross-member cavity ...

WOA14. ... from both ends ...

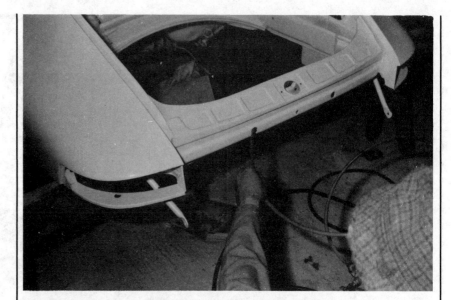

WOA15. ... and around the latch mounting hole panelling.

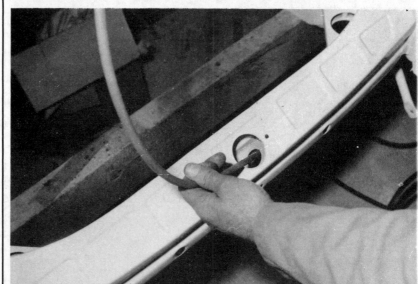

WOA16. When at the rear, inject into the box sections after removing the plastic plugs. All this section was demonstrated by Dave Felton.

On a general level, it will do no harm to spray or paint the entire underbody with a waxed oil. This may not go down too well with Concours judges though, from an appearance or originality viewpoint. *Don't inject rust proofer before painting the car, by the way, or the silicones in it will play havoc with the paint as it is being applied.*

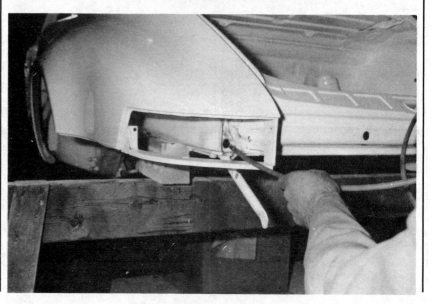

④ Trim

This chapter covers glass removal and replacement, interior trim (including replacement of the headlining) and removal of the electric sunroof. A section covers the removal of the electrically operated door mirrors, fitted to post-75 models and the fitting of a passenger door mirror.

Removal of windshield/rear heated screen

The procedures used for the removal of these two screens are identical. The rear screen is usually heated and greater care is required when removing this glass. Only the removal of the rear screen is covered here, which will give enough information for the removal of the front screen.

RSR1. With a sharp knife, cut through the rubber along the outside edge of the bezel, so that the latter can be pulled out without bending it. Go around the entire screen like this so that the bezel is not damaged.

RSR2. With the knife, cut through the remaining rubber seal as close to the glass and parallel with the surface as possible. The edge of the glass should now be exposed. If removing the front screen, remember to fold the wiper arms out of the way to remove them.

RSR3.   Partially lift the glass from the remaining rubber surround.

RSR4.   Pull apart the spade connectors to the heated screen filament, making a note of what is connected where. Alternatively, the lead to the screen can be disconnected from within the engine compartment and pulled through into the interior. The lead is then removed with the window.

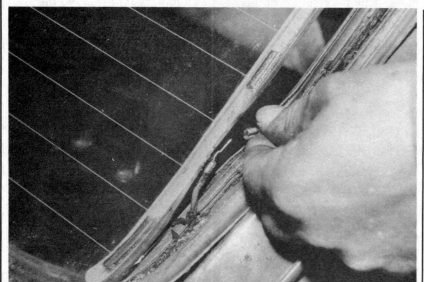

RSR5.   Lift out the glass.

RSR6.   Remove the remaining rubber surround from the window aperture. Note where the wiring goes in the moulding.

Refitting the windshield/rear screen

Again the procedure is largely the same front and rear. The front screen is fitted first.

FSF1. Only a new rubber moulding should be fitted. With the screen supported on a non-scratch surface, fit the new moulding around its edge.

FSF2. Ensure that the surround is positioned correctly in relation to the front/back and the corner locations. The bezel groove faces outwards. It may make fitting easier to smear the moulding with soapy water or glycerine.

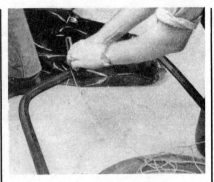

FSF3. Feed a piece of stout cord (string will not be strong enough) into the moulding, starting from the top of the screen and working right around until an overlap of about 300 mm is obtained. That is the easy bit!

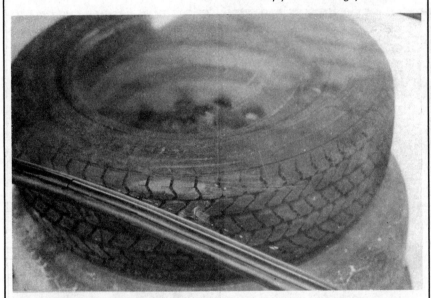

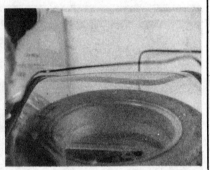

FSF4. Smear the bezel groove with glycerine and insert the bezel into the moulding. Leave about 10 mm gap between the sections at the top and bottom.

FSF5. The screen is ready for fitting. ◄

FSF6. Remove all the remains of the previous moulding, sealer, etc. from the screen recess. If the seam is corroded, patch as necessary and paint with zinc based primer followed by the finish coat. When ready, smear the glycerine around the recess and its groove in the moulding, to help the latter seat properly.

FSF7.   Place the screen with moulding onto the recess.

FSF8.   Push the lower edge into position first, checking that the side to side position is good and then push the top into place.   ➤

FSF9.   When satisfied that the screen is positioned correctly (by looking at the gaps around the inside corners), start to pull the cord out, from inside the car. Ask an assistant to maintain a strong pressure on the screen from the outside, to help seating.

FSF10.   The outside pressure is most important to seat the lower edge.

FSF11.   The reason for needing a strong cord is apparent at this stage.

FSF12. When the screen is in position, with the cord pulled through, go around the inside and out, checking the seating of the moulding on the body and interior trim. With a plastic hammer, lightly tap down badly seated bezel and insert the slide pieces over the bezel gaps. The screen should not need any sealing compound, but if doubts exist about the seal, then inject a suitable cement into the suspect areas.

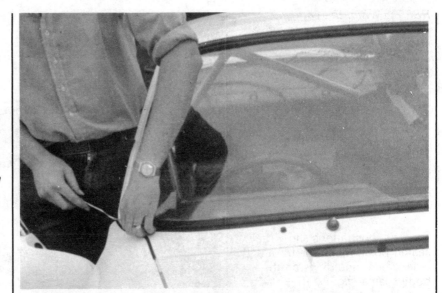

For the rear screen, the procedure takes account of the heating circuitry. The wiring should be positioned around the moulding prior to offering the glass to the car. This applies also to the lead from the engine compartment, if this was removed with the glass.

RSF1. Position the assembly in the body recess, with the top edge going in first. ►

RSF2. Seat the moulding into the recess and begin to pull the cord through from the centre top. Don't let frustration get the better of the job.

RSF3. From inside, pull the moulding lip over the recess seam, taking care not to damage the headlining whilst doing this.

RSF4. Keep constant pressure on the screen from the outside.

RSF5. When the cord is completely removed and the surround is seated, go around the edges and smooth out the headlining and any tucks in the moulding.

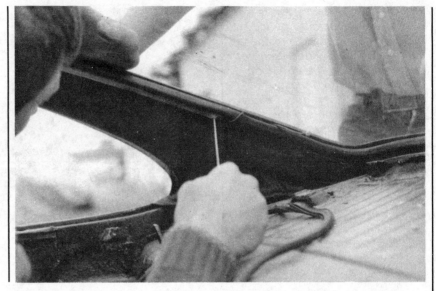

The illustrations show the seated positions of the front and rear screen mouldings on the body seams (fig. 4.1).

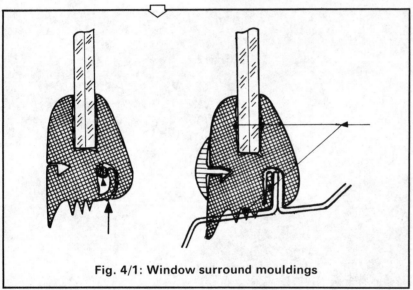

Fig. 4/1: Window surround mouldings

Removal of the rear side screens

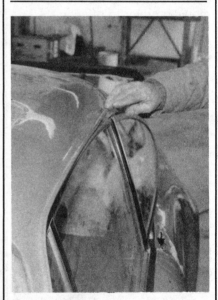

SSR1. Open the side windows to about half way.

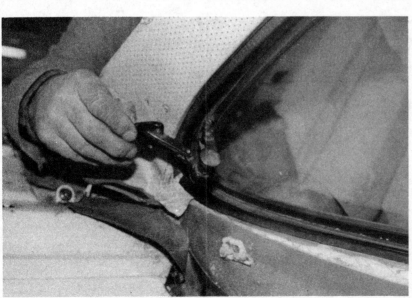

SSR2. Remove the three retaining screws holding the latch assembly.

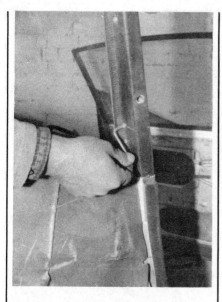

SSR3.   Remove the four socket-head screws that locate the side screen to the door pillar.

SSR4.   The screen will now lift out.

SSR5.   Remove the retaining screws for the trim strip. These may be heavily corroded, especially if the rear wing/fender is also heavily rusted. In this case they are being drilled out.

SSR6.   Remove the black trim from the door pillar seam ...

SSR7.   ... and upper seam. Assembly is the reverse procedure.

Removal of the interior trim

ITR1.   Remove the front screw holding the upper interior trim to the door pillar.

ITR2.   Then remove the two screws retaining it to the inner wing/fender.

ITR3.   The trim strip can now be lifted out.

ITR4. Remove the screws holding the rear safety belt mounts to the rear shelf.

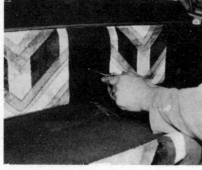

ITR6. Remove the screws retaining the rear shelf trim to the rear wall.

ITR8. Remove the retaining bolts at each outer side of the rear seat backs.

ITR5. The belt mountings should be removed.

ITR7. Lift out the rear shelf trim.

ITR9. The seat backs can now be lifted out.

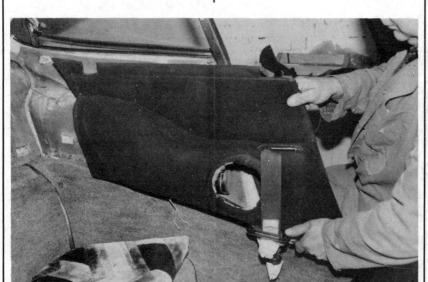

ITR10. At this point, the rear wall sound proofing can also be removed.

ITR11. On 911 models fitted with non-inertia reel seat belts, the trim panels under the side windows can be removed with the side panel. The sound proofing should also be removed.

ITR12. The inertia reel mechanism can then be removed.

The components should be re-assembled in the reverse order, cleaning or replacing as necessary. It is suggested that if carpets are damaged, then new ones can be made using the old items as templates. Edging can be fabricated from leather cloth and sewn or bonded in place. Replacement carpeting etc. is still easily available. For more detailed aspects of upholstery renovation, the reader is directed to one of the specialist motor books on the subject. Home fabrication is perhaps most straightforward when replacing the front luggage compartment carpets. The material can usually be obtained through well stocked motor factors or from certain carpet stores.

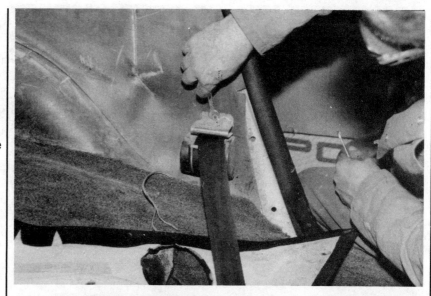

Seat removal

Seat removal is straightforward. Earlier 911 models have socket-head screws retaining the seat frames to the floor structure, whereas later models have hex. head bolts. The hex. heads will need a 0.25 inch drive socket to remove them, since access is limited.

SR2. Now move the seat all the way forward. This will similarly reveal the rear locating bolts, which should also be removed.

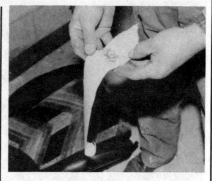

SR4. Wrap all screws in masking tape and secure to the seats to keep them safe. The interior still/body rocker carpets can now be removed.

SR1. Move the seat as far back as it will go. This will reveal four locating bolts (two on each rail) that should be removed.

SR3. Remove the screws retaining the inside tread strip over the sill/body rocker.

SR5. Lift out the tread strip and the protective cover on later models.

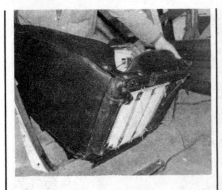

SR6. The seat can now be lifted out. With the seats removed the front carpets can be taken out. Refitting is the reverse procedure.

Electric sliding roof removal

ESR1. Open the roof about 100 mm. ▲

ESR2. If this cannot be done electrically, then open zip at rear of headlining. The drive motor for the roof will be observed and its flexible drive to a reduction gearbox. In the centre of the box is a narrow slotted screw, which if turned, will manually drive the gear and open the roof. If the screw will not turn, it suggests a faulty motor and this should be removed and the screw then turned. For motor renovation, see the section on the door electric window lifts.

ESR3. Remove the screws retaining the aluminium air deflector plates and lift off the components of the deflector.

ESR4. Unclip the sunroof headlining from its front edge. Now open the sunroof as far as it will go and then close it to leave the starting gap of 100 mm. The headlining should be left behind in the cavity, exposing the guides, etc., on the sunroof lower side.

ESR5. Looking upwards from inside the car, note the front and rear guides on each side of the sunroof. Remove the front guides from each side.

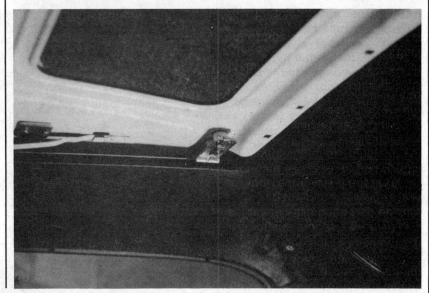

ESR6. Lift and turn sideways the spring catch on each rear guide and then unscrew the rear guides from the roof.

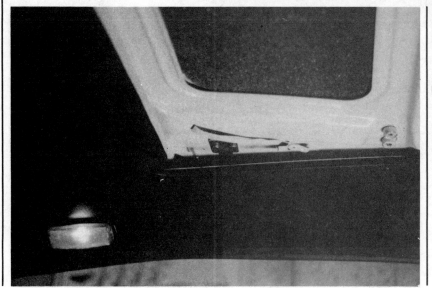

ESR7. The sunroof can now be pulled forwards and upwards, away from the car. Take care not to damage its paintwork, if appropriate.

ESR8.   Unscrew and remove each guide rail spacer and then the rail itself.

ESR9.   The headlining of the sunroof can now be removed. Assembly is the reverse procedure, but do not push the headlining into the cavity too far. Take care also not to soil the headlining on replacement, with grease, etc., from other sunroof renovation work. Check also the operating cables for wear and replace these if necessary.

ESR10.   When rebuilding, replace the velvet strips that seal the edges of the sunroof, before fitting the sunroof panel. The strips should be fitted to the front and sides of the roof opening, as far back as the start of the rear corners.

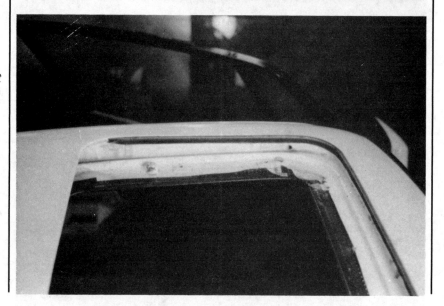

ESR11. *The velvet strip at the back fits the sunroof panel and should extend around the rear corners. When the roof is closed the mating strips should form a seal, with no difference in heights.*

When refitting the guide rails, they must be fed onto the pegs at the rear of the sunroof cavity.

The height of the sunroof can be adjusted by turning the knurled nuts under the front guides, after the location screws have been loosened. The same guides can be used to position the roof from sideways. The rear sunroof height is altered by the adjusting screws in the rear guide brackets.

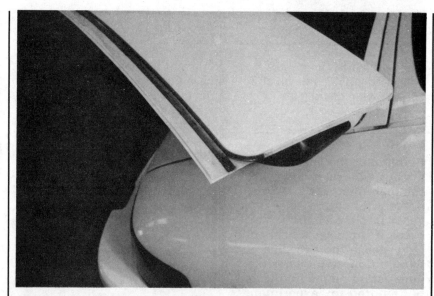

Dash top removal

DTR1. *The dash top can be taken off after removing the screws around the front, adjacent to the luggage bay opening ...*

DTR2. *... and those found beneath.*

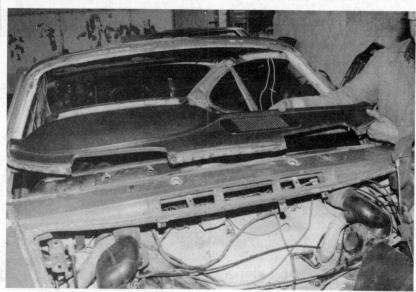

Removal and replacement of headlining – general

There is no doubt that replacing the headlining is a job that requires a lot of forethought and planning. It is necessary to remove all the glass, including the front and rear screens, before work can commence. If the car has a sunroof, this should also be removed (see last section).

However, if a full bodywork restoration is to be done properly, then replacing an old smoke stained and torn headlining can transform the interior's looks.

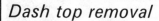

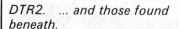

Tool box

Pair of sharp fabric scissors; impact adhesive and a brush to apply it with; craft knife.

Safety

Remember the hazards of impact adhesives and read the manufacturer's safety notes with care. Use in a well ventilated area and take a break if it causes a headache. Don't leave the adhesive lying around where curious youngsters might find it and be tempted to "experiment" with it. Don't leave craft knives lying about with exposed blades.

Removal of headlining

With the glass out, remove the clips that hold the old headlining to the window recesses. Remove the interior roof fittings, making a rough sketch of where they are located relative to the door pillars, etc. Remove the door rubber surrounds.

As the old headlining is removed, note how it fits the roof, where adhesive has been used and the relative position of the sewn seams, stays, etc. If a sunroof model, note where the zip is positioned.

Fitting a new headlining

Before starting to fit the headlining, which would be done after any paint restoration work, ensure that the inside of the car is as clean as possible and that paint dust, etc., is cleaned off the window recesses and adjacent areas. Do not allow adhesive to get onto the hands and transferred to the headlining.

Models without sunroof

Cars not fitted with a sunroof have transverse stays to tension the headlining across the centre roof section. Before the headlining is offered to the car, push the stays into the loops and place the caps on the wire ends.

HL1. Start by clipping the headlining to the door openings on each side in approximately the right location. Stretch the lining forwards to the windshield recess and place clips along the front seam, to the pillars. ▼

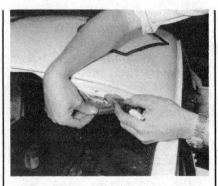

HL2. Stretch the lining back to the rear window recess and similarly clip in position. Don't glue or cut yet!

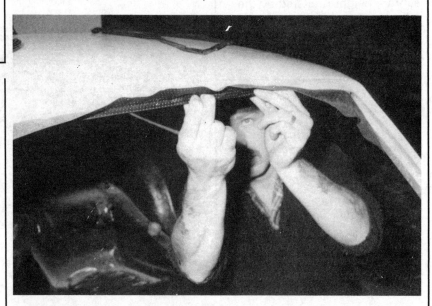

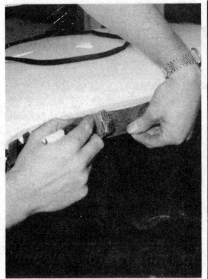

HL3. Tension the lining out to each side, re-clip in place and check that the fit is good around the side windows and rear pillars down to the rear shelf. If happy with the positioning, remove the front clips and apply adhesive along the front strip. The adhesive will take a few minutes to cure, so this is a job that tests patience. Don't rush off to glue another section until the current one is completed. Use the clips to hold the lining in place at the top of the front screen recess, once glued. ◄

HL4. Working towards the rear window, tension the lining evenly out to each side, across the rear window recess and down each quarter. This will involve removing and replacing clips until satisfied and then applying a layer of adhesive.

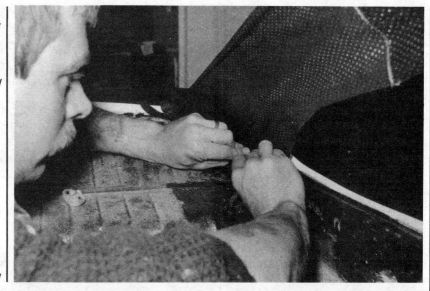

HL5. At the base of each rear quarter, insert the stays into the loops in the lining and tuck the stays under the metal hooks on the shelf (to tension lining). ▼

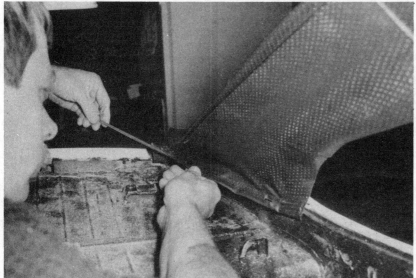

HL6. The rear window recess ▲ will require glueing and clipping (so that the window moulding does not push the lining off the seam).

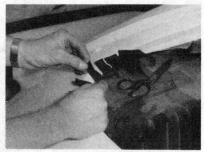

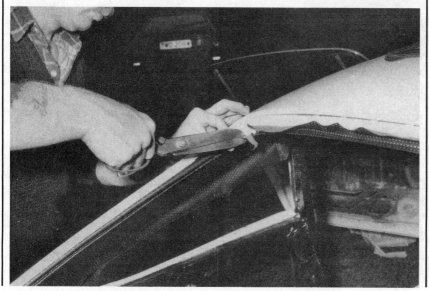

HL7. Careful cutting of the ▲ lining will be necessary around the small radius of the rear side windows.

HL8. When the glue has dried out, trim the excess lining off the front seams around the window recesses, taking care not to trim too much off. A craft knife is useful for this.

HL9. Trim around the door and front screen pillars. If the pillar trim is to be replaced this should be glued in position after the headlining. A small decorative fold back at the top of the leathercloth should be made, so as not to show the cut end of the material.

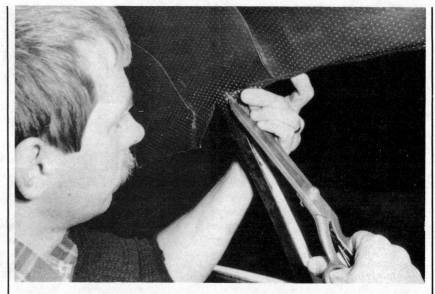

HL10. With the lining in place and trimmed, use the craft knife to cut openings for the interior lights, sun visors, etc. This process involves a lot of feeling around with fingers, so as to cut at the right place. Use the sketch made before removing the old headlining as a rough guide.

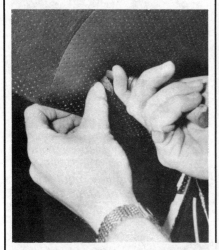

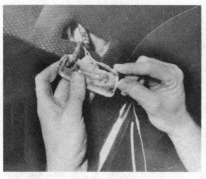

HL11. With the interior lights, pull the leads through the lining and connect to the light assembly.

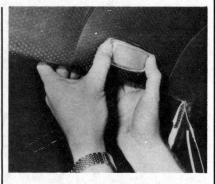

HL12. Push into place, ensuring that the earth side is grounded onto the metal bracket in the roof.

HL13. Tension the headlining to remove any creases or wrinkles.

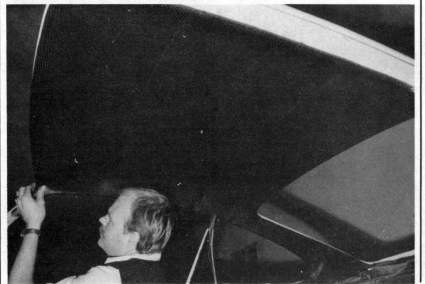

To finish off, the lining can be further tensioned by very careful use of a hair dryer, to pull in loose fabric. This technique should be used with special care as the lining can be damaged beyond repair. Don't expect large folds of material to magically tension itself!

Sunroof models

The procedure is largely the same, except that there are no transverse roof stays to tension the lining. Only cut the roof opening after the rest of the lining is in place and tensioned. Be very careful not to cut out too much, especially at the rear of the cut-out, where the lining is tensioned into the cavity.

It then remains to refit the remaining interior fittings, the door surrounds and the glass, this latter subject being covered in an earlier section.

Electrically operated door mirrors – removal and stripdown

Use a steel rule or knife blade to carefully prise out the mirror from its back plate. Be prepared for the clips to have corroded into the back plate. Breakage of the clips can be avoided if penetrating fluid can be applied to the clips prior to removal. This corrosion also occurs to the heater element leads, where they fit to the mirror.

Remove the three screws that are visible through the back plate. This allows the back plate to be lifted out as a unit after disconnecting the plug. It is suggested that the back plate unit is not dismantled any further, since the mirror motor and adjustment assembly is a sealed unit.

NOTES:
1) Connections between switches and doors are found in front luggage compartment, (behind instruments), on right and left sides.
2) COLOUR CODES:
BL Blue   GY Grey
BK Black   GN Green
BN Brown   R Red
W White   P Purple
Y Yellow

To remove the mirror housing, remove the three Phillips head screws that mount it to the mirror arm.

If it is required to remove the mirror arm and base from the door, it will be necessary to detach the electrical plug from the leads. A note should be made of the location of the leads in the plug, prior to removing the leads, with the aid of a pointed tool.

To remove the base from the door, unscrew the socket-head bolt. The location of this bolt may be visible, adjacent to the door surface or it may be necessary to turn the mirror arm through a right angle to expose the bolt in the base. To investigate the mirror wiring further it will be necessary to remove the door trim. Assembly of the mirror is the reverse procedure.

If the door wiring has been moved, ensure that the leads in the door are held away from the window lift mechanism on reassembly. When assembly of the mirror back plate has been completed, check the functioning of the motor before clipping the mirror into place. This reduces the likelihood of accidental damage to the possible fragile mirror clips, if the mirror has to be removed again.

Fitting a passenger door mirror

Until quite recently the passenger door mirror was an option, rather than a standard fitting to all models. Not everyone sees the need for the passenger door mirror (abbreviated to "pdm" in adverts). Indeed, if driveway width is restricted the extra inches of the second mirror can be important on some models.

This fitting guide assumes that a single driver's door electric mirror is already fitted. The passenger door mirror is available as a retrofittable kit, but fitting involves the removal of both doors. See the Bodywork chapter for advice on door removal.

The passenger door mirror includes three separate wiring harnesses. These are:
   Driver's door harness
   Front compartment floor harness
   Passenger door harness

The first task is to paint the mirror parts in the colour appropriate to the car. See the paintwork section for further information on paint type, colour codings and preparation.

Assemble the mirror base to

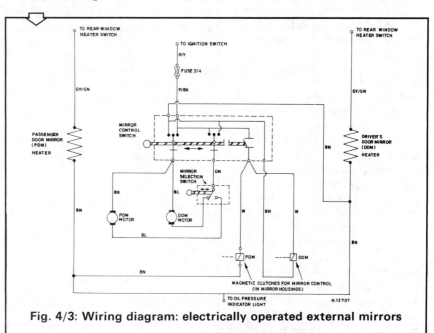

Fig. 4/3: Wiring diagram: electrically operated external mirrors

the arm and tighten to a torque of 15 Nm. This torque should enable the mirror to be turned on the base.

Remove the trim strip from the top edge of the door panel.

Remove the door interior trim, so that the outer panel is accessible.

Drill the holes in the door as shown by Fig. 4/2. Use the reinforcing plate to guide hole location also.

Fit the reinforcing plate to the inside of the door skin using pop rivets.

Fit the passenger door harness to the mirror base and feed into the door.

Fit the mirror base unit to the door.

In order to correctly route the wiring harness the door should be removed by extracting the hinge pins. Alternatively, if the hinge brackets are removed from the door posts, it will be necessary to set the door gaps using the gap gauge illustrated in the Bodywork chapter. This is not an easy job, so consider the work involved before starting to fit the mirror. The harness should exit the passenger door below the existing harness. Ensure the rubber grommet protects the leads around the opening.

With the door removed, drill a hole through to the front compartment and fit a rubber grommet. The door can now be refitted, ensuring the electric window lift harness is reconnected and the new mirror harness is pushed through into the front compartment.

Using the accompanying wiring diagram as a guide, the new harness is attached to the rear window demister switch.

Remove the driver's door and its interior trim. Fit the new harness for operation of the passenger door mirror. This will involve drilling a similar access hole at the front of the door as used on the passenger door. It will also be necessary to drill an access hole to the front compartment, again as performed

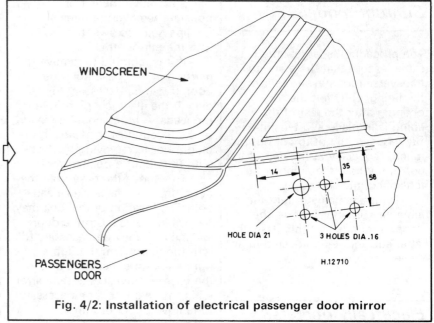

Fig. 4/2: Installation of electrical passenger door mirror

on the passenger side. Refit the driver's door once the holes are drilled and route the harnesses through grommets.

Connect the new harness to the mirror control switch in the driver's door.

The mirror selection switch is fitted under the main instrument cluster, approximately above the ignition switch. It will be necessary to cut a hole in the instrument surround to mount the switch. Connect the leads from the two mirrors and the control switch, as indicated on the wiring diagram.

Connect and tidy up the remaining leads in the front compartment, linking the left and right-hand sides with the selection switch and rear window demister.

Complete the assembly of the new mirror by fitting the

leads to the socket and using the wiring diagram to ensure correct positioning of the leads.

Connect the backplate plug into the socket and attach the backplate to the mirror housing. Check the function of the mirror before installing the mirror glass, to prevent unnecessary stress on mirror clips.

5 Engine and Transmission

Part 1: Introduction and stripdown

It is assumed the reader will now understand the changes in engine and transmission configurations over the life of the 911. Through its remarkable development cycle, the basic layout of the engine has remained unchanged, which suggests far-sighted design by any standards.

It may help to explain the code letter found on earlier 911 models which refer to the engine configuration. The T models, (meaning Touring) were designed as cheaper versions of the range, having carburettors and cast iron cylinders, along with other cost saving features.

An E (standing for Einspritz, or injection) featured mechanical fuel injection, which was introduced from 1968 (for the 1969 model year). The S model was the top model of the range. As one might expect from a Sports version, it featured many modifications from the basic type. It is outside the scope of this book to go into the details of the engine developments and the reader is recommended to read an authoritative text on the subject if he or she wants to know more.

The gearbox also has been changed considerably over the years, mainly to handle the increases in torque. Several features have remained unchanged in principle, such as the synchronising system. This latter was first produced for the 1959 356A and is an example of steady development of a good idea, so typical of Porsche. Dismantling of the gearbox as a whole is considered outside the scope of the average enthusiast, since the work requires specialist tools to assemble the gear clusters.

Engine general arrangement

As noted earlier, the basic engine design is similar in all 911 models, being a six-cylinder horizontally opposed, air-cooled unit. The valves are operated by an overhead cam on each bank of three cylinders. Most important changes to the engine during its life have been to capacity and cylinder materials.

The crankshaft runs in eight main bearings, with the oil being carried in a separate tank. Dual oil pumps in the crankcase respectively scavenge oil from the crankcase and draw oil from the tank for distribution.

The oil pumps are driven by an intermediate shaft, geared off the crankshaft. This intermediate shaft also drives the camshafts by means of duplex (or twin row) chains.

Cooling of the engine is performed by a ducted fan mounted above the engine block. Interior heating is provided by a heat exchanger arrangement around the exhaust pipes.

Tool Box

Before starting a 911 engine stripdown, find out whether any special tools will be required. Listed below are the special tools which the Porsche Club of Great Britain offer on loan to members. These tools would cover a total engine rebuild by the enthusiast.
1. Engine stand (bench mount) P201.
2. Engine stand snap on tools.
3. 46 mm socket ($3/4$ inch square drive).
4. 46 mm crowfoot ($1/2$ isd).
5. 36 mm socket ($1/2$ isd).
6. 32 mm combination wrench.
7. 36 mm combination wrench.
8. 12 mm universal joint socket ($3/8$ isd).
9. 13 mm universal joint socket ($3/8$ isd).
10. 12 mm 12 point socket ($1/2$ isd).
11. 8 mm 12 point socket ($3/8$ isd).
12. 6 mm 12 point socket ($3/8$ isd).

13. 10 mm long hex. socket key ($^3/_8$ isd).
14. 8 mm long hex. socket key ($^3/_8$ isd).
15. 6 mm hex. socket key.
16. 5 mm hex. socket key.
17. Adaptor $^1/_2$ inch male to $^3/_4$ inch female.
18. Adaptor $^3/_8$ inch male to $^1/_2$ inch female.
19. $^3/_4$ inch drive bar.
20. $^1/_2$ inch drive torque wrench (0 to 25 kg f m).
21. Dial gauge (0 to 10 mm)
22. Magnetic dial gauge holder.
23. Porsche tool P222, timing chain holder.
24. Porsche tool P200a, valve spring compressor.
25. Porsche tool P202, camshaft holding tool.
26. Porsche tool P214, chain tensioner clamp.
27. Porsche tool 214b, chain tensioner gauge.
28. Porsche tool P216, No 8 bearing sealer.
29. Porsche tool P10c, valve spring height gauge.
30. Porsche tool PP206, valve guide go/no-go gauge.
31. Circlip pliers, internal and external.
32. Piston ring compressor.

This may seem like a daunting list, but the tools cover most 911 engine variants. For any one type, not all the tools will be needed.

The two engine stands are alternatives and a block and tackle, or some strong helpers will be needed to position the engine in these stands.

The 46mm socket and crowfoot are used to remove the nuts on the ends of the camshafts. P202 can be used to rotate the camshaft during reassembly and valve timing, the latter operation also requiring the dial gauge and holder.

The valve spring compressor has a special collar to hold the valve spring caps. The valve guides can be easily checked for wear with P206 and similarly the valve spring heights are easily checked with P10c.

The piston ring compressor is essential for safe fitting of the fragile rings in the individual barrels.

P214 and P214b are used for refitting the early chain tensioners. It is suggested that if these are out of the car, they may as well be overhauled by a specialist, in which case they will be returned in the compressed position (with safety clips installed.) Alternatively, they could be replaced with the new oil-fed tensioners, of which more later.

The combination wrenches are used for unscrewing the various oilpipe connections. The 12 mm and 13 mm universal sockets are used in certain areas where access is difficult (namely heat exchanger nuts). The 12 point sockets are used at various points on the whole car. A notable engine requirement is the flywheel mounting bolts. The 36 mm socket is used not on the engine, but to undo the wheel hub nuts.

The 5 mm socket key is used for the rocker shaft bolts and the 8 mm socket key will be useful in removing the heat exchangers (with the aid of a long extension).

Not all of the above are essential and the enthusiast will find that his/her existing tools may do most jobs adequately.

There is nothing better for the confidence than to have the right tools for the job and to know that the work is being done correctly.

As mentioned, these tools are available on special loan from the Porsche Club of Great Britain to members only, together with a complete set of factory workshop manuals. A deposit is payable for each, but it is well worth the expense. It is possible to buy certain tools, such as keys sockets, etc. from specialist tool suppliers.

Two other tools which will be useful are a vernier caliper and a metre steel rule. The vernier permits accurate length measurement, for instance, during cam sprocket alignment. Joint sealing compound (like Hylomar), instant gasket compound and thread locking adhesive should also be to hand.

MC1. These Link-Sedan products: a vacuum and fuel pump tester, a dwell tachometer and the 7-function analyser with inductive pick-up, will prove invaluable to the DIY home mechanic.

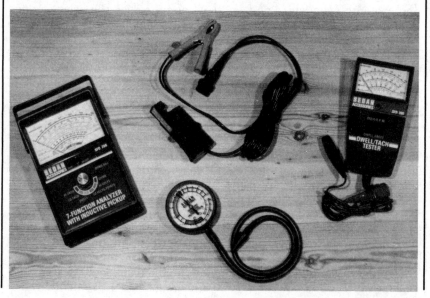

MC2. The same company produces this easy-to-store trolley jack which nevertheless gives an impressive amount of lift due to its ingenious design.

MC3. The cheapest tools available are most definitely not the most economical in the long run. Sykes-Pickavant who have made some of the best tools in the world for many years now also produce Speedline tools which, although very high quality, are a little more affordable. They recommend that if you're buying your first tool set, you should consider going for a $3/8$ inch drive socket set rather than the traditional $1/2$ inch drive. Not only does this cost less but it can also get into more awkward spaces. If you've been put off by cheap $3/8$ inch drive sets shearing off in the past, don't worry! These tools are made to last.

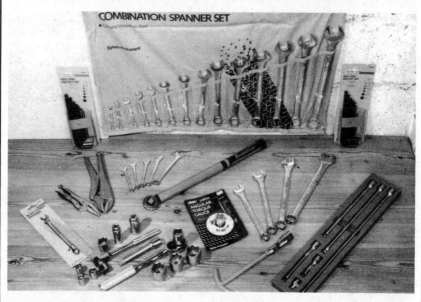

MC4. Compression tester, sparkplug thread chaser, circuit tester, combination feeler gauge, oil filter remover, piston ring compressor, carburettor tool set, and cylinder head stand: all made by Sykes-Pickavant and many of them absolutely invaluable to the home restorer, depending on how much mechanical work you intend carrying out yourself.

MC5. S – P also produce a range of tool chests to compliment their tool selection. The sliding drawer tool chest in the background sits neatly on top of the rolling, floor mounted unit in the foreground.

MC6. Slick 50 emphasise that their products are not an oil additive but an engine, gearbox or bearing treatment. Slick 50 microscopically coats all bearing surfaces with PTFE which significantly reduces friction levels, improves engine economy and reduces wear rates. It really does seem to work! ▼

raised at the rear. The body should be high enough that the engine/gearbox can be rolled out from underneath (say on a trolley jack).

The body should be supported on axle stands when lifted to sufficient height. It may make things easier to remove the rear bumper/valance bodywork before trying to remove the engine.

ER1. Disconnect the battery at its terminals.

Jobs possible with the engine in the car

1. Most accessories fitted to the engine can be removed with the engine in place. These include the oil filter, air cleaner, carburettors or fuel injection (major components) and the distributor.
2. Removal of the oil temperature thermostat and in certain cases the oil cooler.
3. Removal of the cooling fan assembly, including the alternator.
4. Removal of the heat exchangers and silencer. With the silencer removed the chain tensioners are accessible.
5. Removal of the crankshaft oil seal, after removal of the V-belt drive pulley, and silencer.
6. Removal of the rocker covers and then the rocker shafts and arms.

Engine removal

The engine can only be removed as a unit with the gearbox. After removing the connections to the engine and gearbox for oil, fuel and electrics, the car should be

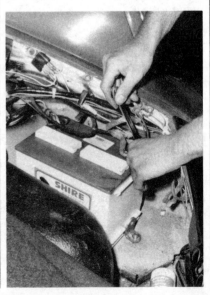

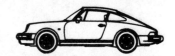

ER2. *Starting at the top of the engine, disconnect the flexible duct from the warm air regulator, if fitted.*

ER4. *Unclip and remove the air cleaner housing assembly from the car.*

ER6. *Similarly, disconnect and note the HT and LT leads from the ignition circuit.*

ER3. *Remove the oil breather pipe.*

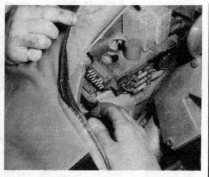

ER5. *Disconnect the plug connector to the alternator at the voltage regulator. With all electrical connections, use a strip of masking tape and a pen to identify where the leads go. It makes reconnection much easier.*

Safety

When disconnecting the fuel lines it is almost inevitable that there will be some fuel spillage. Do not smoke or work near exposed flames. An appropriate fire extinguisher should be available and instantly accessible whilst working on the fuel system.

ER7. *On fuel injection engines, disconnect the pipes from the fuel filter, fuel distributor and the control pressure regulator. Tag each pipe for location. To prevent contamination getting into the fuel system, plug all open pipe ends with tape or rag bungs.*

On carburettor engines, disconnect the pipes from the electric fuel pump. There is no need to disconnect the hoses from the carburettors or the secondary mechanical fuel pump at this stage. Plug all open pipe ends.

The remaining jobs inside the engine compartment are as follows:

Disconnect the throttle linkage at the bellcrank. Remove the oil breather pipe from the filler. Disconnect the lead from the oil pressure switch.

ER8. Drain the engine oil into a suitable container.

ER9. Don't forget to also drain the oil from the tank, which could be up to 5 litres.

ER10. Disconnect the oil hoses from the oil tank. On older models this may be difficult, because of corrosion and a build up of road debris. It may be possible to remove the oil pipes at their ends away from the tank. It may also be that the only way of getting the tank out is to cut through the pipes themselves. In the case of the high pressure pipes, try to cut through the aluminium end fittings without damaging the other fittings. This will reduce the size of the replacement parts cost.

ER11. Similarly remove the oil pipes from the oil cooler at the front right-hand side of the engine. Disconnect the lead to the starter motor.

ER12. Disconnect the hot air ducts that join the heat exchangers at their top front ends to the air mixing valves. Disconnect also the heater control cables from the mixing valves.

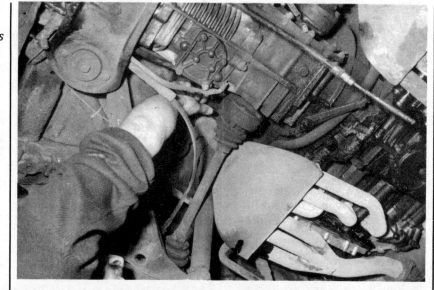

ER13. Disconnect the clutch cable from the clutch release lever.

ER15. Disconnect the leads to the reversing lamp switch, speedometer cable and vacuum hose from its reservoir (if appropriate). On the Sportomatic, disconnect the neutral indicator switch.

ER17. Disconnect the anti-roll bar mounts from the body.

ER14. Disconnect the earth strap which links the engine and body, adjacent to the gearbox.

ER16. If an anti-roll bar is fitted, disconnect this at its connection with the control arm tie bar.

ER18. Remove the anti-roll bar.

ER19. Remove the screws from the cover over the centre tunnel behind the front seats and lift off the cover.

ER20. Pull the rubber bellows towards the front of the car and expose the gear linkage.

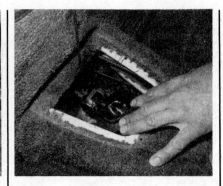

ER21. If fitted, cut the lockwire that secures the lockbolt and then loosen the lockbolt that clamps onto the gearbox selector shaft. Separate the linkage from the selector shaft.

ER22. Check that no other ancillaries are still connected, e.g. electrical connections. On Sportomatic cars, disconnect the oil pipes from the transmission oil pump. If the car is fitted with emission control equipment, the hoses from the air pump must be disconnected together with the air pump filter.

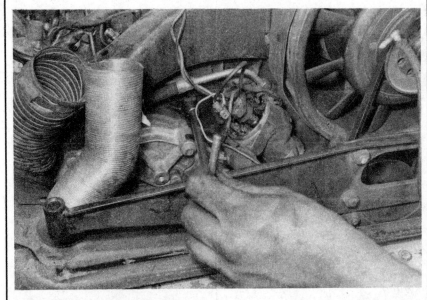

ER23. Place a trolley jack under the engine/gearbox and take its weight. The lifting point should be in front of the oil strainer cover. A piece of hardwood to spread the load on the crankcase is advisable.

ER24. Unscrew the socket-head bolts from the inner couplings of the driveshafts.

ER25.   Pull the driveshafts away from the differential flange. These may need a little gentle persuasion with a plastic hammer to separate them from their flanges. The fibre gaskets on the flanges should be replaced when reassemblng, so it does not matter if these are accidentally damaged at this stage. Wrap the exposed couplings in polythene bags, with an elastic band around the drive shaft to seal them. This prevents the grease from getting out and contamination from getting in.

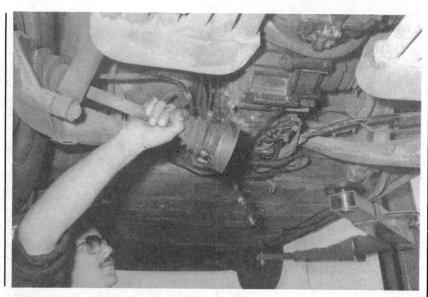

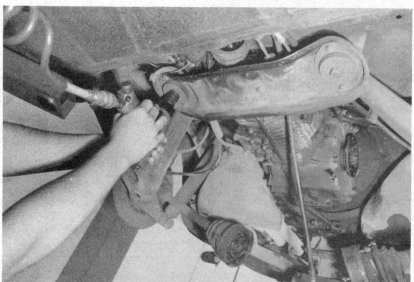

ER26.   After ensuring that the engine/transmission assembly is supported on a trolley jack, remove the two bolts supporting the gearbox mounting to the body.

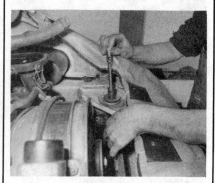

ER27. Remove the two bolts supporting the rear engine cross-member bracket. Carefully lower the trolley jack, checking that there are no connections that have been missed, that will be damaged by the removal.

ER28. When the jack is fully lowered the engine/gearbox assembly can then be rolled out from under the rear of the car (assuming of course, that the body has originally been raised high enough!).

Engine/gearbox separation

At this stage the job is fairly satisfying, since it will be realised how easy it has been to get this far. It is a good idea to take a look around the engine/gearbox prior to separation and identify some of the components.

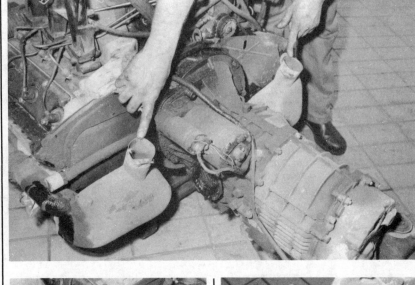

ES1. Note the two heat exchanger outlets to the heater control or mixture valves. ➤

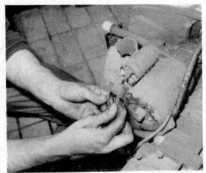

ES2. Note and then remove the connections to the starter motor.

ES3. Tape over or plug the scavenge pipe from the crankcase oil pump.

ES4. Note the position of the earthing strap on the gearbox front casting, if the gearbox is to be dismantled further.

ES5. Remove the connections to the reversing light switch on the front of the casting.

ES6. Remove the bolts retaining the starter motor.

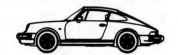

ES7. Remove the bolts around the gearbox bellhousing. On pre 1970 models the engine can now be separated from the gearbox. On later models, the job requires more effort. Turn the flywheel until the first of the three rivet heads comes into view, through the starter motor aperture. It will be necessary to make up three spacers as shown in Fig. 5/1. If using self made spacers, fit socket headed screws (M6 with 10 mm of thread) through each spacer and into the threaded bore of each rivet head in turn. Use an Allen key to tighten the screws, which should relieve the load on the release bearing. On certain 1970/71 models, it is possible to relieve the tension on the release bearing simply by backing off the release fork adjuster. When the

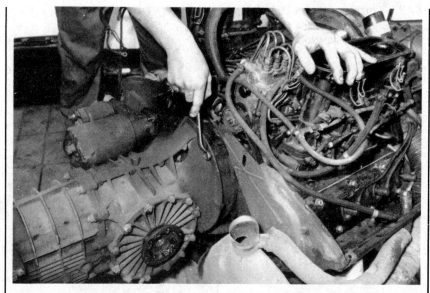

release bearing load has been relieved, use a screwdriver to turn the release bearing through 90 degrees. To do this, insert the screwdriver through the small hole in the bellhousing, on the top right-hand side. This will allow the release lever and fork to be taken out.

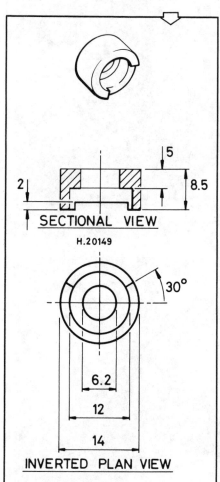

SECTIONAL VIEW

H.20149

INVERTED PLAN VIEW

Fig. 5/1: Clutch rivet head spacers

ES8. The gearbox can now be separated from the engine.

For Sportomatics, remove the nuts holding the torque converter housing to the gearbox. Disconnect and remove the intermediate lever from the actuating lever by removing the cotter pin. The torque converter housing can now be pulled from the gearbox, disengaging the clutch release fork from the release bearing as it comes away.

Removal of engine ancillaries

EA1. Remove the throttle control rods and linkage. On carburettor models the carburettors can also be removed complete with their manifolds. With fuel injection engines, the injection pump (if appropriate) and fuel distributor must be removed.

EA2. Remove the nuts securing the induction pipes to the cylinder heads.

EA3. *Unscrew the nuts holding the fuel delivery pipes to the top of the fuel distributor.*

EA4. *Remove the braided pipe on the inside face of the fuel distributor.*

EA5. *Remove the smaller oil pipe below the braided one.*

EA6. Unscrew the nuts mounting the fuel distributor to the crankcase.

EA7. Pull off the toothed belt drive.

EA8. Unclip the throttle linkage from the right bank of induction pipes.

EA9. *Lift out the fuel distributor.*

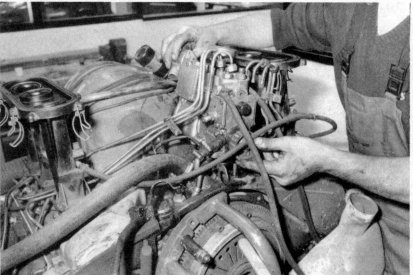

EA10. *Unscrew the fuel injectors at the cylinder heads. Be careful not to damage the pipes during this operation. Lock the injector in place with a second spanner whilst undoing the connector.*

EA11. *Remove each bank of induction pipes.*

For cars fitted with the K-Jetronic system, the procedure is largely the same, except that there is a different layout of components. The mixture control unit can be removed once the throttle linkage, ducting, inlet pipes and injector assemblies are removed. You are strongly advised not to dismantle the fuel injection system further unless professional assistance is available. This is because the system is carefully set up using electrical diagnostic equipment, to ensure correct mixture, fuel consumption, etc.

EA12. *Remove the strap bolts which secure the alternator to the blower housing.*

EA13.   Remove the cooling duct mounting bolts from the top of the crankcase.

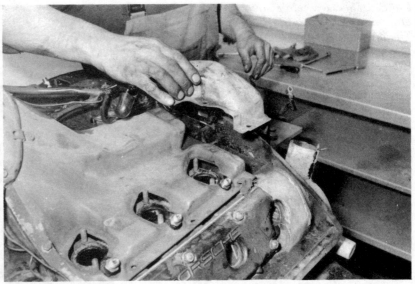

EA14.   Remove the oil cooler air duct, if this is a separate component. ▲

EA15.   Remove the blower pulley nut and V-belt. The pulley should be locked using a C-spanner if possible, whilst releasing the nut. Note the spacer washers behind the pulley and bag the parts, so that they are not separated or lost.

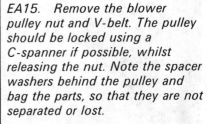

EA16.   Lift up the forward ▲ section of the blower ducting and release the blower earth strap and the alternator wires if still connected in this area.

EA17.   The blower ducting can now be removed.

EA18. This is where a special engine stand comes in useful! The engine has been turned over to give easy access to the heat exchanger flanges. It is very easy to say here that the heat exchangers should be unbolted and removed. In practice, it is likely that penetrating oil and a certain amount of patience will also be necessary. Access to the nuts is poor in some cases and corrosion may make removal very difficult. As a last resort be prepared to destroy the nut (by splitting) to get the exhaust off. A universally jointed socket on the end of an extension will overcome most of the access

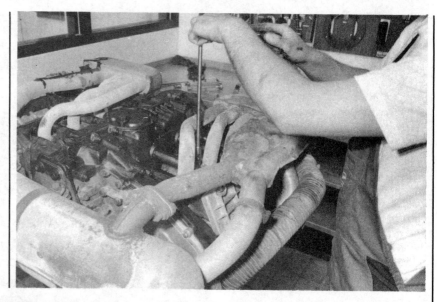

problems, although the flange to number three cylinder may still give problems. In this case, if (8 mm) socket-headed nuts are fitted, use a $^3/_8$ inch square drive socket with an 8 mm hex. head, fitted to a universally jointed extension, to remove the nuts.

EA19. Loosen the straps holding the silencer to its rear mounting bracket. ◄

EA20. Push the straps off the bracket. ▲

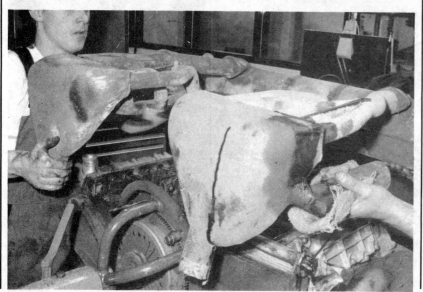

EA21. The complete heat exchanger/silencer system can now be lifted off the engine.

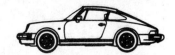

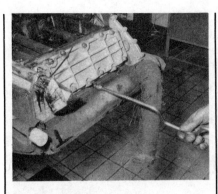

EA22. Remove any remaining sheet metalwork around the sides of the engine.

EA25. Remove the rear engine mounting bracket.

EA27. Lift off the oil cooler. Be careful not to drip oil everywhere as this is removed. Have a pan ready to leave the cooler in, to drain out residual oil.

EA23. After removing the fuel pump drive pulley if fitted, from the end of the left-hand camshaft, remove the sheet metal cover at the front of the engine.

EA26. Remove the bolts securing the oil cooler to the crankcase.

EA28. Mark the position of the distributor body relative to the crankcase and remove from the engine.

EA29. Unscrew the nuts holding the rocker covers.

EA24. Remove the remaining sheet metal from the rear of the engine. Be careful not to damage the flexible ducting on removal and store this in a place where it is not likely to be accidentally damaged.

EA30. Remove the rocker covers. Wrap these in an old rag, so that they are not scratched or damaged whilst in store.

This completes the removal of the ancillaries. It is a good idea at this stage to wash the engine block down with paraffin/ Kerosene or water soluble solvent.

Removal of timing chains and sprockets

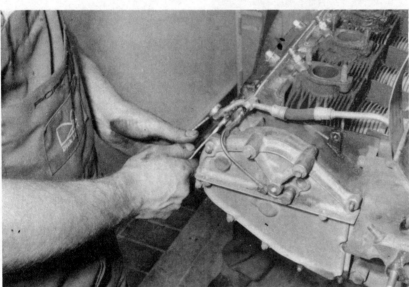

TCR1. This engine has the later engine oil-fed chain tensioners fitted. The first job therefore is to remove the oil lines that feed the tensioners. It is best to remove the short oil feed pipes completely.

TCR2. Remove the nuts that ▲ secure the chain case covers, then use a plastic hammer to dislodge the gasket, if necessary. Remove the chain case cover.

TCR3. Turn the V-belt pulley until the Z1 mark on the pulley aligns with the mark on the crankcase.

TCR4. When the pulley is aligned, check that the centre punch marks on the end faces of the cams are vertical. It is important to set the crankshaft up in relation to the cams, so that there is no danger of valves digging into the piston crowns during later operations with the chains removed.

TCR5. Remove the tensioners and their idlers.

TCR6. Removing the camshaft ▲ sprocket nuts will require a 46 mm socket and, done correctly, Porsche tool P202, to hold the camshaft in position.

TCR7. Remove the sprocket dowel pins, by screwing an M4 x 10 bolt into the threaded centre of the pin. They fit into one of the holes drilled around the sprocket.

155

TCR8. Remove the outermost plastic chain guide slippers from their mounting pins. It is not necessary at this stage to remove the inner ones, which are retained by bolts.

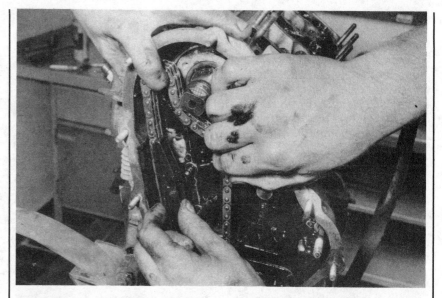

TCR9. Pull off the sprocket and drive hub from the camshaft: note the thrust washers that align the driven with the drive sprocket.

TCR11. Remove the three bolts from the sealing flange and pull off the flange, seal and gasket.

TCR13. Don't forget the nuts inside the cases as well!

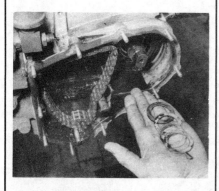

TCR10. Remove the Woodruff keys from the camshafts, shown here with the spacers.

TCR12. Remove the bolts holding the chain cases to the crankcase.

TCR14. Remove the chain cases over the chains.

Removing the cylinder heads

The next task is to remove the cylinder heads. For a full strip down, each cylinder head should be dismantled and inspected. It is possible to remove the camshaft housing and remove an individual head, if it is known it has a problem.

CHR1. If just one cylinder head is to be removed, then unscrew ► the rocker shaft bolts using a 5 mm Allen key. These shafts can only be pushed out if the valve spring pressure is off them. This means turning the camshaft independently of the crankshaft. Mind those pistons! Remove the rocker assemblies, labelling them for their position.

CHR2. Unscrew the camshaft housing nuts evenly and lift the housing off the cylinder heads. Remove the nuts from the relevant cylinder head and pull the head off its barrel. ►

CHR3. If the bank of three cylinder heads is to be removed, it is not necessary to unscrew the housing nuts. Remove the cylinder head nuts and tap the head assembly lightly with a plastic hammer to break the gasket seals. ◄

CHR4.   Lift off the bank of three heads, complete with camshaft housing.

CHR5.   Pull off the oil return pipes and check for signs of leakage or damage along their lengths. Corrosion of these pipes is not out of the ordinary.

CHR6.   The professional touch: if the engine is on a rotary stand, these collars will prevent the barrels sliding off while you're working on other parts of the engine.

Removal of pistons, flywheel and crankshaft

PFC1.   Unclip the cooling air guide plates from around the barrels. Again bag these parts after cleaning, so as not to lose them.

PFC2.   If the barrels are not to be left in place, remove them carefully. Hold the piston as it slides out of the bottom of the barrel.

PFC3.   Remove a circlip from one side of each piston, so that the gudgeon pin can be tapped out.

PFC4   Tap the pin out. Whilst doing this take care not to stress the piston or con rod. On early models the pins are an interference fit and will need to be sweated out. If the pistons are to be scrapped, then a blow lamp could be used to heat them. If the pistons are to be used again, try pouring boiling water over the pistons, or wrapping the pistons in rags dipped in boiling water. If the crankcase is not to be split, take great care not to let water inside. (You might try wrapping the rag in a plastic bag.)

PFC5.   Remove the oil strainer cover and strainer from the underside of the crankcase.

PFC6.   Remove the crankcase breather casting from the top of the crankcase.

PFC7.   Unscrew and lift out the oil thermostat, which is positioned next to the breather casting.

PFC8.   The next job is to remove the clutch and flywheel. The clutch pressure plate is removed by evenly loosening the mounting bolts connecting it to the flywheel.

PFC9.   On older cars, the flywheel can be prevented from turning by locking the starter ring gear with a screwdriver. On later cars, a locking plate should be used, which screws into a gearbox location hole and two of the clutch mounting holes in the flywheel. See fig. 5/2 for a simple solution.

If the flywheel has not been removed for many years, this can be a difficult job. For a start, the bolts used are the 12 point (Fillister) socket-head type (the right equipment is a 12STSM 12A socket key from Snap On Tools). Secondly the bolt threads will probably have become corroded, or worse, a thread locking adhesive may have been used at some earlier stage in the engine's life. Either way, don't expect the bolts to be reusable after removal. An easy and final solution, if a high power MIG welder is available, is to weld on hex. nuts to difficult bolts and use a conventional socket or even a Stillson wrench to loosen the

extended bolts. It is strongly recommended that a gas welder is not used for this drastic action, as it will spread heat excessively into the flywheel and may cause distortion. Don't worry about the centre bearing during removal of a difficult flywheel, the whole boss assembly can be replaced. Even if a MIG welder is used near the flywheel, check it afterwards for flatness and other damage. On Sportomatic models, the driveplate bolted to the crankshaft should be locked to prevent the crankshaft turning.

PFC11.   Remove the case bolts/nuts that are fitted behind the flywheel . . .

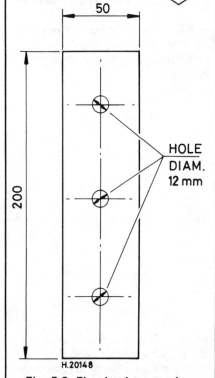

50

200

HOLE DIAM. 12 mm

H.20148

Fig. 5.2: Flywheel to gearbox flange locking plate

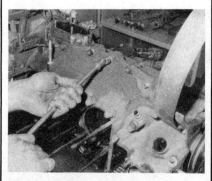

PFC10.   Remove all the crankcase nuts that hold the two halves together.

PFC12.   . . . and the ones at the front of the crankcase.

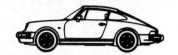

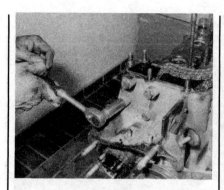

PFC13. Remove the bolts holding the inner chain guide slippers.

PFC15. Remove the two domed nuts that are accessed through the oil cooler flange. Remove also the through-bolt that is located inside the chain housing.

PFC16. Unscrew the long crankcase bolts . . .

PFC14. On removal of the slippers, note how the longer end is closer to the sprocket and that the snap fitting with the bolt is only on one hole.

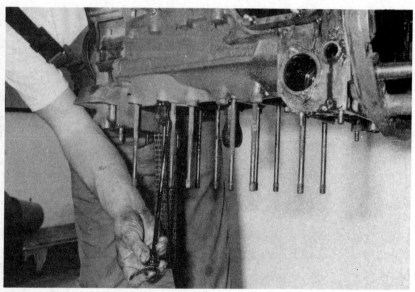

PFC17. . . . and carefully withdraw from the crankcase.

PFC18. This picture shows the crankcase bolt assemblies, complete with sealing rings at each end.

PFC19.   Take a look around the crankcase to see if any nuts or bolts have been missed that hold the two halves together. Tap the case lightly to break the gasket joint.

PFC20.   Pull the two halves apart, feeding out the con rods and timing chain from the half being lifted.

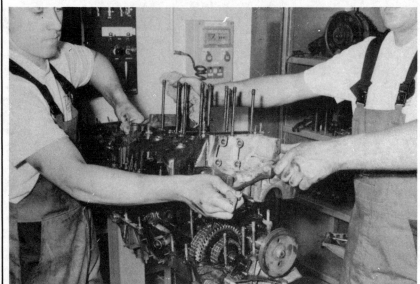

PFC21.   The oil pump nuts can be removed after opening out the lock tags.

PFC22. The pump and the intermediate shaft can be lifted out. When removed, the intermediate shaft can be separated from the pump. ➤

PFC23. The crankshaft assembly, complete with connecting rods, can now be lifted out. It should be placed on a clean surface and prevented from rolling off. ▲

At this point the engine is largely dismantled. It is a good idea to clean up the work area and wash your hands. Handling and assembly of many of the engine internal parts should be performed with cleanliness in mind.

During reassembly, it is useful to have a jar of new engine oil and a small brush handy. This should be used to coat bearing surfaces and other rubbing parts before assembly. The oil film will protect against corrosion during the rebuild, as well as helping when the engine is cranked over for the first time after completion.

Part 2: Engine inspection

Inspection of the crankcase halves

The major components should be checked for wear and renewed or cleaned up as necessary.

Clean off all the old jointing compound from the faces of the two halves. Use a stout round brush to clean out the oilways and flush out these and the inside of the case halves with petrol. Wipe clean after flushing. Clean out the oil strainer mesh and the crankcase filter mesh.

Check for cracks, stripped threads and other damage. A specialist will be able to fit thread inserts if any threads are damaged. Cracks can be welded up assuming they are not too serious.

E11. Check the main bearings for wear, if the surface is scored, the wear uneven or the copper is showing through, then replacement will be necessary. Check also for movement of the shells in their journals. If the evidence of such movement is found, then seek specialist help. ◄

E12. Note the way the main bearings fit to the crankcase. ▲

E13.   Ensure that all oilways are clear, the crankshaft oil passages can be cleared with a long probe. You should also inspect the crank surface visually. Any signs of scoring necessitate a regrind.

Inspection of the crankshaft and intermediate shaft assemblies

The crankshaft should be checked with a micrometer for wear of the main bearing journals and the connecting rod journals. To inspect the big-end journals the connecting rods will have to be removed from the crankshaft. As the rods are taken off, keep the mating bearing caps in the correct relationship with the rod. Note which way round the rods assemble to the crank. The micrometer should be used to look for out of roundness or taper. The journal surfaces should be inspected for scoring also. If you are unsure about what is seen, or don't have the right micrometer, take the crank to a specialist.

Out of roundness or taper more than 0.01 mm on any journal means the crank should be reground. Undersize bearings will also be required. This is clearly a job for the specialist, who will also supply the correct fit of bearings.

If no regrind is necessary, it is suggested that the bearings are still replaced at the existing size. They should be assembled with new engine oil.

The oil seals on No. 8 bearing insert should be replaced whilst the engine is stripped. The old oil seal should be prised out with a screwdriver and replaced. Ensure that the new seal is seated squarely in its journal and given a smear of new engine oil prior to reassembly to the crankshaft. The O-ring seal should also be replaced (Fig. 5/3) and similarly given a smear of new oil.

Replacement of the end oil seal can be done without splitting the crankcase, if a serious oil leak is present. A bolt with a large washer can be screwed into the pulley mounting hole in the end of the crankshaft. The bolt is tightened to draw the seal squarely down into the bearing insert.

Whilst the connecting rods are off, check the wear of their little-end bearings. These latter can be pressed out if necessary and new ones fitted. The gudgeon pins should be a tight sliding fit and will not require reaming.

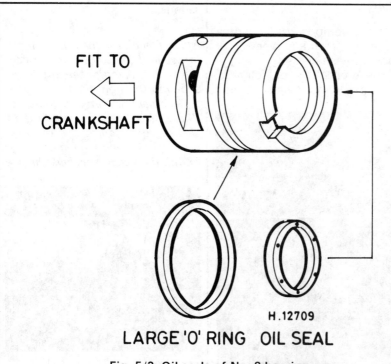

FIT TO ← CRANKSHAFT

H.12709

LARGE 'O' RING   OIL SEAL

Fig. 5/3: Oil seals of No. 8 bearing

E14. When reassembling the connecting rods, use new bolts and torque to the correct setting. **Note:** *it is essential that the numbers on the rods and their case should face one another and be the same. Inspect the teeth of the distributor and intermediate shaft drive gears on the crankshaft for wear or damage. Again, consult a specialist if unsure.*

E15. With the intermediate gear separated from the oil pump, inspect the sprocket and aluminium gear for wear.

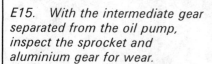

E16. This photo shows the aluminium gear of the intermediate shaft. The wear, though not enough to mean replacement, is enough to give an audible rattle at idle speeds. This type of wear is more likely on 2.7 and early 3.0 engines. If the wear on the gear has been giving an objectionable noise or if damage to the aluminium gear teeth is obvious, then the whole shaft assembly should be replaced.

E17. Inspect the intermediate shaft bearings for wear. If the bearings are scored or the copper is showing then they should be replaced. If wear in the oil pump is suspected, then the unit must be completely replaced.

Inspection of cylinders, pistons and rings

Through its production run the materials used for cylinder bore material have varied. The early models used cast iron liners, with aluminium barrels. Aluminium was later used with specially treated "Nikasil" bores, which enabled the bore size to be increased by eliminating the relatively thick cast iron liner (first seen on the Carrera RS). The later 2.7 range saw a reversal of the conventional arrangement, when plain aluminium cylinders were used. Special iron coated pistons were fitted. These "Alusil" cylinders were cheaper than the Nikasil type and gave good service. For the later 3.0 litre engines though, the Nikasil type were used once more.

E18. Barrels which have a cast iron liner can be rebored, but the later aluminium types should be replaced when over tolerance.

The bores should be checked with an internal micrometer, although clouds of blue smoke behind the car will have said something about the condition of the bores. The bore should be measured about 30 mm above the base of the barrel. The clearance between bore and piston should not exceed 0.1 mm. If in doubt, take the piston/barrel assemblies along to a specialist, who will check their condition.

Cylinder Barrel Mark	Installed Height, (mm)
5	Up to 1972: 82.000 to 82.225
	1972 onwards: 85.400 to 85.425
6	Up to 1972: 82.225 to 82.250
	1972 onwards: 85.425 to 85.450

Fig. 5/4: Barrel installed height symbols

E19. The barrels in any one bank should have the same installed height between the crankcase joint and the cylinder head joint. This is noted on the barrel by a symbol as shown by fig. 5/4.

The pistons are selected so that their marking matches the mark on its accompanying barrel.

Fig. 5/5 shows the markings to be found on the pistons and is a quick method of determining the bore size on cast iron linered models.

It is recommended that new piston rings are fitted at the time of a full rebuild, even if the bores are found to be satisfactory. Whether old or new rings are used, check the compression ring installed gap by fitting them in turn to their barrels. The ring should be squared in the barrel using a ringless piston as a guide and positioned about 30 mm from the base of the barrel. Measure the ring gap, using a feeler gauge on the new rings. If the measurement is not within the range stated in the specification table (fig. 5/6), then file the ends of the ring with a fine file or emery paper. Keep the

Engine	Ring end gap, (new)	Wear limit
2.0 litre	0.30 to 0.45	1.00
2.2 litre	0.30 to 0.45	1.00
2.4 litre	0.30 to 0.45	1.00
2.7 litre	0.15 to 0.45	1.00
3.0 litre Compression:	0.1 to 0.2	0.80
Oil scraper:	0.15 to 0.30	1.00

Fig. 5/6: Piston ring installed gaps

Pistons and cylinders will be either standard or oversize. The size of the assembly can be established from the symbols stamped on the piston crown and barrel skirt. The symbols for a given piston or barrel should match.

Standard piston and cylinder diameters, (all dimns in mms)

Marking:	0	+1	+2	+3
Cylinders				
1965-67	80.000-80.010	80.010-80.020	–	–
1968-69	80.000-80.010	80.010-80.020	80.020-80.030	–
1970-73	84.000-84.010	84.010-84.020	84.020-84.030	–
1974-77	90.000-90.010	90.010-90.020	90.200-90.030	–
1978-on	95.000-95.007	95.007-95.014	95.014-95.021	95.021-95.028
Pistons				
1965-67	79.925-79.935	79.935-79.945	79.945-79.955	–
1968 911S	79.945-79.955	79.955-79.965	79.965-79.975	–
1968 911L	79.955-79.965	79.965-79.075	79.985-79.995	–
1968-69:				
911T, (Mahle)	79.965-79.975	79.975-79.985	79.985-79.995	–
911T, (Schmidt)	79.955-79.965	79.965-79.975	79.975-79.985	–
1969 911E	79.945-79.955	79.955-79.965	79.965-79.975	–
1969 911S	79.935-79.945	79.945-79.955	79.955-79.965	–
1970-73				
911T, (Mahle)	83.952-83.967	83.962-83.977	83.972-83.987	–
911T, (Schmidt)	83.965-83.975	83.975-83.985	83.985-83.995	–
911E	83.955-83.965	83.965-83.975	83.975-83.985	–
911S	83.945-83.955	93.955-83.965	83.965-83.975	–
1974-77 911, 911S				
Nikasil	89.965-89.975	89.975-89.985	89.985-89.995	–
Alusil	89.952-89.967	89.962-89.977	89.972-89.987	–
1978-on	94.463-94.977	94.970-94.984	94.977-94.991	94.984-94.998

Oversize piston and cylinder diameters

Markings:	0KD1	1KD1	2KD1
Cylinders			
1965-67	80.500-80.510	80.510-80.520	–
1968-69	80.500-80.510	80.510-80.520	80.520-80.530
1970-73	84.250-84.260	84.260-84.270	84.270-84.280
Pistons			
1965-67	80.435-80.445	80.445-80.455	–
1968 911S	80.445-80.455	80.455-80.465	80.465-80.475
1968 911L	80.455-80.465	80.465-80.475	80.475-80.485
1968-69			
911T, (Mahle)	80.865-80.875	80.875-80.885	80.885-80.895
911T, (Schmidt)	80.455-80.465	80.465-80.475	80.475-80.485
1969 911E	80.445-80.455	80.455-80.465	80.465-80.475
1969 911S	80.435-80.445	80.445-80.455	80.455-80.465
1970-73			
911T, (Mahle)	84.202-84.217	84.212-84.227	84.222-84.237
911T, (Schmidt)	84.215-84.225	84.225-84.235	84.235-84.245
911E	84.205-84.215	84.215-84.225	84.225-84.235
911S	84.195-84.205	84.205-84.215	84.215-84.225

Oversizes were not available in pistons or barrels after 1973
Note that in 1965-67, an oversize of −1 was available as follows:
Cylinders: 80.490-80.500, Pistons: 80.425-80.435

Fig. 5/5: Piston symbols

end faces of the ring square to one another.

The compression ring/groove clearance is next checked by fitting the rings and measuring the gap between the edge of the ring and the side of the groove with feeler gauges. If the ring is tight in its groove, then fine emery should be used to rub the ring down. Do this on a flat surface such as a sheet of glass. Place the emery (or a self adhesive fine grit sanding disc) on the glass and rub the ring lightly and evenly down onto it.

Finally, assemble the piston rings to the pistons so that the word TOP is uppermost on all rings. Each ring should be fitted using a feeler gauge placed behind the ring and moved around the piston. This method ensures the ring is not overstressed as it is opened out to fit around the piston crown and also eases passage of the ring over the other grooves. Fit the rings so that the gaps are placed at equally spaced intervals around the piston.

Inspection of flywheel

On earlier models, check the starter ring gear for wear or damage, replacing the flywheel if damage is found.

If the clutch driven plate shows uneven wear or scoring, it can be machined by a specialist. Compare the differences between the earlier and later types of flywheel, (see fig. 5/7). The central bearing can be replaced at this stage, if it has been damaged or is worn. The old bearing should be tapped out using a flat faced round drift of approximately the same diameter as the bearing. Before fitting the new bearing, ensure the journal is not damaged or deformed (especially if the flywheel was difficult to remove from the crankshaft). Use the drift to evenly tap the new bearing into place, taking great care to seat

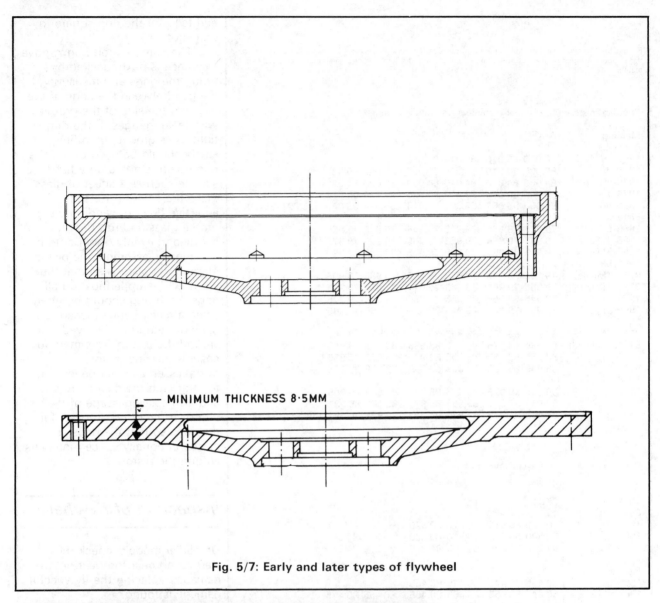

MINIMUM THICKNESS 8·5MM

Fig. 5/7: Early and later types of flywheel

the bearing squarely into its journal.

Inspection of camshafts and housings

EI10. Inspect the camshaft lobes for wear and the bearing faces for scoring or uneven wear. If a problem is suspected consult a specialist. Check the camshaft oilways for blockage and use a long probe to clear, if necessary.

EI11.   Check the bearing face of the cam where it runs on the front oil seal. The face should not be excessively grooved. It is possible to shift the position of the oil seal by a small amount, to run on a different circumference of the bearing face, if some wear is found. The seal should be replaced on rebuilding.

Closely examine the camshaft housings for cracks and clean off the remains of old jointing compound. This is especially important on the mating faces with the cylinder heads. On early models equipped with fuel injection, the bearing on the front of the left-hand camshaft should be checked for wear and replaced if necessary.

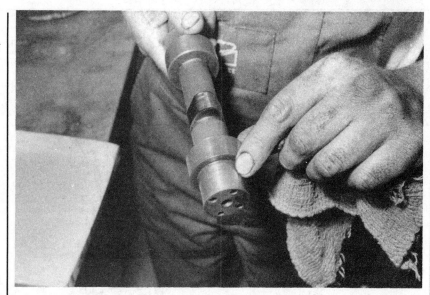

Inspection of rocker shafts and arms

The rocker shafts are retained in the camshaft housing by expansion of their ends as the centre bolt is tightened. This expansion also provides an oil seal, so cleanliness of these components is important. The rocker arm lobes should be free of score marks and obvious wear.

Inspection of cylinder heads

EI12.   Probably the easiest way to approach work on the cylinder heads is to work on one at a time. A scraper that does not damage the aluminium should be used to remove the worst of the carbon deposits from the combustion chamber and port area. A rotary wire brush held in an electric drill can be used to give a final polish on the surfaces.

A valve spring compressor will be required to remove each valve. Be careful not to lose the valve collets whilst working on the head.

Use paraffin to clean up the outside of the head and thoroughly clean off any remaining loose debris before starting reassembly.

Check the head for distortion by holding a steel straight edge on the head surface. Use a feeler gauge to measure any irregularity. If any gap exceeds 0.15 mm then the head should be replaced. If you are in any doubt about the flatness of the heads, it would be sensible to have them checked by a specialist.

Inspection of valves and valve guides

If any more than an imperceptible sideways movement is possible between the valve stem and guide then both valve and guide should be replaced. This is a job for a specialist. Again, if you are unsure then take advice on how much sideways movement is acceptable.

Examine the valve heads and their respective seatings in the head for pitting or burning. If the pitting is slight regrind the valve

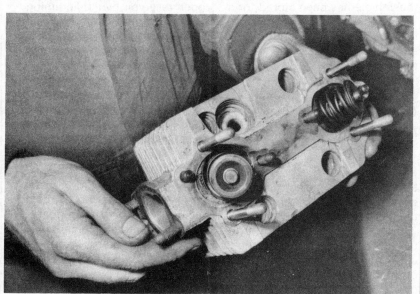

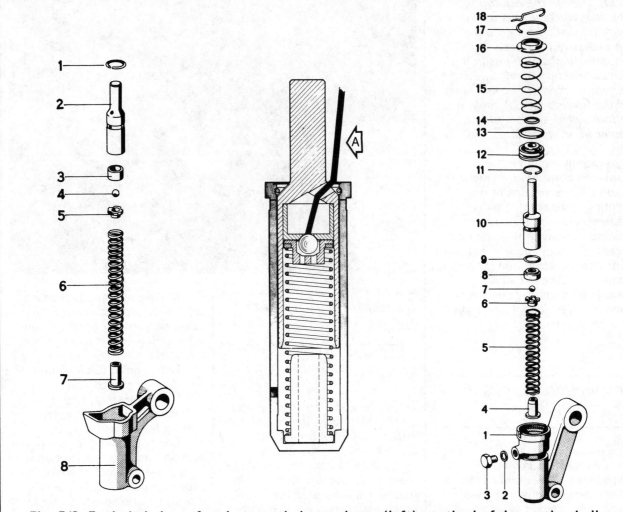

Fig. 5/8: Exploded view of early-type chain tensioner (left), method of depressing ball using a piece of wire A (centre), later type (right)

seat using coarse then fine valve grinding paste. Any worse than slight damage and the assembly should be taken to a specialist for inspection and possible new seats and valves.

Clean up the valves in the same way as the head in order to remove the carbon deposits, etc. Do not use a scraper or wire brush on 3.0 litre or Turbo engine valves. Any scratching of the stems may set up stress points which, coupled with the high temperatures may cause the valve head to break off during running. Only chemical cleaning methods should be used on these valves.

Valve springs are very expensive to replace as a complete set. Replacement

should be considered though, if the vehicle has been stored for a long time, or if certain springs have become permanently set at a lower uncompressed length than the others.

Chain tensioners – early types

Fig. 5/8 shows sketches of the three principal types of timing chain tensioners used through the life of the 911 (to date!).

Generally speaking, if the tensioner can be moved by the index finger pressing on the top of the piston, then it should be overhauled or replaced.

Until approximately 1970, open reservoir hydraulic timing chain tensioners were fitted to all 911 models, which used a hydraulic damper to control movement.

From about 1970 through to 1984, the second type, a self contained hydraulic tensioner was a standard fitment. This type was reliable for about 30,000 miles when driven hard. In normal road use and with care, these tensioners could probably be taken for many thousands of miles more. However, sudden failures were quite common with these tensioners and so guards were developed which could be clamped on the piston stem. It is important to state that these

guards were developed by non-factory sources and have never been approved by the factory as an accessory or replacement part. The guards prevented sudden collapse of the tensioner, so allowing, at worst, the chain to jump the camshaft sprocket and a valve to hit a piston. The problem could be that without very regular checking, it was possible to drive without realising a tensioner had failed. The guard would then be subject to the whip forces of the chain and eventually the single clamp bolt could slip and disaster would follow.

It is not proposed to go into the overhaul of the early tensioners since these have been superseded by much better designs, which can be retrofitted in all but the very earliest 911 models.

Chain tensioners – 1984 Carrera type

It is claimed that the tensioners introduced from 1984 are the answer to all our dreams. Unlike the previous types, the latest model is supplied with engine oil which tensions a mechanical spring arrangement. The oil-fed tensioners can be retrofitted by the competent enthusiast to any post' 1968 911. This procedure will be covered at the reassembly stage.

Part 3: Engine reassembly

A gasket set is available that covers an entire engine rebuild. It is strongly advised that all gaskets are renewed on reassembly.

The key words with any engine rebuild are cleanliness and patience. Don't try to rush through the work; speed comes with knowledge. A build mistake

due to rushing in the early stages may only be discovered when the engine is in the car and ready to be started. That is going to waste a lot more time than if the subject was carefully researched and the work understood beforehand.

Rebuilding a 911 engine can be a satisfying experience, so know what is to be done, keep everything clean and just stop work when impatience or irritation creep in.

Crankcase

ERC1. Fit the main bearing shells into the two crankcase halves. Ensure that the tags on each shell are seated in the slots provided in the castings (see also photo EI1). Ensure also that any oil passages to the main bearings line up with the holes in the shells.

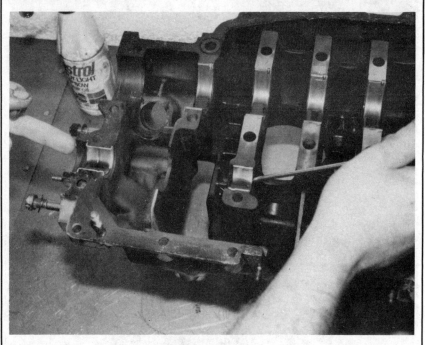

ERC2. As previously mentioned fit new intermediate shaft bearing shells to each crankcase half, if these are required.

ERC3. There is a total of four sealing rings to be fitted to the oil pump. The first of these is fitted into the recess provided in the right lower crankcase. This will eventually mate with the oil pump. Note in this photo the flanged No.8 main bearing shell. This bearing controls crankshaft endfloat.

ERC4. Fit new linkless timing chains to the intermediate shaft sprockets, if there is any doubt as to the age or wear of the original chains.

ERC5. With the intermediate ▲ shaft reassembled to the oil pump, fit the whole assembly into the right-hand crankcase, feeding the relevant timing chain through the opening in the crankcase. Ensure the sealing ring, placed in the crankcase earlier, has not become dislodged.

ERC6. This photo shows the three remaining oil sealing rings to be positioned once the oil pump is in place in the right-hand crankcase. Tighten the oil pump nuts and bend up the locking tabs.

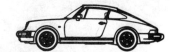

Assemble the connecting rod big-end shells to each paired rod and cap. Apply a light film of new engine oil to the faces of the shells and assemble to the crankshaft, using new connecting rod bolts, as the old ones will have stretched. Make sure that each rod is assembled in the same orientation as taken off and with the same bearing cap (keep the numbers adjacent). Fit each rod and cap assembly to the same bearing journal and with the same shells, if these have not been replaced. Tighten the big-end bolts to the specified torque.

Fit the main bearing insert for No. 8 bearing to the crankshaft, complete with new oil seals. The bearing insert will locate on a dowel in the right-hand crankcase half. It will help fitting if a mark is scribed on the insert showing where its locating hole is.

Fit the crankshaft oil seal at the flywheel end.

ERC7. Apply a light film of new engine oil to the main bearing caps. Lower the assembled crankshaft into the right-hand crankcase. Ensure the No. 8 main bearing inset is located properly in its journal and that the dowel pin has located in the correct

hole in the insert. It must not locate in the oil passage to the bearing. Make sure the crankcase is clear of the bench, to allow the connecting rods of cylinders 4, 5 and 6 to hang straight down. This allows the main bearings to seat correctly.

ERC8. Check around the crankcase mating faces for any traces of old sealing compound. Wash the faces with paraffin again if necessary before drying with a cloth. When everything is clean and you are satisfied that all the components are assembled and positioned correctly, apply a film of instant gasket compound to all the sealing faces of the left crankcase half.

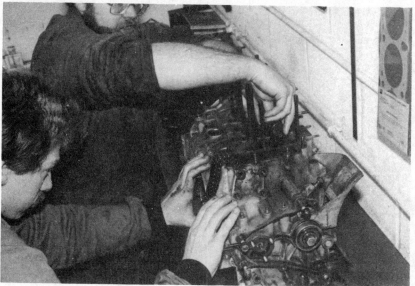

ERC9. Bring the left-hand crankcase down onto the right-hand assembly. At this stage another pair of hands could help by holding up Nos. 1, 2 and 3 con rods and the timing chain for the left bank. If help is not available, then rod and chain props will be needed (available as special tools). Alternatively, thread a piece of string through each of the small ends of the rods and through the chain and hold these up with one hand. Locate the crankcase half correctly to its opposing half.

ERC10. Ensure that nothing has become trapped between the mating faces of the crankcase halves as they are pressed together.

ERC11. The main bearing tie-bolts should be fitted with new oil seals at each end. The washer should be put on the bolt first, with the washer's smooth face towards the crankcase. The sealing ring is then pressed on to form a seal between the washer and the crankcase.

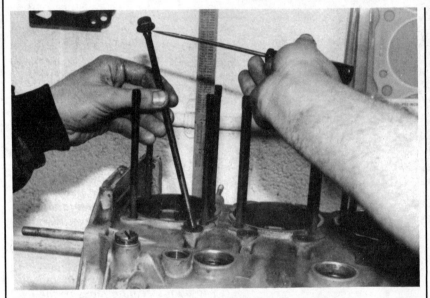

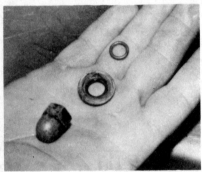

ERC12. This photo shows the tie-bolt seal, plain washer and nut, assembled to the bolt in that order. The washer smooth surface should be towards the crankcase.

ERC13. Install the nuts finger tight at this stage. The two domed nuts located within the oil cooler flange are assembled in the same way, with the oil sealing rings trapped by the plain washer.

ERC14. Fit also the plain nut and washer onto the stud in the chain housing. There is no seal on this nut.

ERC15. Tighten the tie-bolts and the stud nuts progressively to the specified torque. Ensure even loading of the crankcase by

tightening the bolts to half torque then three-quarters torque before final tightening. When one bolt is set, move on to another at the opposite end of the crankcase and so on such that the castings are not distorted by having all the bolts at one end fully tightened, whilst the other end is loose.

Fit plain washers and new self-locking nuts on all the crankcase flange studs and tighten these to the required torque. Don't forget the nuts/bolts required at the flywheel flange.

The crankshaft pulley can now be fitted along with its securing bolt and washer.

Flywheel, pistons and barrels

The flywheel needs to be fitted carefully. The flywheel/crankshaft are balanced. The flywheel can only be fitted in one particular position, this being achieved by an asymmetric arrangement of the mounting holes so it cannot be assembled incorrectly. The flywheel also locates over the front flange of the crankshaft, so that the two items are centred. The number of mounting bolts was six until the 1978 models, when the number was increased to nine. The good news was that the tightening torque was reduced from 14.6 kg f m to 9.0 kg f m!

Use new Fillister (12 point socket) headed bolts and tighten them progressively up to the specified torque. The correct 12 point socket will be necessary for this operation. When tightening to the high torque levels of earlier models, take care not to let the socket key slip out of the nut as this can result in injury. Do not smear the face of the crankshaft flank or the mating face on the flywheel with oil. Wipe all contamination from these faces. Lightly lubricate the bolts with oil before fitting. Do not use a thread locking adhesive.

Assemble the pistons as described previously. It is assumed here that the pistons are the type that have sliding fit gudgeon pins, although earlier models have an interference fit. With the interference fit types the piston should be soaked in boiling water prior to fitting to its rod.

The larger valve recess on the piston crown is always towards the inlet valve or the top of the engine; always check that piston orientation is correct.

FPB1. If new pistons are fitted, fit the circlip to one side of the gudgeon pin hole.

FPB2. Ensure that the return on the circlip sits in the recess provided in the piston. Check that the ring gaps are equally spaced around the piston circumference.

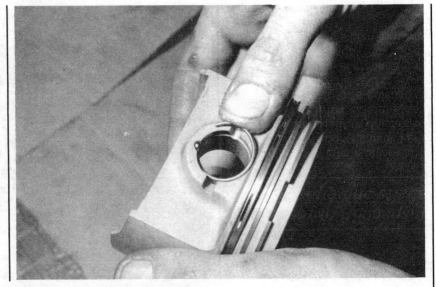

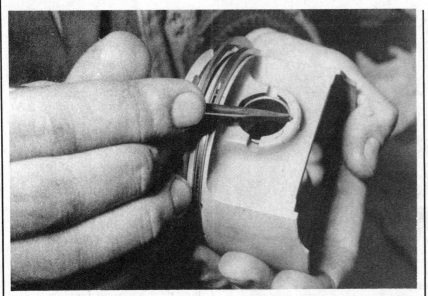

FPB4. If the liners are cast iron or Nikasil and were found to be in acceptable condition (ie not needing reboring or replacement), it will help the seating of new rings to glaze-bust the bores. This is done by lightly rubbing 1200 dry paper in a circular motion on the working areas. This is not necessary on Alusil bores. Wipe the bores when glaze-busted with a tissue or clean cloth and wet the bores with new oil. ▼

If the engine has Alusil barrels, then take particular care with the more brittle chrome plated rings. If resistance is met when tightening the piston ring compressor, then it is likely that the rings are not seating properly in the grooves. Remove the ring compressor and check it out. The oil scraper rings on this type are in three parts. Check that the expander ring is seated correctly before fitting the upper and lower parts of the scraper rings.

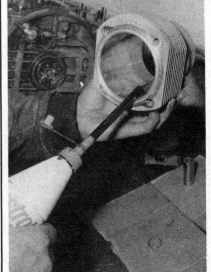

FPB3. Lubricate the piston rings with new oil. ➤

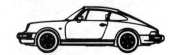

FPB5. Use a piston ring compressor to seat the rings in their grooves.

FPB6. Slide the piston into the correct barrel (from the bottom), checking again that the recesses in the piston are in the correct position.

FPB7. Push the piston in only far enough to just cover the rings.

FPB8. Check the fit of the gudgeon pin in the little-ends. Lubricate before assembly.

FPB9. Fit a new copper washer at the crankcase/barrel face.

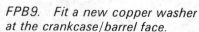

FPB10. Offer the piston and barrel up to the crankcase.

FPB11. Feed the gudgeon pin into the piston and little-end.

FPB12.   When the gudgeon pin is pushed up to the fitted circlip, fit the second circlip, checking that it is seated correctly.

FPB13.   Slide the barrel down onto the copper washer.

FPB14.   The barrel is now ready to receive a new cylinder head sealing ring. With older models, where the head sealing gasket locates on the barrel studs, ensure that the perforations are towards the cylinders. Repeat this procedure for the remaining piston/barrel assemblies.

FPB15.   Install the air deflector plates and clips around the barrels, taking care to position them correctly. (Note that these were coded on removal so that they can be replaced in the correct location).

Assembly and fitting of cylinder heads

This assembly sequence assumes that the cylinder heads and all their associated components have been checked, cleaned and replaced if necessary.

CHF1. Lubricate the valve stems and insert them into their original seats. If new valves are being fitted, these will need lapping to their new seats.

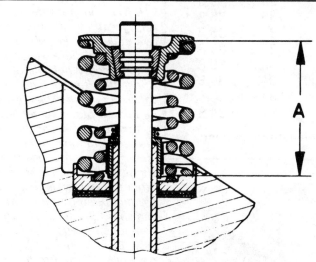

Fig. 5/9: Valve spring sectional drawing

CHF2. Note the difference in size between the inlet valve (the larger) and the exhaust. Fit the washers which determine the outer valve spring installed length, see fig. 5/9.

CHF3. Fit the spring seat and new valve stem oil seal. If Porsche tool 10c is available check the installed heights of new valve assemblies (or if the shim washers have become mixed). If this tool is not available check the heights with a caliper after fitting the springs. Check the height against the spec. given in fig. 5/10.

Engine	Valve	Length
2000, (1991cc)	Inlet	35.7 to 36.3
	Exhaust	35.7 to 36.3
2000T, (1991cc)	Inlet	40.5 to 41.0
	Exhaust	40.5 to 41.0
Eng. No. 911001 on	Inlet	34.7 to 35.3
(1991cc)	Exhaust	34.7 to 35.3
911T, (2195cc)	Inlet	35.7 to 36.3
	Exhaust	35.7 to 36.3
911E, (2195cc)	Inlet	35.7 to 36.3
	Exhaust	34.7 to 35.3
911S, (2195cc)	Inlet	35.2 to 35.8
	Exhaust	34.2 to 34.8
911S, 911T, (2341cc)	Inlet	34.7 to 35.3
	Exhaust	34.7 to 35.3
911E, (2341cc)	Inlet	33.7 to 34.3
	Exhaust	33.7 to 34.3
911, (2687cc)	Inlet	34.7 to 35.3
	Exhaust	35.2 to 35.8
911S, (2687cc)	Inlet	34.7 to 35.3
	Exhaust	35.2 to 35.8
Carrera, (2687cc)	Inlet	35.2 to 35.8
	Exhaust	34.2 to 34.8
Carrera, (2994cc)	Inlet	34.2 to 34.8
	Exhaust	34.2 to 34.8

Fig. 5/10: Valve spring installed length table (mm)

CHF4. Fit the valve springs (two per valve). If relevant, fit the close coils of the outer spring to the cylinder head. Locate the spring retainer.

CHF5. Compress the valve springs sufficiently to insert the two collets. A dab of grease helps locate these. Release the compressor. When the other valve is installed, tap the ends of each valve stem with a hammer and hardwood block, to settle the components. Repeat the valve fitting operations to the remaining cylinder heads. It is suggested the cylinder heads are fitted to the barrels first, followed by the oil return pipes and the camshaft housings. The rocker components must not be assembled before fitting the camshaft housing to the cylinder heads. Check that the head sealing rings are correctly seated in the barrels and lower each head onto its barrel. ◄

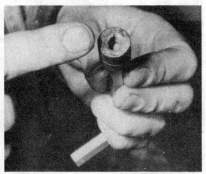

CHF6. Put a smear of grease onto the cylinder head washer.

CHF7. "Stick" it to the nut.

CHF9. Smear the faces of the camshaft housing that mate with the cylinder heads with a jointing compound (like Hylomar).

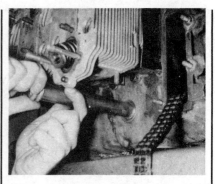

CHF11. Fit each return pipe to the crankcase, wetting each sealing ring with some new oil or grease to improve the seal.

CHF8. Install these using the correct Allen key. Repeat for all the head nuts. At this stage only finger tighten the nuts.

CHF10. Fit new O-ring seals to each end of each oil return pipe (two per bank).

CHF12. Fit the camshaft housing and install the washers and nuts, again finger tight.

CHF13. Tighten the cylinder head nuts progressively up to specified torque.

CHF14. Then tighten the camshaft housing nuts progressively up to torque. Don't tighten all the nuts on one barrel and move on to the next, go from opposite sides of the bank and tighten evenly.

1   2   3   4   5

9   4   3   2   1

8

7

6

5

1	Plug	1	Plug
2	Gasket	2	Sealing ring
3	Spring	3	Spring
4	Plunger	4	Plunger
5	Plug	5	Valve body
6	Gasket		
7	Spring		
8	Plunger		
9	Body		

Fig. 5/11: Oil pressure relief valve types

182

OF1. *Fit the oil breather casting, using a new gasket.*

OF2. *After cleaning it thoroughly and fitting a new O-ring to the body, install the oil thermostat in the top of the crankcase. It can only be fitted one way.*

Fig. 5/11 shows the components of the oil pressure relief and the oil safety valves. If the uncompressed spring length is less than 70 mm, then fit new springs. Use a new aluminium sealing ring, if one was fitted previously.

After checking that the two sealing rings are in position on the crankcase, fit the oil cooler to its flange. Use new self-locking nuts if these were used previously.

Clean the components of the crankcase oil strainer, removing any debris from the mesh. Refit the strainer so that it fits around the oil pick-up tube to the pump. Fit a new gasket to either side of the cover plate. Refit and tighten the nuts. Fit and tighten the oil drain nut.

Checking intermediate shaft endfloat

A steel rule or similar straight edge and feeler gauges will be needed for this job, which is necessary on early engines. The aim is to measure the projection of the intermediate shaft relative to the crankcase flange face. By simple calculation the thickness

of shims between the case and end cover can be found. An endfloat of 0.08 mm to 0.12 mm is required (see fig. 5/12). If a dial gauge is available, check the float by moving the shaft back and forth and compare with the thickness of the shims. Adjust these as required to give the free movement. On later engines the intermediate shaft is recessed relative to the cover plate. This later type does not require shims on the end cover.

Do not fit the cover or shims at this stage, since the camshaft sprockets must be aligned first.

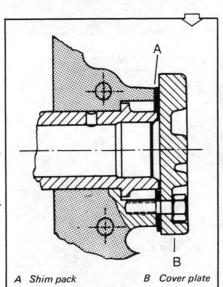

A Shim pack *B Cover plate*

Fig. 5/12: Intermediate shaft/cover gasket

Fitting camshafts and rocker assemblies

CRA1. *If the old chain guide slippers are undamaged refit these into the crankcase, so that their longer ends from the mounting studs are closest to the sprockets.*

CRA2. *Clean off the remains of any previous jointing compound from the crankcase and chain case faces. Apply a smear of new jointing compound to the faces and locate a new gasket on the crankcase face.*

CRA3. Refit the chaincase slippers, again with their longest sides towards the cam sprockets.

CRA4. Feed the chains through the opening in the chaincases and fit the cases to the crankcase.

CRA5. Refit the nuts to the chaincases. Where self-locking nuts were used previously, these should be replaced with new items. Note here the two standard nuts inside the case.

CRA6. Thoroughly clean the camshaft bearing journals in the camshaft housings and apply a film of new oil to the journals. Similarly, clean the cams. Slide each cam into its correct housing. Note that the cams are different. As a guide note that the left-hand cam has a drive take-off at its front end. Note also that the left-hand cam centre bearing is ahead of the middle two lobes, whereas the right-hand one has its centre bearing behind them. The camshaft should turn freely at this stage. If it is binding, loosen the housing nuts and retighten progressively to the correct torque, so that the cam is free to turn.

CRA7. The rocker assemblies should be thoroughly cleaned. The shafts seal against their journals in the camshaft housing, so cleanliness here is important.

CRA8. Check the assembly and fit of the rocker on its shaft. Lubricate the parts with new oil.

CRA9.   Start with the centre rockers. Slide the shaft in and locate the rocker arm in its correct position, engaging the cam and valve stem. Slide a feeler gauge between the cam housing and the rocker. Push the shaft in until the feeler gauge picks up the groove in the shaft. Remove the gauge and push the shaft in about another millimetre or so. See fig. 5/13 for the general arrangement.

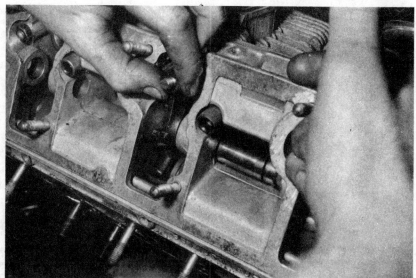

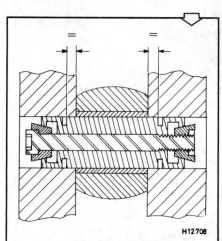

Fig. 5/13: Location of rocker shaft in cam housing

CRA10.   Fit the cones and then each nut and bolt. Tighten to the specified torque, without moving the shaft.

Repeat this procedure for the remaining rockers. It will help to back off the adjusters on the rockers, since the cam will need to be turned to enable all the rockers to be fitted. When turning the camshaft, be wary of digging a valve into a piston. Turn the crankshaft if necessary, to match the cam rotation. When the rockers are all fitted, it may simplify the valve timing work later to bring the centre punch marks on the ends of the cams back to the vertical. Similarly, turn the crankshaft again, so that the "Z1' mark on the pulley aligns with the vertical groove on the crankcase. Be careful to avoid valve contact with the pistons.

CRA11.   Fit a new paper gasket to the camshaft front bearing face. Use jointing compound to improve the seal. Fit a new O-ring to the aluminium sealing flange, also shown here.

CRA12.   Fit the flange to the camshaft housing.

CRA13.   Locate the thrust washer and spacer(s).

CRA14.   Locate the Woodruff key in its groove in the camshaft. Repeat for the other camshaft.

CRA15.   Fit the sprocket flanges to each camshaft.

CRA16.   Although the sprockets are common, the one on the left bank is fitted with its recess ► towards the rear of the engine. The right-hand sprocket is fitted the other way round. An easier way to understand this positioning is to think that the left sprocket needs to be further forward, since its drive sprocket on the intermediate shaft is in front of the right side drive sprocket (and the intermediate gear).
     Feed the chains onto the driven sprockets.

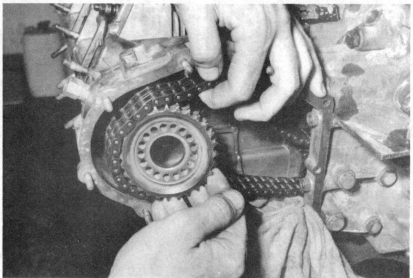

CRA17.   Left-hand sprocket installed. Don't fit the nuts until the sprocket alignment has been checked, but ensure the sprockets are correctly seated.

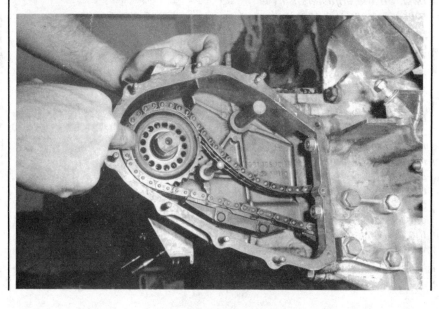

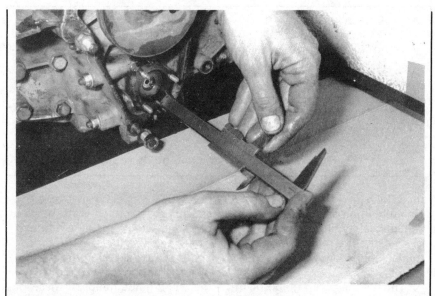

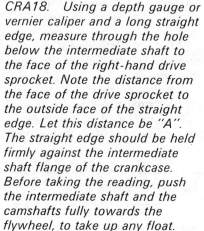

CRA18. Using a depth gauge or vernier caliper and a long straight edge, measure through the hole below the intermediate shaft to the face of the right-hand drive sprocket. Note the distance from the face of the drive sprocket to the outside face of the straight edge. Let this distance be "A". The straight edge should be held firmly against the intermediate shaft flange of the crankcase. Before taking the reading, push the intermediate shaft and the camshafts fully towards the flywheel, to take up any float.

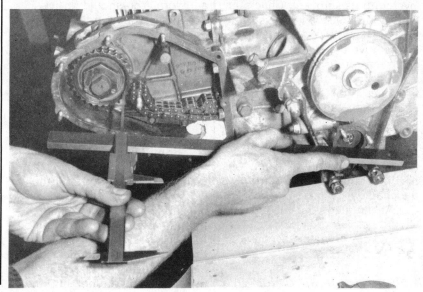

CRA19. Measure the distance from the face of the driven sprocket, in this case the left-hand side, to the rear of the straight edge. With the left side, it is not possible to measure to the face of the drive sprocket, so 54.8 mm is added to the dimension "A" above to compare with the driven sprocket dimension. See fig. 5/14.

For the right side driven sprocket, compare the centre dimension "A" directly. The maximum difference between drive and driven sprockets should not exceed 0.25 mm. If a misalignment is found, correct

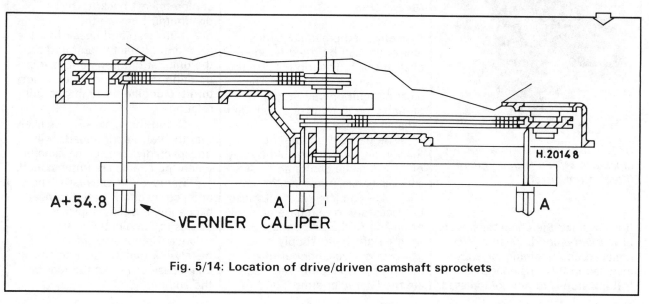

H.2014 8

A+54.8   A   A

VERNIER CALIPER

Fig. 5/14: Location of drive/driven camshaft sprockets

the spacers between the driven sprocket flange and its thrust washer.

Refit the intermediate shaft end cover, with its spacer shims, if necessary.

If the camshaft nuts are refitted, only hand tighten them at this stage as they will need to be removed for valve timing later.

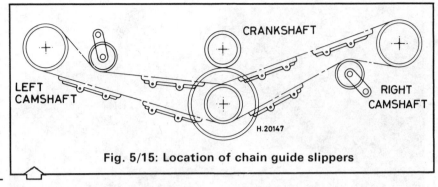

CRANKSHAFT

LEFT CAMSHAFT

RIGHT CAMSHAFT

H.20147

Fig. 5/15: Location of chain guide slippers

Chain tensioners

If early mechanical chain tensioners are to be re-used and the engine is being built up on a rotating engine stand, the heat exchangers should be refitted at this stage. This is because the early tensioners are open at their tops and their oil will run out if they are turned over. It has been previously noted that use of the early type tensioner is not recommended, when much more reliable replacements are available.

Refitting pre-84 chain tensioners

CT1. *This shot shows a pre '84 tensioner, with a failure "guard" fitted to the piston.*

It is assumed the chain tensioners have been reconditioned or replaced and retaining clips are installed in the tensioner pistons. If the pistons are not compressed,

then this should be done carefully in a bench vice and suitable safety clips installed.

Ensure the remaining chain guide slippers are correctly fitted (see fig. 5/15).

Install the chain guide pivot lever with its sprocket. Check the lubrication holes face upwards.

Fit the right-hand tensioner and remove the clip, allowing the chain tension to be taken up.

Only position the left-hand tensioner at this stage. Don't fully tighten the retaining nut as it will have to be removed to tighten the cam nut. Its safety clip should not be removed, but a wedge inserted temporarily between the piston and idler arm, to tension the chain.

At this stage the valve timing should be checked. This is covered after the next section.

Retrofitting post-'84 oil-fed tensioners

As mentioned previously, these tensioners can be fitted to any post-'68 911. The job is feasible for the average enthusiast. The most difficult operation will probably be to remove a corroded exhaust silencer.

The parts to update the tensioning system are sold by any official Porsche centre and specialists like Autofarm, in the UK, as a complete kit. It may also be necessary to purchase an extension to the oil connection for the right-hand supply pipe, ask your specialist about this.

An optional purchase also are the later idler arms, fitted to

post 1980 models. However, spacers are supplied with the basic kit, which enable continued use of the existing arms.

It would also be prudent to take the opportunity of replacing the chain guide ramps, if these are worn. You should fit five black ramps and, in the lower right-hand side, a brown one. On early engines, the black ramps may give a higher noise level and fitting all brown (lower height) ramps will reduce this noise.

The car should be raised on axle stands and the engine oil drained out.

Bring number one cylinder to top-dead-centre by turning the crankshaft pulley nut until the "Z1" mark aligns with the crankcase split line. To ensure that number one and not number four cylinder is at TDC, follow the plug lead from number one cylinder (at the rear left side of the engine as you look into the compartment) back to the distributor. Remove the distributor cap and check that the rotor arm contact is pointing at the number one segment. If it is pointing in the opposite direction, turn the engine through one full rotation.

Doing this makes it less likely that the valve spring loads will unexpectedly turn the camshafts when the chains are untensioned.

Remove the exhaust silencer at its connections with the heat exchangers. It may improve access to remove the lower rear valance. Remove the sheet metalwork that attaches to the chain case covers at the rear of the engine.

TF3.   Similarly, remove the right-hand side camshaft oil feed pipe.

TF4.   Fit the replacement right-hand feed pipe. As noted at the beginning, on certain models it may be necessary to use an extension connector, where the pipe exits the crankcase.

TF1.   Undo and remove the oil supply pipe from behind the distributor to the top of the left camshaft housing.

TF2.   Fit the replacement pipe provided with the fitting kit, as shown. The oil connections should use new aluminium washers to ensure a good, leak-free seal. The tapered aluminium sealing ring that fits the straight-in pipe at the crankcase should be fitted in the same way as the item it replaces, with the small edge towards the crankcase.   ▶

TF5.   Remove the chain case covers to reveal the chain assemblies. Note the tensioner guard fitted to this pre-'84 tensioner.

TF6. Starting with the right ►
side, remove the tensioner. Be
careful not to disturb the
relationship of the drive and
driven sprockets. The chain
should not be allowed to slacken
excessively. The chain can be
supported by inserting a block of
wood under the idler arm or by
wrapping wire around the chain,
both at the driven sprocket and
the drive sprocket ends. If a cam
is allowed to move relative to its
drive sprocket, it may then be
necessary to re-time the cam, as
discussed in an earlier section.

At this stage fit new chain
ramps, if this is necessary. Fit the
ramps so that the longest ends
point towards their adjacent
sprockets. If one of the centre
ramps falls into the crankcase, it
can be retrieved by opening the
sump cover. When fitting the
central ramps make sure they are
engaged on their mounting bolts
and not misaligned to the chain.
One bolt only clicks each ramp
into place, the other acts only as
a support. If the right side centre
ramps are to be changed, the
engine should be jacked up and a
support placed under the rear of
the crankcase. This will allow the
rear engine mount to be removed
and give access to the ramp
fitting bolts.

TF7.   The spacer washer has
been positioned on this pre-'80 ▼

idler arm. Note here that the
chain is slack, since this engine
has been rebuilt and has not yet
had the valve timing set. If the
new tensioners are being fitted in
place of the older types, not in
the course of a full rebuild, the
importance of keeping the chain
tensioned at all times to preserve
existing valve timing has been
noted and is more important on
the right-hand side, with number
one cylinder at TDC, since the
cam is much more likely to move.

If new type idler arms are to
be fitted, ensure that the open
edge in the idler sprocket shaft is
facing upwards, see next photo.

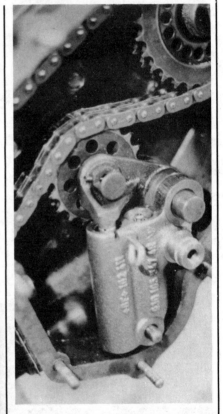

TF8.   Fit the tensioner, complete
with safety pin in place. When
satisfied with the location of all
the components, fit the tensioner
fastening nut, with spring washer,
if required. Remove the safety
pin, followed by the clamp wires,
if these were used.

TF9.   Remove the old left-hand tensioner, again taking care not to let the chain go slack. Fit the spacer washer to the idler shaft if necessary.

TF10.   Slide on the new tensioner and when the locating nut is fitted, release the safety pin. Fit the small red O-ring seals on the oil feed stubs into the tensioners.

On early model cars, it will be necessary to replace the two top left-hand chain cover fitting studs, with the two provided in the tensioner kit. This will enable the left-hand chain cover provided with the kit to be fitted (it is designed to fit all models of 911 and accommodates an air pump mounting flange on that cover). Use a "Mole" type wrench to remove the old studs and fit the new studs using a thread-locking adhesive. Be careful not to damage the threads when using the wrench.

TF11. Completed tensioner installation.

Clean off any remains of old sealing compound from the chain case flanges and cover faces. Locate a new sealing gasket on each chain case flange.

Ease the chain covers over the O-ring seals as the covers are fitted to the chain cases.

Evenly tighten down the chain covers.

Use new aluminium washers to fit the oil feed lines from the cam housing lines.

It will be necessary to cut a small slot in the rear engine sheet metal cover that attaches to the chain cases. This will allow the right-hand tensioner feed line to clear the cover on reassembly. Tin snips will be suitable for the job and the slot should be filed afterwards to eliminate any sharp edges.

On completion, refill the engine with oil and when warmed up check for leaks around the new connections.

It will be found that the new tensioners smooth the engine note when idling, otherwise no difference will be noticed. The old tensioner guards can be consigned to the garage museum!

Valve timing

VT1.   This is the stage where the "Z1" mark on the pulley should align with the crankcase joint. This places number one cylinder at top dead centre (TDC). The centre punch marks that are stamped on the end faces of the camshafts should also be vertical.

VT2.   With the cams and crankshaft so positioned, find the hole in each camshaft sprocket that perfectly aligns with the holes in the flanges behind them. Fit the dowel pin to each of these aligned holes.

Locate the spring washers and camshaft nuts and tighten to the correct torque. The left-hand chain tensioner location nut can now be fully tightened. Remove the wedge between the piston and the idler follower and release the safety clip.

Adjust the clearances on number one cylinder inlet valve (on the top bank of valves, nearest the left-hand timing chain) to 0.1 mm. The method of adjusting valve clearances is described in the next section.

Use a dial gauge, fitted with an extended probe and fitted so that its probe rests on No. 1 inlet valve spring retaining cap. Preload the probe so that it does not lose contact with the valve cap when the spring is compressed.

Compress the plunger of the left side chain tensioner (using a screwdriver) and wedge a thick washer between the plunger and the tensioner sprocket to prevent the latter dropping. Repeat this on the right side.

Turn the crankshaft, using the pulley bolt, through 360 degrees or one full rotation. Align the "Z1" mark.

No. 1 inlet valve will be opened. Read off the amount the valve has opened from the dial gauge. Check this reading against fig. 5/16.

Any out of tolerance readings will require the camshaft nut to be removed again and the dowel pin taken out from the camshaft sprocket, using an M4 bolt. The cam should then be turned slightly until the correct valve movement is shown on the dial gauge. Refit the dowel pin into a different hole in the sprocket, which has become perfectly aligned with another hole in the rear flange. Refit the washer and camshaft nut.

Turn the crankshaft, by the pulley nut, a full two rotations and realign the "Z1" mark. Check the dial gauge reading again and compare with the data of fig. 5/16. If the amount of valve opening movement is still not correct, repeat the nut removal and reposition the dowel pin as above. When satisfied with the No. 1 inlet vlave movement, fit the dial gauge to measure No. 4 inlet valve and check this. Adjust as above, if necessary. Remove the wedges from the chain tensioner plungers when the adjustment is completed.

Engine	Dial Gauge Reading
2000, (to engine 909927)	Ideal: 4.3 Allowed: 4.2 to 4.6
2000, (from engine 90927)	Ideal: 3.15 Allowed: 3.0 to 3.3
2000S	Ideal: 5.2 Allowed: 5.0 to 5.4
2000T	Ideal: 2.5 Allowed:2.3 to 2.5
2.4T	Ideal: 2.6 Allowed: 2.4 to 2.8
2.4E	Ideal: 2.9 Allowed: 2.7 to 3.1
2.4S	Ideal: 5.2 Allowed: 5.0 to 5.4
'74 911	Allowed: 0.7 to 0.9
'75 911	Allowed: 0.5 to 0.7
'74-on 911S	Allowed: 0.40 to 0.54
'74-on 2.7 Carrera	Allowed: 5.0 to 5.4
'76-on 3.0 Carrera	Allowed: 0.90 to 1.10
'78-on 911SC	Allowed: 1.4 to 1.7

Fig. 5/16: No.1 inlet valve overlap table

Adjustment of valve clearances

The valves should be set cold. The crankshaft should be aligned so that the "Z1" mark on the V-belt pulley lines up vertically with the crankcase joint, with No.1 cylinder at TDC and No.4 on overlap. If the clearances are being adjusted with the engine in the car and the distributor fitted, check that No.1 and not No.4 is at TDC. This is done by noting which plug lead the rotor arm is pointing to when the distributor cover is removed. Turning the crankshaft is far easier with the spark plugs out. To adjust the valve clearances, remove the four rocker covers.

Use a feeler gauge to set both inlet and exhaust valve clearances to 0.1 mm. The clearance is measured between the end of the valve stem and the cap on the end of the rocker adjusting screw. The feeler should be a firm sliding fit. Adjust the rocker screw using a ring spanner and correct size screwdriver. When the clearance is correct, lock the nut without moving the screw.

The valves clearances can be most easily checked by doing them in the firing order, namely 1 – 6 – 2 – 4 – 3 – 5. The crankshaft pulley is marked into thirds, so turning the pulley until the next mark aligns with the split line brings the next cylinder in the above sequence to TDC, with both its valves closed.

Fitting the distributor

The "Z1" mark should align with the split line on the crankcase and No.1 cylinder should be at TDC (not No.4). To check this, there should be clearance on No1's valves and No.4's should be loaded. If No.1 cylinder is at overlap, turn the crankshaft through 360 degrees.

A new O-ring should be fitted to the distributor body before refitting. With No.1 cylinder at TDC, insert the distributor into the crankcase. Use previously made centre punch marks to roughly position the distributor so that the rotor arm points towards No.1 distributor cap segment. Use the cap with its plug leads for this. Pinch up the clamp nut.

Turn the crankshaft so that the rotor arm moves towards No.5 segment. Use a small timing light to determine when the points just begin to open as the crankshaft is then turned in the opposite direction towards No.1 segment. A sidelight bulb connected to a battery and switched across the contact breakers will be satisfactory. When the bulb goes out, the points are just opening.

If necessary, loosen the clamp nut and adjust the distributor position to get the correct static timing (see specifications). When set, the correct mark on the V-belt pulley should align with the crankcase split line. As a rough guide 1 mm at the rim of the pulley is equivalent to one degree of ignition advance, but don't use this to set the timing. As an example, an engine with 5 degrees ATDC static timing should have the breakers just opening when the crankcase split line is aligned with a point 5 mm to the right of the "Z1" mark on the pulley.

With the static timing set, the dynamic timing should be adjusted, using a strobe. When the strobe is shone onto the corrrect timing mark on the pully, it should align with the crankcase split line at the specified rpm. See fig. 5/17 for these figures. Where the dynamic timing is checked at 900 rpm, the vacuum line should remain connected. For checks at 6000 rpm, the vacuum line may need to be disconnected. For models with Capacitative Discharge System, or CDS ignition, connect up the strobe

Firing Order: 1-6-2-4-3-5
Number one cylinder is rearmost on the left of the engine when viewed from the back of the car.

Coil Ignition Systems: Dwell angle: 40 +/− 3 degrees.
                                          Distributor points gap: 0.4 mm, (0.016 in.)

Capacitative Discharge Systems, (CDS):
Dwell Angle – Bosch distributor: 38 +/− 3 degrees
               Pre '73 Marelli: 40 +/− 3 degrees
               '73-on Marelli: 37 +/− 3 degrees
Distributor Points Gap –Bosch: 0.3 mm. (0.012 in.)
               Pre '73 Marelli: 0.4 mm. (0.016 in.)
               Post '73 Marelli: 0.35 mm, (0.014 in.)

Ignition Timing

Year/Model		Static	Idle, (with Strobe)	6000 rpm, ditto
1965		0 deg TDC	–	–
1966-911		5 deg BTDC	–	32-33 deg BTDC
-911S		5 deg BTDC	–	30-31 deg BTDC
1967-911		5 deg BTDC	3 deg ATDC at 850-950 rpm	18-32 deg BTDC
-911S		5 deg BTDC	–	30-31 deg BTDC
-911T		5 deg BTDC	–	28-32 deg BTDC
1968-911S		5 deg BTDC	–	30 deg BTDC
-911E		0 deg TDC	–	30 deg BTDC
-911T		5 deg BTDC	–	30 deg BTDC
1969-911S		5 deg BTDC	–	30 deg BTDC
-911E		5 deg BTDC	–	30 deg BTDC
-911T		0 deg TDC	–	35 deg BTDC
1970-911S		5 deg BTDC	–	30 deg BTDC
-911E		5 deg BTDC	–	30 deg BTDC
-911T		0 deg TDC	–	30 deg BTDC
1971-911S		5 deg BTDC	–	30 deg BTDC
-911E		5 deg BTDC	–	30 deg BTDC
-911T		5 deg BTDC	–	32-38 deg BTDC
1972-76		–	5 deg ATDC at 850/950 rpm	32-38 deg BTDC
1974-75	2.7 Carrera	–	TDC at 850/950 rpm	–
1974-77 911		–	5 deg ATDC at 850/950 rpm	–
1976-on	3.0 Carrera	–	5 deg ATDC at 850/950 rpm	–
1978-81 911SC		–	5 deg BTDC at 850/950 rpm	–
1981-on 911SC		–	25 deg BTDC at 4000 rpm	

All ignition timing at 6000 rpm are with vacuum line disconnected, if appropriate. All timings at 850/950 rpm are with vacuum line connected, except 1967 911, (which should be disconnected).

As a guide, one degree approximates to one millimetre moved at the circumference of the crankshaft pulley.

Fig. 5/17: Ignition timing – static and dynamic

only to the fusebox. Connecting the strobe to the ignition transformer may damage the transistorised switches. Rotate the distributor after loosening the clamp nut, if further adjustment is needed. Consult the handbook for your model to find out what type of ignition system you have. Generally, the CDS systems are easily recognised by a high pitched tone from the engine compartment when the ignition is turned on.

Finishing off the engine rebuild

The major work of the rebuild has now been completed.

The assembly of the remaining components is straightforward and will not be described here. The following notes will be useful:

To reduce the chance of oil leaks, fit new gaskets to the rocker covers and chaincase covers.

Align the cooling fan and alternator correctly in the mounting clamp. Tighten the clamp bolts before fitting the plastic cooling air guide that fits to the back of the fan and the crankcase. Be very careful to reconnect the alternator connections exactly as they came off.

When refitting the cooling fan drive belt, tension the belt to give about 15 mm movement at mid way between the pulleys. The tension can be adjusted by adding or taking out shims from behind the pulley flange.

When refitting the rear engine mounting, check that it is positioned horizontally, relative to the engine. Use a known point on the rear of each cylinder bank to equalise the height of each end of the mounting.

The clutch is assembled to the flywheel as a reverse of the removal.

To prevent any imbalance from an off-centre clutch plate, it will be necessary to refit the three spacers to the tapped rivets on the pressure plates of certain cars. This will hold the pressure plate off and allow the centre plate to be aligned. Use a suitable mandrel to centre the plate relative to the flywheel and pressure plate.

The engine and gearbox should be refitted as one unit to the car, when all the ancillaries have been fitted and checked over for tightness, etc.

If new bearings or piston rings have been fitted, allow these to seat correctly in the first few hundred miles. Change the oil and filter after 500 miles and recheck for leaks, etc.

6 Mechanical and Electrical Components

Fuel systems

The 1973 911T was the last 911 to use carburettors. The 911's carburettor supplier changed several times and fig. 6/1 shows this.

Fuel injection

Mechanical fuel injection was introduced in the 1969 model year to the 911S. This same type of fuel injection later appeared on the 911E and other higher performance models, such as the

Carrera RS. System descriptions will not be given here as these can be found in a number of other texts.

From the 1974 model year all 911 models (with the exception of the 2.7 Carrera) have used K Jetronic fuel injection, this system being less complicated

YEAR	MODEL	CAPACITY	CARBURETTOR OR FUEL INJECTION TYPE
1965-67	911	1991cc	SOLEX 40PI, (TWO, TRIPLE CHOKE)
1965-67	911	1991cc	WEBER 40IDAP 3C AND 3CI, (N. AMERICA)
1965-67	911L	1991cc	WEBER 40IDA 3C AND 3CI
1965-67	911S	1991cc	WEBER 40IDA 3C AND 3CI
1965-67	911T	1991cc	WEBER 40IDA 3C AND 3CI
1968	911S	1991cc	BOSCH MECHANICAL FUEL INJECTION
1968	911T	1991cc	WEBER 40IDT 3C AND 3CI*
1969-71	911T	2195cc	ZENITH 40 TIN**
1969-71	911E	2195cc	BOSCH MECHANICAL FUEL INJECTION
1969-71	911S	2195cc	BOSCH MECHANICAL FUEL INJECTION
1972-73	911T	2341cc	ZENITH 40TIN (EUROPE ONLY)
1972-73	911E	2341cc	BOSCH MECHANICAL FUEL INJECTION
1972-73	911S	2341cc	BOSCH MECHANICAL FUEL INJECTION
1974-78	911	2687cc	BOSCH K JETRONIC FUEL INJECTION
1974-75	911S	2687cc	BOSCH K JETRONIC FUEL INJECTION
1974-77	Carrera	2994cc	BOSCH K JETRONIC FUEL INJECTION
1974-84	Turbo	2994cc	BOSCH K JETRONIC FUEL INJECTION
1978-84	911SC	2994cc	BOSCH K JETRONIC FUEL INJECTION
1984-date	Carrera	3164cc	BOSCH MOTRONIC ENG. MNGMT. SYSTEM
1984-date	Turbo	3299cc	BOSCH MOTRONIC ENG. MNGMT. SYSTEM

* With Sportomatic Weber 40 IDS 3C.
** Certain 1969-71 models have Weber 40 IDTP 3C/3CI or 40IDTP 13C/3CI.

Fig. 6/1: Table of fuel system types

than the mechanical type.

From 1984, the Motronic "engine management" system was adopted.

The fuel system components should not be dismantled by the enthusiast. It is a job for the trained professional. Most 911 models will require their fuel systems to be set up on an electronic diagnostic facility.

The enthusiast will be able to do certain diagnostic checks, if a problem occurs. These tests should be confined to assessing whether fuel is being pumped from the tank to the induction system, or whether the warm start device (1972-on models) is functioning.)

Refitting the mechanical system fuel distributor

When refitting the pump after an engine rebuild, it will be necessary to adjust the delivery stroke adjustment to the position of the crankshaft. Turn the crankshaft pulley bolt so that the "Z" mark aligns with the crankcase split line and the distributor rotor arm points towards number one segment on the cap.

Then turn the crankshaft through one complete rotation. Continue past the "Z" mark until the "FE" mark aligns with the split line.

N.B. If the engine is in the car, use a small mirror to align the marks on the pump pulley and pump body. If the marks will not align when the belt is fitted, the driven sprocket on the fuel pump or the drive sprocket on the end of the cam will need to be adjusted. You can adjust either depending on accessibility.

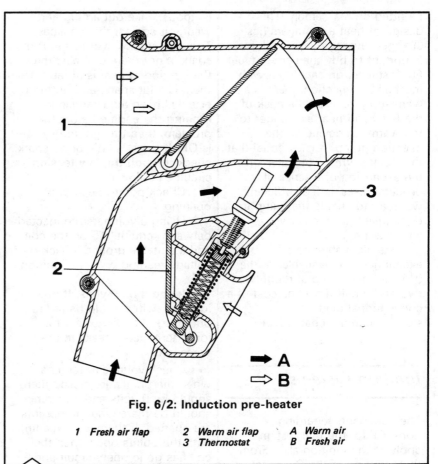

Fig. 6/2: Induction pre-heater

1 Fresh air flap	2 Warm air flap	A Warm air
	3 Thermostat	B Fresh air

Induction pre-heater

This device can be the cause of warm-up problems for 1972-on fuel injected engines. It contains a thermostat (see fig. 6/2), which maintains intake air at a constant level of approximately 45 degrees C. The device aims to improve warm-up and exhaust emissions.

Warm air is drawn from the left-hand heat exchanger and can be mixed with fresh air drawn from within the engine compartment. The thermostat controls the air mixing. When the engine is cold the flap should be positioned so that all the induction air is being drawn from the heat exchanger. The closed ambient air inlet can be checked with the fingers. When warmed up, the flap will have opened. The extent of opening will be determined by the outside air temperature. If the thermostat fails the complete pre-heater must be replaced.

Fuel pumps

When the car receives its more detailed maintenance (say an annual inspection) the fuel filter should be removed and either replaced, if a separate component, or cleaned. Clean out the pump housing and reassemble, checking that no leaks are possible.

Exhaust systems

The complexity of the heat exhanger system used on the 911 means replacement of these is a relatively expensive business. If the heat exchangers and silencers are removed, new gaskets should

be fitted on reassembly. The design of heat exchangers has changed over the years and it is important to buy the correct type. For instance, on cars fitted with mechanical injection, there is a warm-up pipe from the neck of the left-hand heat exchanger to the warm-up device on the injection pump. It is essential that this device, which operates on the expansion of a series of bi-metal discs, is fed sufficient warm air to enable the pump to be regulated to the correct temperature.

Stainless steel heat exchangers are available for the 911, but are priced at roughly two and a half times the cost of a conventional mild steel/aluminium coated type.

Ignition systems

The comments regarding non-DIY for the fuel system apply to the ignition also. From the adoption of the Capacitative Discharge System (CDS), the ignition requires matching with the fuel system accurately. If problems are suspected, then a specialist using diagnostic test equipment will get to the problem quicker. If you are unsure which ignition system you have fitted to your 911, consult the handbook. CDS ignition can usually be identified by a high-pitched tone from the engine compartment, when the ignition is turned on.

Coil ignition

Prior to 1969, conventional coil ignition was used. It is not considered that the enthusiast will require a description of how this system works, but a few fault finding comments might be helpful. Consider the situation when the engine will not start when turned over, (ie the battery

is good). Take out a plug and wedge it against the crankcase. Turn the engine over again. If the spark is not there or weak, then the ignition system is at fault. If there is a fat spark, and nothing else has been adjusted since running the engine before the problem, then the ignition system is OK. If there is little or no spark, check through the low tension circuit as follows:

Check points clean and opening.

Using a voltmeter connected between terminal 15 on the coil and a suitable ground, check the voltage reading with the ignition on.

It shold be 9 volts. If not the ignition switch could be at fault, but check the wiring first for loose terminals, breaks in the wires, etc.

Check voltage at terminal 1; when the points are closed there should be 0 volts and a reading should be there when the points are opened. If there is no reading with the points open, then the coil has gone open circuit and should be replaced.

Check the voltage across the points; when the points are closed there should be 0 volts. With the points open, there should be a reading. If there is no reading with the points open then replace the condenser.

With these checks completed and the fault not found, check the high-tension circuit as follows:

Pull off the HT lead from the centre of the distributor and wedge the end (don't hold it) about 2 mm from the crankcase. Turn the engine over; there should be a large spark. If not, the coil should be replaced.

Turn the ignition off and replace the centre HT lead to the distributor. Check that centre electrode is contacting the rotor arm. There should be no cracks in the cap or signs of electrical tracking (shorting to earth/ground). Clean all the contacts on the plug lead segments. Check the rotor arm for

secure location.

Check the plug leads for signs of damage and that the plugs themselves are clean and gapped correctly.

Capacitative discharge system

A short description of how this system works may be helpful. The principal advantage of this system over the coil arrangement is better high speed spark generation and a more precisely timed ignition. The system offers a stronger spark, since a higher voltage is used than in the coil system, and it allows a larger spark plug gap.

A condenser within the CDS unit is charged to 350 to 400 volts. When the distributor points open, the trigger unit operates a thyristor (or switch) which discharges the capacitor into the primary winding of the coil. The voltage induced in the secondary winding of the coil then produces the spark. A centrifugal advance and retard is retained from the coil system. No points condenser is fitted as the highly inductive primary voltage is not switched by the points in this system.

Great care should be taken not to remove the ignition coil or CDS unit when the ignition is on because there is danger of severe, even fatal electric shock, particularly if the storage capacitor is known to be defective.

As mentioned earlier, it is suggested that fault finding on CDS will be outside the scope of the average enthusiast.

Front suspension and steering

It is advised that you have any work you have carried

out on the suspension or **steering checked over by a specialist, before using the car on the road.**

The front suspension is of the MacPherson strut type, with a single lower wishbone each side.

With the exceptions noted below, all 911 models have torsion bars damped by telescopic shock absorbers. The bars are adjustable for ride height. 1969 911E models used a self-levelling type strut, although this became only an option for 1972.

No attempt is made here to describe the different types of suspension struts that have been fitted to the 911, since production began. The reader is directed to an authoritative history of the model for specific details, and to the Haynes Owners Workshop Manual for specific dismantling/assembly differences.

Rack and pinion steering is used on all 911 models. Needless to say its layout has been changed since the first models. Check the steering components for any signs of wear, especially the ball joints that fit the wheel hub steering arms. Replace these if wear is detected. The rack is maintenance-free and if wear is found, the unit should be replaced.

If splits are found in the flexible boots around the rack, inspect the rack very carefully for wear. The rack should be cleaned and repacked with a general purpose grease containing molybdenum disulphide, before fitting new flexible boots.

Front suspension removal

Never work on a Porsche suspension system unless you are trained and competent to do so. If you are not, take the car to a specialist. This following section is for information only.

The car should be raised on a lift or at least axle stands so that the front wheels are clear of the ground. **Never use a jack of any type to support the weight of the car whilst working underneath. Support the body safely using at least axle stands.** If axle stands are used, support the weight of the body at the recommended points only, using blocks of wood between the body and stands to distribute the load.

Remove the front road wheels.

FS1. Note how the tops of the suspension struts mount into the body turrets. On this post '68 model, the three socket-head bolts, when loosened, allow movement of the strut relative to the body. This permits adjustment of the camber (by moving the strut from side to side) and the castor (by moving the strut forwards or backwards). The camber and castor will need re-setting if the suspension is removed. This requires specialist equipment. In order to position the struts in approximately the same position on reassembly, it will be useful to make aligning marks on the single and double hole pressure plates next to the strut apertures in each turret. These marks should be made **before** loosening the socket head bolts.

It must be repeated that this will only give an approximate setting and should be checked using the correct equipment after reassembly.

The socket-head bolts should be tightened to 4.7 kg f m (34 lb f ft) and the pressure plates re-sealed with permanently elastic sealer.

FS2. With the positions of the pressure plates noted and the socket-head bolts removed, lift the plates off the turret. On pre '69 models, fold back the lock tab on the top of the suspension strut. Use a C-spanner to stop the notched washer from turning and take off the hexagon nut. The strut can now be pushed downwards and clear of the turret.

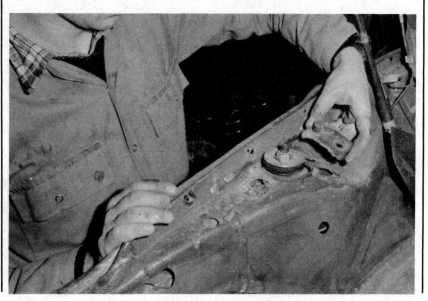

FS3. From inside the wheel arch push down the strut until it can be pulled outwards from the turret.

FS4. An example of poor workmanship – a self-grip wrench clamped to the pipe will prevent excessive brake fluid leakage, but can damage the wall of the pipe in a way that will only show itself later, probably at the moment when you need the brakes rather urgently. Companies such as Sykes-Pickavant make a tool specifically for the job, available from good tool and accessory stores.

FS5. Remove the flexible brake pipe connection at the strut end, inspecting the pipe for any signs of perishing or leakage. Your specialist will replace this if suspect in any way.

FS6. Remove the split pins from the steering arm ends and then take off the castellated nuts.

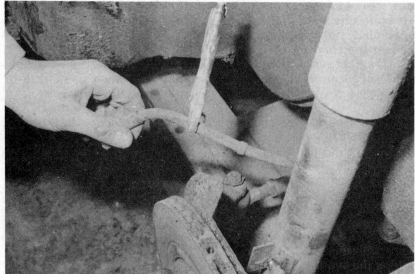

FS7. Separate the steering arms from the kingpins by using a ► proprietary balljoint separator. If the ball joints are to be re-used, be careful not to damage their rubber boots. If the boot is split already or any relative movement has been detected between the steering arm and the kingpin, the ball joint must be replaced. If these are replaced the toe-in will need re-setting before the car is driven again.

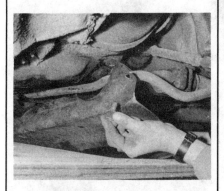

FS8. With the front of the car safely supported as described earlier, remove the bolts holding the spray guard in position on the front underside.

FS9. This is a post '74 front anti-roll bar, showing the removal of one of the two mounting bolts which locate the auxiliary supports of the reinforcing

crossmember. Once the two bolts are removed the anti-roll bar can be pulled out from the mountings on the top of each lower wishbone. Pull out one side and then the other. It will be noted that it is a straightforward job to uprate this type of anti-roll bar. Consult a specialist for possible alternatives. As an example, post '74 models of 911 and 911S had 16 mm bars as standard, with the Carrera model having 20 mm bars. Later models use larger diameters still. The flexible bushes should be checked for splitting or wear and replaced if wear is detected between bar and bush. On reassembly, smear

glycerine or a suitable rubber lubricant on the mating surfaces.

The anti-roll bar arrangement on pre '74 cars used a transverse rod with twin levers and link rods connected to the lower wishbones. The bar passed through the front compartment to the rear of the petrol tank. On dismantling, check the condition of all the flexible bushes and replace if cracked or worn. Check also the sheet metal levers for signs of corrosion and replace if necessary.

FS10.▲ There is one reinforcing crossmember retaining bolt, on each side to hold the crossmember to the body. Do not confuse the retaining bolts with the smaller torsion bar adjusting bolts near them. The torsion bar adjusting bolts should not be moved during suspension removal, unless the wishbone is to be removed.

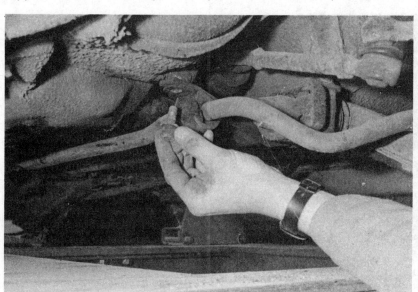

Owners of pre '72 models will have noticed that the front suspension configuration is different in detail. The procedure for removing the front suspension is the same. On 2.7 Carrera models, the reinforcing crossmember is a forged alloy component, rather than a steel tube.

FS11. *Remove the bolts from* ▶ *the torsion bar front mounting brackets and remove the brackets. This one looks as though it's in such bad shape that it has fallen out!*

FS12. *Support the front suspension assembly before . . .*

FS13. *. . . removal of the bolts holding the crossmember to the steering rack.*

FS14. *Lower the suspension assembly away from the body, checking as it is lowered that no parts remain attached.*

FS15. *The complete front suspension ready for cleaning and then inspection. Check the wishbones for rust attack, especially around the anti-roll bar mountings and the forward facing areas. Replace if cracked or damaged by rust. The front suspension struts should be inspected for signs of leakage and replaced if this is found or if the struts are known to be defective. Consult your model specification for the type of strut used. It is possible to uprate the shock absorber units, but this may require replacement of the lower strut/kingpin assembly, which is expensive.*

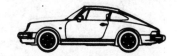

As a guide the strut manufacturer may be identified by its colour. Boge or Porsche types are black, Koni are red and Bilstein are green. Consult a specialist for the most economic set-up for your planned use.

FS16.   A front strut assembly removed from the wishbone. Note the good condition of this brake disc. It is free of scoring and heavy wear.

Ventilated discs were introduced to the 911 from the 1969 model year.

Adjustment of Koni shock absorbers (red casing)

It may be useful to note that rebound damping is adjustable on Koni shock absorbers as fitted to certain models of 911. Consult your model specification to establish what make is fitted. Generally, if they are Konis then the casing will be coloured red (under all that mud!).

912 models were adjusted to the softest settings and early 911 types have the struts set one turn harder, or one full turn counter-clockwise.

The struts can be adjusted on the car, but the front wheels must be removed and the strut top mounting must be removed from the body turret. Follow the procedure given at the start of this section to do this.

Unlock the hexagon nut at the top of the strut and remove the nut, checking the rubber bushings for wear.

Push down the plunger and external casing to the limit of its travel and turn the plunger rod to the left (clockwise), until you can feel its adjusting lug engage with the slot in the base of the bottom casing.

With a felt pen or similar mark two aligning points on the upper and lower casings for

reference.

To establish what the existing setting is, turn the top casing and plunger rod all the way to the left (clockwise) and then back to the original position.

To harden the damping, turn the outer casing and plunger rod to the right (counter-clockwise), at least half a turn or more. The adjustment range is two and a quarter full turns.

When satisfied with the adjustment, pull the upper casing and plunger upwards to release the lug. Repeat the same adjustment on the other side, so that the damping rates are the same on the one axle line.

The shock absorbers can now be refitted to the turrets.

Inspection of front wheel and brake assembly

Never work on a Porsche braking system unless you are trained and competent to do so. If you are not, take the car to a specialist. In such a case this following section is for information only.

Make sure the car is supported securely on axle stands during this work and that the rear wheels are chocked.

Remove the road wheels. Remove the brake pads by pulling out the clips and tapping out the retaining pins. Note how the cross spring is assembled.

Remove the brake pads from the caliper, marking their position if they are to be re-used. The pads may be wedged in the caliper and need tapping out with a hardwood drift and hammer. Be careful not to damage the disc or the pad, if the latter is to be reused.

If new pads are to be fitted without overhauling the caliper, push the pistons back into the cylinders as far as they will go. This should be below the surface of the caliper casting. Whilst doing this, check that the brake fluid reservoir does not overflow. If the caliper is to be stripped, it will help with piston removal if these are left as far out of their cylinders as possible at this stage.

If a piston will not move, it may be seized. The caliper should be removed and attempts made to free the piston by lifting its rim with wide bladed screwdrivers on each side of the piston. If the piston cannot be freed, a new caliper will be required. If the piston is forceably removed, it may be found that there is corrosion on the piston, in which case a new assembly will be required.

Undo the brake pipes to the calipers and drain the fluid into a suitable container.

Undo the caliper bolts and remove the caliper and brake dust shield. Clean up and inspect the caliper. Hold the caliper in a vice, using jaw protectors. Prise out the clamping ring from around the piston gaiter. Remove the gaiter.

If a high pressure air supply is not available to force out the pistons, then it may be possible to insert two screwdrivers under the rim of a piston and lever it out. Take care when removing the piston in this way not to damage the caliper or piston. The piston must be levered out squarely. Inspect the pistons for damage or corrosion. Minor corrosion should be cleaned off with fine emery cloth. Heavy pitting of the piston will mean a new caliper will be required, since leakage may occur past the piston seal and onto the brake pads.

With the piston removed, pull out the sealing ring in the cylinder. Inspect the cylinder for signs of damage or corrosion.

If the caliper is stripped it should be carefully cleaned using methylated spirit or clean brake fluid. It should be rebuilt with new seals, etc. Assembly is straightforward. If appropriate, align the two halves of the front calipers using new seals, bolts and washers. Tighten these bolts to 3.4 kg f m torque. Progressively tighten the bolts nearest the wheel centre first working out to the other two.

Fig. 6.3 shows an easily made gauge, which should be used by your specialist when refitting the caliper pistons. Position them before pushing into the cylinder as they can be difficult to turn.

When the calipers have been renovated, they should be put in an oil-free place, whilst renovating the remainder of the wheel assembly parts.

Prise off the hub bearing cap and loosen the clamp screw

enough to remove the nut and thrust washer.

Remove the brake disc from the hub. If appropriate, mark the way the brake carrier fits to the hub and then remove the brake carrier from the hub.

Inspect the discs for cracks, scoring or uneven wear. Check the discs for minimum thickness, appropriate to your model. Your Specialist will advise on their condition.

Inspect the front wheel bearings for wear or excessive play, which may have been evident whilst driving. Look especially carefully if there is evidence the bearing has been

running without sufficient grease, if the bearing track is pitted or if the grease was heavily contaminated.

Check also whether the seals have been leaking, especially if the stub axle track they run on is grooved. If leakage is occuring and grooves are found then the stub axle may need to be replaced. If it is suspected that any parts of the assembly need replacement, remove the hub from the car and have the job done by a specialist.

The front wheel bearings use general purpose grease, but it is important careful not to get this on the brake components. The

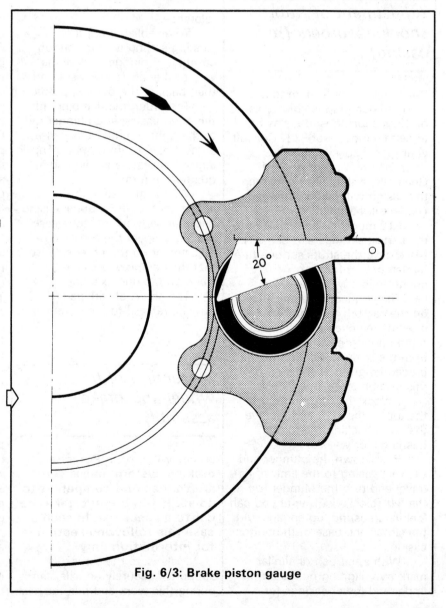

Fig. 6/3: Brake piston gauge

hub should be packed so that stub axle cavity is filled, the bearings are fully wetted with grease and the sealing lips are lubricated.

Refit the parts in the reverse order, tightening the clamp nut to 1.5 kg f m to seat the bearings. Turn the hub whilst tightening the nut.

Loosen the nut again, so that the thrust washer can just be moved with a screwdriver point. There should be no detectable sideways play in the bearing, but the wheel should turn freely.

Tighten the Allen bolt, without moving the clamp nut. Refit the grease cap. Your specialist will now refit the brake caliper and complete the assembly, before bleeding the brakes as described in the *Haynes Owners Workshop Manual* for the model.

Brake master cylinder

Do not attempt any work on the master cylinder unless you are trained to do so. When this work is carried out by a specialist, this section is for the reader's general information only. Only Porsche factory-approved parts should be used when overhauling the braking system.

Access to the master cylinder is gained from under the car, which should be supported on axle stands.

There have been several types of master cylinder on the 911.

From 1968 a dual circuit system was introduced which used a tandem master cylinder and a two-tank brake fluid reservoir. Such a system offered obvious safety advantages. American models saw the introduction of a brake servo in the mid 'seventies, which eventually was fitted to European models. This eliminatd the

famous heavy brake pedal of the 911 and made the car more acceptable to the less enthusiastic driver.

Only the dual master cylinder will be discussed here. An exploded view of this is shown in fig. 6.4. The procedure for overhauling the single cylinder is largely the same, but with fewer components.

If a problem is suspected with your braking system, have the car immediately checked out by a specialist.

An easy check on the status of the master cylinder and caliper seals can be made by pressing the pedal hard, whilst the car is stationary. In cycles of about a

couple of seconds, release the pressure slightly and then re-apply the pressure. The pedal should not progressively go to the floor. If it does then worn seals or a corroded master cylinder will be to blame.

Corrosion in the master cylinder and the caliper cylinders is caused by water carried in the brake fluid. The water gets there from the atmosphere, so regular (annual) changing of the fluid will reduce corrosion, if the procedure is observed from new.

This description of master cylinder stripdown is given for information only.

Detach the throttle pedal from its pushrod, at the driver's

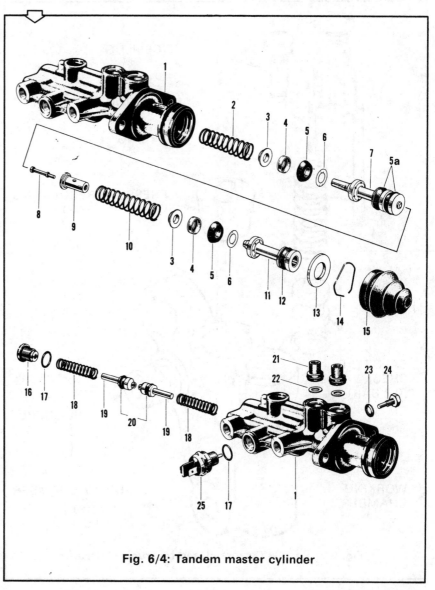

Fig. 6/4: Tandem master cylinder

footwell.

After removing the floor mat, remove the nut that holds the floorboard in place. Lift out the floorboard.

Pull back the dust boot from the master cylinder, in the area behind the brake pedal. Whilst in this area, check the movement of the brake pedal with the master cylinder disconnected. If the action is rough or stiff, replace the shaft and bushings only with factory-approved parts.

After the brake fluid has been drained into a suitable container, remove the undershield that covers the steering rack and front suspension crossmember.

Disconnect the brake lines to the master cylinder. Note whether any of these should be replaced.

Remove the nuts that mount the master cylinder to the body and withdraw the whole assembly.

After cleaning up the exterior of the master cylinder, remove the lock ring and the stop plate from the brake pedal end. Remove the primary piston assembly.

Take out the secondary piston stop bolt, which is positioned about half way along the outside of the cylinder body on its side.

Use an air line to force out the secondary piston. Apply the air line to one of the bleed nipples, covering the outer nipple and outlets to prevent loss of air pressure. Take great care to wrap the assembly in an old cloth so that, if the piston releases unexpectedly, it will be caught in the cloth. If the piston falls out of the caliper it may be damaged.

Put the primary piston in a vice and compress the spring using a jaw clamp. Undo the stroke limiting bolt. Remove the components from the primary piston.

Reassemble the master cylinder in the reverse order.

Before starting, lay out all the parts on a clean work area and understand how they all go together, especialy the orientation of the flexible seals (see fig. 6/4). Check again for any signs of corrosion or pitting in the cylinder bores that will reduce the efficiency of the braking system. It should be rebuilt using only a factory supplied master cylinder reconditioning kit, discarding all the old seals, etc. It is vital that the working area and hands are completely clean when handling the brake parts. Have a lint-free cloth or paper tissues handy to clean up individual parts and wash these only with new brake fluid or methylated spirit. It will ease assembly of the new parts to lubricate all the seals with new brake fluid, before fitting them.

After refitting to the car your Specialist will use new brake fluid and bleed the whole braking system, as described in the *Haynes Owners Workshop Manual*.

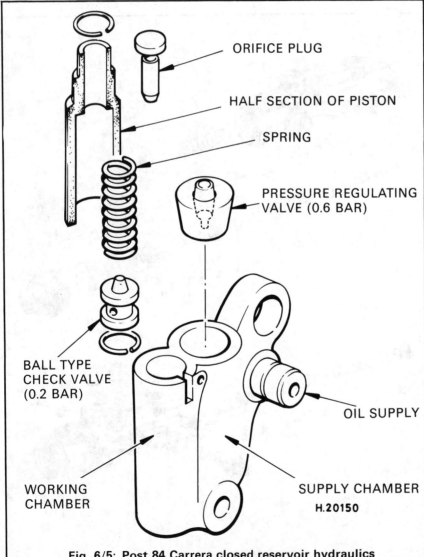

Fig. 6/5: Post 84 Carrera closed reservoir hydraulics

ORIFICE PLUG

HALF SECTION OF PISTON

SPRING

PRESSURE REGULATING VALVE (0.6 BAR)

BALL TYPE CHECK VALVE (0.2 BAR)

OIL SUPPLY

WORKING CHAMBER

SUPPLY CHAMBER
H.20150

Rear suspension

The rear suspension is of the control arm type, with torsion bars and telescopic shock absorbers.

Adjustments to the rear suspension (like the front suspension) enable variation of

ride height, camber and castor. It is recommended that such adjustments are only done by a trained specialist who has access to accurate measurement equipment, which is required to set the angles of the rear spring plates. For the same reasons, removal and refitting of the torsion bars is considered outside the scope of the average enthusiast.

Early 911 models were fitted with Hookes-type Nadella drive shafts from the transmission to the rear hubs. These type of joints are now something of a collector's item, due to their rarity. From 1968, Lobro drive shafts were adopted. At the same time the wheelbase was increased without moving the location of the engine/gearbox.

The rear suspension and drive shafts do not need routine maintenance. It should be noted that the Lobro couplings should only be packed with a lithium based molybdenum disulphide grease.

Overhaul of the brakes was

covered in the section on the front suspension. The rear brakes differ in that a small drum is designed into each hub for the handbrake. The shoes should be checked for oil contamination and wear.

Replacement of the bearings or bushes in the control arm or wheel hub should be performed by a specialist with the right equipment.

Adjustment of the handbrake

The maintenance and adjustment of the handbrake should be carried out by a trained specialist. The following is given for information only.
Adjustment of the handbrake can be performed on each rear wheel. Figure 6/6 shows the configuration. The handbrake lever operates two cables through

a balance bar, the cables connecting to the drum brake in each rear wheel. Before adjustment of the handbrake, inspect the cables for any signs of corrosion, fraying or other damage. If the cables are suspect, have them replaced by a specialist. The inner cables should be lubricated with grease, but in such a way that there is no possibility of any grease reaching the other braking system components.

Chock the front wheels and lift the rear wheels clear of the ground.

Support the car on axle stands as described in previous chapters.

Remove the rear road wheels.

Let the handbrake off, so that the hubs can turn freely. If there is any load in the handbrake cables, with the handbrake released, back off the adjusting nuts, so that the tension is just released from the lever.

Turn the hub assembly until

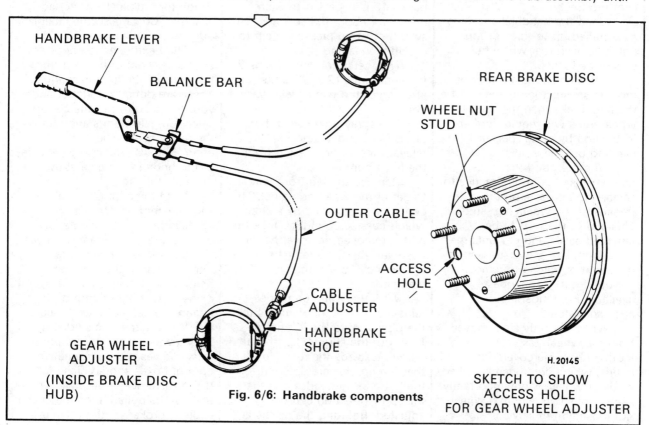

HANDBRAKE LEVER

BALANCE BAR

REAR BRAKE DISC

WHEEL NUT STUD

OUTER CABLE

ACCESS HOLE

CABLE ADJUSTER

HANDBRAKE SHOE

GEAR WHEEL ADJUSTER

(INSIDE BRAKE DISC HUB)

H.20145

Fig. 6/6: Handbrake components

SKETCH TO SHOW ACCESS HOLE FOR GEAR WHEEL ADJUSTER

it is possible to just see the small adjusting gear wheel through the small hole in the hub. A small light will be useful to get the hub positioned correctly for this.

Use a screwdriver to turn the gear wheel adjuster, through the hole in the hub, so as to just prevent the hub from being turned by hand. Repeat this for the other side.

Inside the car, lift the rubber boot and carpet trim so that the handbrake balance bar can be seen through the inspection holes to the rear of the lever. If necessary, adjust the balance bar so that it is at right angles to the handbrake lever, by moving the adjuster nuts at the wheel hubs. When the balance bar is positioned correctly, tighten the adjuster locking nuts.

If the balance bar position has had to be adjusted, re-position the gear wheel adjusters as described above so that each rear wheel is just prevented from turning.

Now loosen each gear wheel adjuster enough so that the hubs can turn freely.

When the handbrake lever is now pulled up to three or four notches, each rear wheel hub should be locked.

If this adjustment does not provide satisfactory operation of the handbrake then the cables or wheel hubs will require further inspection by a the specialist carrying out the work.

When refitting the roadwheels, it is good practice to smear copper paste on the threads of the wheel hub studs. This allows the nuts to be removed easily and prevents the studs from being overstressed in the event of having to remove a corroded nut. Copper paste is available from most motor accessory stores.

When the nuts are removed from the wheel, take care not to let them become covered in debris, which could damage the studs or wheel. More importantly, such debris can lead to a wheel nut loosening in service.

Only tighten the wheel nuts using a torque wrench, set to the correct figure. The correct wheel nut torque is given in the General Data section of this book.

Removal and refitting of headlamp washer parts

Headlamp washers first appeared on the 911 for the 1976 model year. The nozzles were very noticeable projections to the front impact bumpers and were replaced for the 1980 model year by almost-flush units on the top surface of the front bumper. The principal of operation remained the same on the later system.

Pressing the switch on the instrument panel operates the electrically driven water pump which is fitted to the front compartment lock panel. The pump is controlled by a relay, fitted next to it. When the switch is pressed a valve opens and water under pressure, (about 2.8 bar or 40 psi) passes to each nozzle for about 0.3 seconds. The switch must be pressed again to continue washing.

The water container holds 2 Imperial pints, (2.2 US pints) and also serves the windshield washer system.

The spray nozzles can be taken out by removing the relevant indicator housing from the front bumper.

Remove the left front wheel to get at the water container. The container is attached by a strap which passes around it. Once the bolt is removed, remove the filler hose and the threaded cap.

Remove the container rearwards.

With the water container removed there is now access to the pipework to the left nozzle. Push out the spring clip of the nozzle, towards the rear. Note that the nozzles are different for the left and right sides and that the spray direction can be adjusted. Refitting the nozzle is

the reverse procedure. Before tightening the water container strap, make sure that the strap is properly seated on the bracket under the headlamp bowl.

To remove the washer pump, disconnect the electrical plug at the pump body and pull off the water hoses, having noted which hose goes where on the pump. The pump can be lifted out after loosening its locating strap.

Heater control adjustment

On pre '74 cars the heater control was placed next to the handbrake lever. Poor heater operation could be due to several factors, not least of which will be that the heater exchangers have rusted out and need replacement. If the heat exchanger jackets are rusted so far that there are holes present, the heating will be poor. See photograph R15 in the Body Inspection section of the Buyer's Guide for a typically corroded example. Check also the flexible ducting for splits.

The next items to check are the heater control boxes at the top ends of the heat exchangers. These are difficult to get at and you will need to put the car up safely on axle stands and remove the rear wheels. The heater control boxes attach to each side of the body in the area above the drive shafts.

Note the control cables to each heater box. On pre '74 models there was a single lever to operate the heater control valves. On later models, before the introduction of the automatic heating controller, two levers made it possible to control the heating to each side of the car.

When either the single or both levers are pulled up, the rotary valves on the respective control boxes should close fully. If the valve does not move when the lever is pulled, then either the cable is broken or the valve is

corroded beyond use.

New heater control boxes are available and are fitted to the body by three nuts. If a new heater control cable is to be fitted, lift the carpet around the handbrake and remove the flexible boot. Remove the cover from the gearshift link rod tunnel. Remove the bolts holding the handbrake mounting plate.

Lift up the handbrake assembly to reveal the control cable attachments. Unclip the heater cables from the base of the heater control lever(s). Loosen the clamping nut on the heater control box and pull the cable through.

Replacement is the reverse procedure, remembering to smear the inner cable with general purpose grease before fitting.

To set the heater control lever(s), push the lever(s) fully down and tighten the cables at this position at the rotary valves. When the lever(s) are pulled up fully the rotary valves should be fully closed.

Where there are two heater control levers, the longer cable goes to the left-hand heater box.

No details are given here for repairing problems with the automatic servo system used from the '76 model year. By following through the checks listed above, it is a fairly straightforward job to find out whether the heater mechanical components are functioning correctly.

If the heater operates satisfactorily by hand, then there may be a problem with either the sensors fitted next to the heater control boxes, the interior temperature sensor (above the interior mirror) or the servo-motor with its adjacent printed circuit board. Ask a specialist to check these parts for you.

Torque wrench setting – engine

	kg f m	lb f ft
Crankcase section bolts	3.5	25
Crankcase nuts (M8)	2.5	18
Flywheel nuts	14.6	106
Crankshaft pulley bolt	7.7	56
Connecting rod bolts	5.0	36
Cylinder head bolts	2.9	21
Camshaft sprocket nuts	9.8	71
Rocker arm shaft nuts	1.8	13
Pulley to alternator nut	3.9	28
Spark Plugs	2.5	18
Blower housing clamp bolts	0.8	6
Fuel injection pump pulley	2.5	18
Fuel lines to injectors	1.1	8
Clutch pressure plate bolts	3.5	25
Transmission to engine bolts	3.9	28

Torque wrench settings – chassis etc

Rear suspension and driveshafts

	kg f m	lb f ft
Rear axle control arm nut	12	87
Radius arm (trailing arm) nut	9	65
Camber eccentric bolts	6	43
Tracking (toe-in) eccentric bolts	5	36
Shock absorber attachment – M12	7.5	54
Shock absorber attachment – M14	12.5	90
Halfshaft castellated nut	30/35	253/217
Halfshaft flange Allen bolts – Nadella	4.7	34
Halfshaft flange Allen bolts – Lobro M8	4.3	31
Halfshaft flange Allen bolts – Lobro M10	8.3	60
Bearing cap bolts	4.7	34

Front suspension and steering (not exhaustive)

	kg f m	lb f ft
Shock absorber strut upper mounting	8	58
Strut upper mounting plate	4.7	34
Auxiliary support to body	9	45
Fanbloc attachment bolt	4.7	34
Steering unit attachment bolt	4.7	34
Wheelbearing clamp nut to axle	1.5	10
Balljoint to shock absorber strut (nut)	2.2	16
Balljoint to shock absorber strut (bolt)	4.5	33
Steering wheel attachment	7.5	54
Balljoint to steering knuckle	4.5	33

Braking system

	kg f m	lb f ft
Master cylinder attachment nuts	2.5	18
Brake disc/hub nuts (front)	2.3	17
Caliper carrier plate (front)	4.7	34
Brake caliper attachment (front)	7.0	51
Brake caliper attachment (rear)	6.0	43
Hyraulic connections	2.0	15
Bleed nipples	0.3	2
Wheel nuts	13	94

7 Modifications

The subject of modifications to a Porsche 911 is a vast one and could almost be the subject of a book in itself! With the assistance of independent Porsche specialists and experts on Porsche modification, Autofarm, Lindsay Porter presents an overview, a kind of taster of what can be achieved. The latter part of this chapter illustrates some of the areas that can be modified on a 911 and shows an actual 911S Targa being modified with fibreglass panels ready for hill climb competition.

Two points have to be made here. One, and the most important, regarding safety. Before modifying a 911's bodywork, it is essential to ensure that the basic structure is sound or that it has been restored in the manner described through the rest of this book. Also, the fitting of fibreglass panels for road use cannot be recommended by the author because of the loss of strength involved in removing steel panels. And while still on the subject of safety, note that modification of any car from its original spec. could make the car more difficult to use or less comfortable to own and could compromise the car's safety. Do ensure that whatever modifications you may have in mind are discussed very thoroughly with your supplier who, if they have a reputation

like that of Autofarm, will be fully able to guide you along the right, safe and responsible lines.

The second point relates to the value of the car because, as pointed out later in this chapter, the owner who runs a heavily modified car may lose out in terms of value and will nullify the manufacturer's anti-corrosion warranty.

Very few restoration projects are carried out without some modification or other being added to the car's original spec. Some sports cars seem candidates for more dramatic uprating and the Porsche 911 is among them. The principal reason is doubtless that the Porsche 911 has been remorselessly improved over the 24 years during which the car has been produced whilst, in addition, very many later parts can be fitted to earlier cars. Indeed, it is said that the very earliest 2.0 litre 911 could have its engine whipped out and the whole thing replaced with a 3.3 litre Turbo! Not that anyone would do such a thing, of course. For a start, how would the car get round a corner at the speeds generated by the Turbo unit? And how would it stop? And for another, the historic value in an early car would be destroyed in spite of the fact that the conversion would cost an absolute fortune to carry out.

The last points raised, those of cost and the value and originality of the 'original' car, are among the major reasons for *not* carrying out modifications to an earlier 911. On the other hand, it is sometimes not very much more expensive to fit later parts than it is to fit original ones, while their performance and appearance can be very much better. Also, the owner of a Porsche 911 may very rightly feel that, since the car belongs to him or her and to no-one else, they can do what they like with it! That sort of attitude prevailed in the case of Peter Gorton whose early 911, turned into an RS Carrera look-alike, is pictured here. Peter bought a virtually scrap car and proceeded to turn it into exactly the car *he* wanted to be seen driving in, doing 90% of the work himself and even succeeding in fitting replica panels that were not supposedly made to fit his car. It just goes to show that, since all motor cars are made up from bits and pieces to start off with, there's nothing to stop anyone from adapting or fitting any other bits and pieces, provided they have the time and/or money to enable them to do it. The question then becomes one of 'how far should I go?' The answer has to lie with the tastes and interests of the individual. If the questioner then wants to look at the value of the car after it has

been modified, the answer becomes slightly different. If you want to retain the potential for originality, only fit bolt-on, bolt-off parts so that the original status quo can be restored 'on demand', as it were.

Engines

When the author quizzed Autofarm, Hertfordshire-based independent Porsche specialists, about 911 mods. in general, they started with engine modifications, breaking them down into four sections, and that's how they will be examined here. Autofarm partner Josh Sadler, who has competed very successfully in 911s for more years than even he probably cares to remember, and who must know as much or more about the subject as anyone, started off with:

Engine Capacity

Josh claimed that the only realistic option when it comes to modifying a Porsche 911 engine lies in uprating to another engine's specifications. He says that there are alternative cams available in the United States but he has tried them and finds that production cams are so well sorted, that there's little or no improvement to be had from fitting the American variety. Alternative 'factory' cams are available, which Josh describes as being 'very revvy' but they are, as one comes to expect from Porsche parts, very expensive indeed and, unless the intermediate gear on the crankshaft is modified to take the extra strain imparted by these higher-lift variety of cams, the original has an unfortunate tendency to fall apart! Ports and manifolds fitted to production cars are quite nicely gas flowed, so there's little or no advantage to be gained from working on those areas and although you

could fit larger ports and manifolds from a model of Porsche so equipped, it's not the sort of thing you would do in isolation rather than as part of a general engine uprating. For instance, improvements to the 'in' side of breathing are not terribly useful unless teamed up with improvements to the 'out' side.

The 911's exhaust system is not just the bit of wiggly pipe fitted to most conventional cars; it's a major (and expensive) piece of plumbing taking into account things like heat exchangers to suit the air-cooled engine's heating system. Autofarm have had big-bore exhaust systems manufactured and will sell you one for a not inconsiderable sum!

But to return to Josh Sadler's original point about the need to go for added capacity if you want extra performance: Autofarm have analysed just about all of the options that are available to the enthusiast and have included not only the larger 'production' capacities in their repertoire of parts but also capacities that Porsche may have used for competition purposes and even capacity options that Autofarm have developed themselves. Very broadly speaking, Autofarm claim that a Porsche's engine evolution breaks down into three stages, based on the distances between adjacent cylinder head studs. You have:

80 mm, built from 1964–77, including all production cars from 2.0 to 2.7 litres.
83 mm, from 1974–75 which, since they were used only for the 3.0 litre RS and RSR are as rare as hens' teeth!
86 mm from 1978–on. These include 3.0, 3.2 and 3.3 litre and include Turbo models.

Ignoring, for obvious reasons, the middle category, this leaves two sets of engine up-rate options. The first is for engines with 80 mm stud distances and the options available are as follows. Broadly speaking, any of these crankcases can be increased to any of these capacities:

	Production			Non-production		
Bore (mm)	80	84	90	90	92	93
Stroke (mm)						
66	2.0 litre	2.2 litre	–	–	–	–
70.4	–	2.4 litre	2.7 litre	2.7 H.C	2.8 litre	2.9 litre

Points to bear in mind are that:
– early crankcases will require machining for barrels over 90 mm.
– no alternative pistons are available for 2.7 litre K-Jetronic injection system engines.
– there are actually yet more 'special' capacities available if you should want them, such as 2.5 litres, with either crank.

Actually, having said that any of these options can be done, you may have to bear in mind that there could be all sorts of compatibility problems with ancillary components. The main ones to watch are: con. rod clearance; distributor mounting; oil pipe diameters; piston oil cooling jets; cylinder head joints; compression ratios; clutch strength and more besides. You could end up writing a book about the minutiae of the nuts and bolts, but the easiest way around the problem is to depend on the practical experience of your supplier.

The 86 mm stud separation engines give the following options, bearing in mind that the 74.4 mm crank shown will only fit 1978-on engines:

– no 100 mm pistons are available for K-Jetronic or Motronic injection engines or for Turbos.
– no larger bore pistons are available for the 3.0 litre Turbo.

	Production		Non-production		
Bore (mm)	95	97	97	98	100
Stroke (mm)					
70.4	3.0 litre	–	3.1 litre	3.2 litre	3.3 litre
74.4	3.2 litre	3.3 litre	–	3.4 litre	3.5 litre

Obviously, the cost of building a modified engine will be greater than that for a simple rebuild, but owners often uprate when rebuild time comes round, saving at least some of the cost. But before contemplating the building of a more powerful engine, do consider whether the car's basic chassis will take it or whether extensive modifications will be necessary to brakes or other chassis components. Once again, you should seek the advice of your specialist supplier because there are simply too many possible variations on the theme to even begin to detail them here.

Engine Induction Systems

Josh Sadler recommends using larger carburettors, fitting American Weber kits, complete with inlet manifolds, air cleaners and linkages. But if you want to stick with injection (always assuming that your 911 comes with it in the first place), the best one to use is the mechanical system. The *very* best are the 'factory' racing mechanical injection systems with 50 mm butterflies, but these are so rare as to be not worthy of realistic consideration. Autofarm, however, can modify the mechanical injection system's inlet stack, offering a bigger bore and larger (45 mm) butterflies. This improves the breathing and is really as far as you can go, dimensionally, without losing correlation with the system's original injector pump.

If a 911 is fitted with the later, K-Jetronic or Motronic injector systems, there's not much you can do except go in for an engine capacity increase, throw them away and fit carburettors. They are based on an air flow measuring system and, as a result, their electronic 'black box' becomes all confused if a hotter cam is fitted, leading the car to 'kangaroo' its way down the road. It is possible for a specialist like Autofarm to have someone hack into the black box and re-program it. But avoid this path if the car is under warranty, of course.

Exhaust Systems

It is only necessary to fit a larger bore exhaust system if the inlet system is fitted with a larger-bore carburettor or mechanical injection inlet stack. The early, pre-1975 exhaust layout improves all K-Jetronic injection engines, while a non-standard simplified silencer releases more power, especially on early cars. It will be necessary to go to an independent supplier to purchase such non-standard parts. It is also possible to purchase stainless steel systems at somewhat high cost, which may not improve the exhaust system as such but which last a lot longer than a mild steel system, which is expensive enough in itself!

Cylinder heads and camshafts

2.0 litre engines used several different valve sizes, but it is probably true that owners of the early 2.0 litre engines won't be much bothered about doing anything but sticking with their original spec. In any case, if real improvement *should* be wanted, it would not be worth swapping around between the standard 2.0 litre valves. 2.2 to 2.7 litre engined cars all used the same size valves while 3.0 litre-on valves are all the same. Theoretically, 3.0 litre-on valves can be squeezed into early heads, although with considerable difficulty and in practice, virtually no one has bothered trying it!

2.2 litre-and-on engines can have their ports enlarged to 43 mm as used on the race engines. A 2.4T can be uprated to E spec. and an E cam and ports, while an S-spec. can be obtained with S cam and ports but the correct S pistons and injection will then also be demanded. A lot of money will also be demanded for this swap and it may be considered financially impractical, according to Josh Sadler.

Turbo

Finally there's what many must regard as the ultimate engine mod., the fitting of a turbo. It isn't possible to fit a Porsche Turbo to a non-turbo engine, although there are American aftermarket turbo kits available. Josh Sadler's recommendation, however, is that if you want to go the turbo route, look for a second-hand turbo engine complete, which (theoretically!) 'drops in' to any 911!

If you feel really ambitious, you can tune a turbo engine just as you can a normally aspirated unit, although the whole thing is, naturally, a good deal more complex. The one thing you can't realistically do, however, is set up a turbo engine on a rolling road because you can't get an accurate reading: the intercooler requires a very large air flow to enable it to operate efficiently and this can't properly be achieved while the car is static. But this is getting us well beyond the scope of our brief!

Gearboxes

As with engine modifications, the

numbers of gearbox variables are immense while the potential for gearbox 'swaps' is also huge. The moral, once again, is to consult your specialist about which 'boxes will fit your particular 911. From 1972 to 1986, what is essentially the same 5-speed gearbox was used all through. These gearboxes will fit into earlier cars with the exception of short wheelbase 911 models where one would encounter rather severe problems when attempting to couple the different sizes of driveshafts.

Suspension

In principle, 911 suspension systems are simple to uprate although geometry changes are far too complex for the owner to dabble with and the consequences of faulty dabbling could be catastrophic!

In brief, you change the torsion bar settings to lower the car and change the components to stiffen it. Later anti-roll bars are stiffer than earlier ones and are a direct swap and, similarly, lower specified cars have thinner anti-roll bars than higher specified cars. If you have a 911T, it's simple to fit a 911S's anti-roll bar in place of the original. Late Carreras have thicker bars still. But in the case of all anti-roll bars, they should be fitted only as matching pairs.

Shock absorbers dampers: rears are bolt-on telescopics; fronts are inserts and all are simple to uprate with stiffer capacity units. Once again, the rule when selecting precisely which units can (and just as importantly, should) be fitted to which car is to have a session with your specialist supplier.

Brakes

"In a nutshell," says Josh Sadler, "you improve brakes by bolting on later ones . . . " 911 models without ventilated discs can be fitted with later, ventilated discs, although the early, small cast-iron M-type calliper-equipped cars require a change of strut in order to accept the bigger, later callipers. S models, incidentally, have alloy callipers while the others have cast-iron, but all pre-1976 alloy callipers have, according to Josh, probably seized up and become useless by now. You could (but *mustn't*) fit the 'big caliper' 3.3 Turbo front callipers, since you can't also fit the matching rear brake set-up, and the braking balance would be ruined – yet another instance of where it is necessary to discuss your proposed mods. with those who know. Another brake swap option is to go for non-Porsche ventilated aftermarket discs, or even the Autofarm-developed four-pot bolt-on calliper conversion could be fitted.

Bodywork

Most popular Porsche body conversions involve making the car look like one of the more exotic models of 911. Carrera and Turbo flares can be bought in steel or fibreglass; front spoilers and bumpers are frequently swaped, again for 'original' or fibreglass replica parts while, since all engine lid apertures are the same, the whole range of lids and spoilers can be bolted into place. Space prevents a fuller exploration of what can be done in terms of body styling, but suffice it to say that body mods. are among the most popular ways of changing the specification of a 911. However, it is very important to take specialist advice when considering fitting a non-standard rear spoiler. It can make the car dangerous at speed if not balanced by the correct front air dam.

Clearly, the 911 is one of the most 'modifiable' cars on the road – which must make it tough for anyone attempting to purchase an original 911! – and there's virtually no limit to what can be achieved, except that imposed by the depth of the owner's pocket.

MOD1. Autofarm produced this attractive 935 style 911 SC with 928 flat front headlight conversion.

MOD2.   At the rear, its stunning black coachwork enveloped an engine uprated to a 3.2 litre high compression unit. The dramatic spoiler complements the wide flares and tyres.

MOD3.   Air intake louvers let into rear wheel arches add another dramatic touch and are beautifully executed.

MOD4.   BBS wheels can make a large impact upon the visual appeal of the 911.

MOD5.   These non-standard mirrors blend aerodynamically with the 911's bodywork.

MOD6.   Peter Gorton with his DIY Carrera look-alike, fitted with a whole panoply of fibreglass panels on a home-restored 'tub' or body shell.

MOD7.   The excellent fit of these panels reflects the hundreds of hours and huge sum of money that Peter put into his pet project. The dent he once put into the roof when driven mad with frustration at the difficulty of making panels fit properly in the early hours of one winter's night has since been panel-beaten out!

MOD8.   A new sill/body rocker welded in place before attempting to fit any modified sheet metal work.

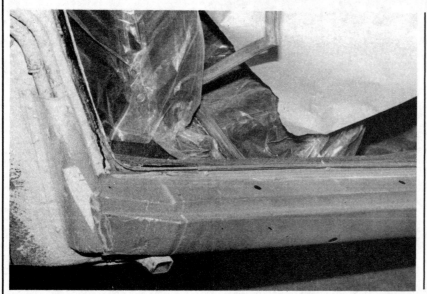

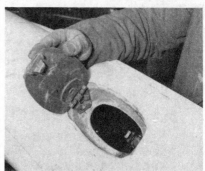

MOD10.   Before fitting, the fuel filler flap is fitted in place.

Fitting front fibreglass flared wings/fenders

Safety
Always wear an efficient particle mask when drilling or sanding fibreglass; the glass fibres, if inhaled, can be injurious to health. Wear gloves and goggles when handling fibreglass resin, hardener and mat.

MOD9.   A 'glass wing/fender is offered up to the restored 911 body shell prior to fitting.

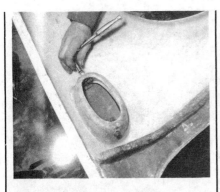

MOD11. Beware! This sort of thing takes time! You'll have to work out correct positions, drill holes in the panel in appropriate places and often use no little ingenuity in order to make the flap fit properly.

MOD14. . . . slotting them if you wish to match those in the steel wing/fender. (See appropriate restoration section.)

MOD17. Those you can't drill in situ, you'll have to drill after marking out carefully.

MOD12. With the wing/fender held in place, mark the position of the mounting holes adjacent to the screen pillar.

MOD15. You'll need a socket set with a universal joint extension on it in order to do up this bolt.

MOD18. Rather than using the spring nuts used for steel wing/fenders, you may be better off using regular nuts and bolts with large flat washers between nut and fibreglass, to spread the load.

MOD13. Take the wing/fender back off and drill out the holes . . .

MOD16. Hold the front of the wing/fender in place and drill through the holes in the flitch panel.

MOD19. Ken Wright, the Classic Car Restorations panel beater carrying out this work, fits up the wing/fender. He looks askance at the fit of the rearmost part of the 'glass wing/fender . . .

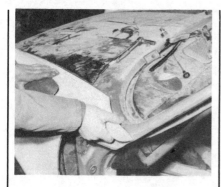

MOD20. . . . but finds that the mounting bolts have pulled it nicely into position.

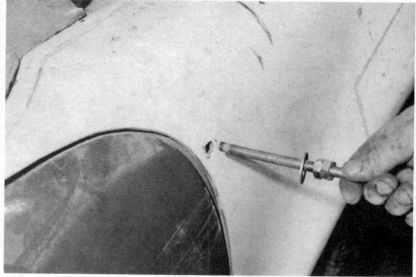

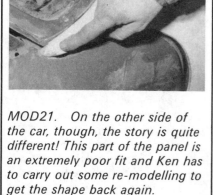

MOD21. On the other side of the car, though, the story is quite different! This part of the panel is an extremely poor fit and Ken has to carry out some re-modelling to get the shape back again.

MOD23. Ken makes up a special bolt to pull the panel into position while he fixes it top and bottom before taking the bolt back out again and filling the hole. This kind of improvisation is the sort of thing you almost expect to have to do with fibreglass panels which **never** fit as well as steel.

MOD24. The base of the wing/fender was clamped in place . . . ➤

MOD25. . . . while the A-post holes were positioned . . .

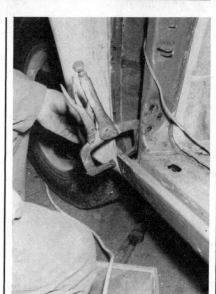

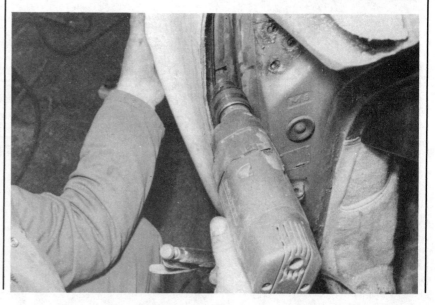

MOD22. The curvature of the wing/fender where it meets the door is also all wrong.

MOD26. . . . being drilled out with the panel removed, yet again. These panels really do take a lot of time!

Fitting rear fibreglass flared wings/fenders

MOD29. This shot shows a full rear wing/fender having been fitted with an authentic steel flare by Dave Felton's restoration shop.

MOD30. Back to the 'glass wings/fenders: Ken offers up the rear wing/fender and draws around it carefully.

MOD27. Before finally bolting them in place, the luggage bay cover must be fitted and the panel gaps aligned as well as possible, just as for steel panel (see appropriate restoration section).

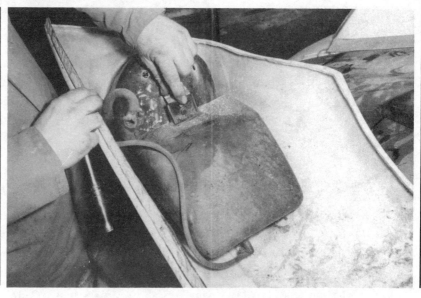

MOD31. Then he removes the new panel and draws another line a couple of inches 'in'.

MOD28. At some stage, whilst the wing/fender is off the car, it will have been necessary to fit the washer bottle brackets and the bottle itself. When? Please yourself!

MOD32.   He cuts along the innermost line, using here a pro. workshop's air chisel.

MOD33.   The surplus steelwork is removed completely. Heavy duty industrial gloves strongly recommended here!

MOD34.   Ken cleans up the edge of the steel with a sanding disc . . .

MOD35.   . . . and finds that part of the lower front section is corroded. This is typical of such work; you invariably uncover more problems than you have bargained for.

MOD36.   Ken MIG welds in the repair patch panel he has fabricated from sheet steel.

MOD37.   The next job is to go around the cut edge, using a hammer and dolly to turn a 90 degree flange over.

MOD38.   The flange is then turned right over and carefully hammered flat to provide a neat, strong seam.

MOD39.   The 'glass flare is re-offered up . . .

MOD40.   . . . and a few locating holes drilled right through fibreglass and steel.

MOD41.   The panel can be pop-rivetted in place.

MOD42.   Ken also chose to use nuts and bolts because, while the pop rivets were fine for holding the panel on initially, they didn't pull the flared panel tight to the steel wing/fender.

MOD43.   Before going further, the replacement side skirt was offered up and temporarily fitted to ensure the correct placement of the new wing flare.

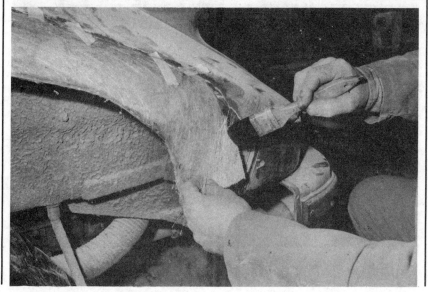

MOD44.   After sanding off all paint and wiping the panel down with spirit wipe to remove any grease Ken started by painting resin (follow the supplier's instructions regarding hardener quantity, etc) onto the edge of the steel panel, then placed a strip of mat upon the panel and stippled more resin into it.

MOD45. Then the 'glass flare was bolted back on (mucky job, this!) and more mat and resin stippled over the top of the joint, and yet more added beneath to make a strong, sealed joint.

IMPORTANT! Fitting fibreglass panels reduces the strength of the car. They should only be used as in the case of this 911, on off-road cars. Such panels also dramatically reduce value!

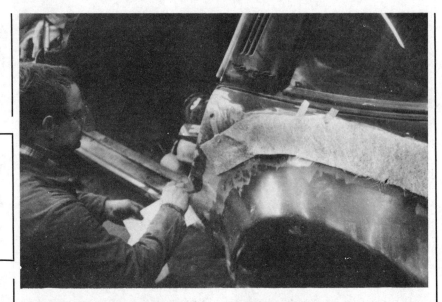

MOD46. The bolts could be unbolted, once the resin had 'cured' and any pop-rivets still left in place drilled out.

MOD49. . . . followed by as much hand sanding and filling as is necessary to gain a smooth, blemish-free surface.

Bumpers and air dams

MOD50. Ken offers up the new (non-original) air dam . . .

MOD47. Then, it's a matter of adding filler to give a smooth surface . . .

MOD48. . . . sanding off obvious lumps and bumps . . .

MOD51. . . . securing the fibreglass panel to the mounting holes on the car's body. In fact, in this case, the mounting holes didn't line up and new mounting brackets had to be fabricated and fitted.

MOD52. A far more expensive option (although not on a lightweight competition car, of course) would be to use genuine Porsche components. ►

Side skirts

MOD53. Ken removed the old sill/body rocker extensions.

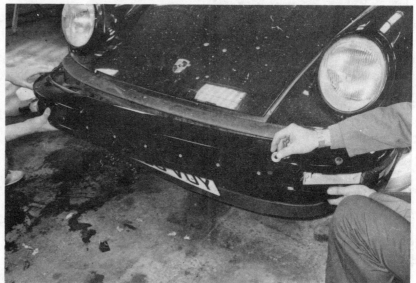

MOD54. Then he clamped the new side skirts in place, marked the hole positions . . . ◄

MOD55. . . . and drilled through with a tapping size drill.

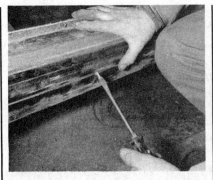

MOD56. The new side skirts were held on with the self-tapping screws provided.

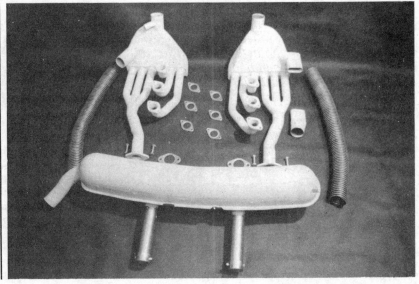

MOD59. 'Independents' such as Autofarm market exhaust conversions, this one being for a late 911.

MOD60. Viewed from beneath, this big-bore system is fitted to what Autofarm call their '3.5 litre shopping racer'!

Other modifications

MOD57. Mechanical mods. ▲ were discussed earlier in this chapter. Here are two heads with two different port sizes.

MOD58. High lift cams can necessitate a change of valve (intermediate) gear.

MOD61. A stainless exhaust system costs an arm and a leg but could provide good long-term value.

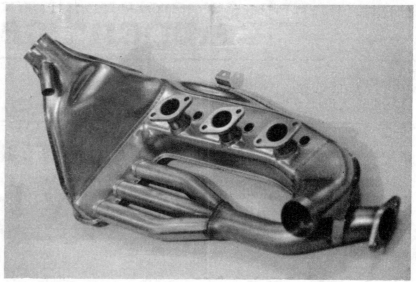

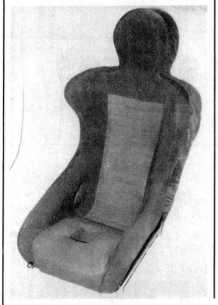

MOD62. This race seat is an ideal example of the kind of bolt-in, bolt-out mod. that need not change the car's value – provided that you hang on to the originals!

Appendices

1 Workshop Procedures and Safety First

Professional motor mechanics are trained in safe working procedures, whereas the onus is on you, the home mechanic, to find them out for yourself and act upon them. However enthusiastic you may be about getting on with the job in hand, do take the time to ensure that your safety is not put at risk. A moment's lack of attention can result in an accident, as can failure to observe certain elementary precautions.

There will always be new ways of having accidents, and the following points do not pretend to be a comprehensive list of all dangers; they are intended rather to make you aware of the risks and to encourage a safety-conscious approach to all work you carry out on your vehicle.

Be sure to consult the suppliers of any materials and equipment you may use, and to obtain and read carefully operating and health and safety instructions that they may supply.

Essential DOs and DON'Ts

DON'T rely on a single jack when working underneath the vehicle. Always use reliable additional means of support, such as axle stands, securely placed under a part of the vehicle that you know will not give way.

DON'T attempt to loosen or tighten high-torque nuts (e.g. wheel hub nuts) while the vehicle is on a jack; it may be pulled off.

DON'T start the engine without first ascertaining that the transmission is in neutral (or 'Park' where applicable) and the parking brake applied.

DON'T suddenly remove the filler cap from a hot cooling system – cover it with a cloth and release the pressure gradually first, or you may get scalded by escaping coolant.

DON'T attempt to drain oil, automatic transmission fluid, or coolant until you are sure it has cooled sufficiently to avoid scalding you.

DON'T grasp any part of the engine, exhaust or catalytic converter without first ascertaining that it is sufficiently cool to avoid burning you.

DON'T allow brake fluid or antifreeze to contact vehicle paintwork.

DON'T syphon toxic liquids such as fuel, brake fluid or antifreeze by mouth, or allow them to remain on your skin.

DON'T inhale dust – it may be injurious to health (see Asbestos below).

DON'T allow any spilt oil or grease to remain on the floor – wipe it up straight away, before someone slips on it.

DON'T use ill-fitting spanners or other tools which may slip and cause injury.

DON'T attempt to lift a heavy component which may be beyond your capability – get assistance.

DON'T rush to finish a job, or take unverified short cuts.

DON'T allow children or animals in or around an unattended vehicle.

DON'T park vehicles with catalytic converters over combustible materials such as dry grass, oily rags, etc., if the engine has recently been run. As catalytic converters reach extremely high temperatures, any such materials in close proximity may ignite.

DON'T run vehicles equipped with catalytic converters without the exhaust system heat shields fitted.

DO wear eye protection when using power tools such as an electric drill, sander, bench grinder, etc., and when working under the vehicle.

DO use a barrier cream on your hands prior to undertaking dirty jobs – it will protect your skin from infection as well as making the dirt easier to remove that long term contact with used engine oil can be a health hazard.

DO keep loose clothing (cuffs, tie, etc.) and long hair well out of the way of moving mechanical parts.

DO remove rings, wrist watch, etc., before working on the vehicle – especially the electrical system.

DO ensure that any lifting tackle used has a safe working load rating adequate for the job, and is used precisely as recommended by the manufacturer.

DO keep your work area tidy – it is only too easy to fall over articles left lying around.

DO get someone to check periodically that all is well, when working alone on the vehicle.

DO carry out work in a logical sequence and check that everything is correctly assembled and tightened afterwards.

DO remember that your vehicle's safety affects that of yourself and others. If in doubt on any point, get specialist advice.

IF, in spite of following these precautions, you are unfortunate enough to injure yourself, seek medical attention as soon as possible.

Fire

Remember at all times that petrol (gasoline) is highly flammable. Never smoke, or have any kind of naked flame around, when working on the vehicle. But the risk does not end there – a spark caused by an electrical short-circuit, by two metal surfaces contacting each other, by a central heating boiler in the garage 'firing up', or even by

static electricity built up in your body under certain conditions, can ignite petrol vapour, which in a confined space is highly explosive.

Always disconnect the battery earth (ground) terminal before working on any part of the fuel system, and never risk spilling fuel on to a hot engine or exhaust.

It is recommended that a fire extinguisher of a type suitable for fuel and electrical fires is kept handy in the garage or workplace at all times. Never try to extinguish a fuel or electrical fire with water.

Fumes

Certain fumes are highly toxic and can quickly cause unconsciousness and even death if inhaled to any extent. Petrol (gasoline) vapour comes into this category, as do the vapours from certain solvents such as trichloroethylene and those from many adhesives. Any draining or pouring of such volatile fluids should be done in a well-ventilated area.

When using cleaning fluids and solvents, read the instructions carefully. Never use any materials from unmarked containers – they may give off poisonous vapours.

Never run the engine of a motor vehicle in an enclosed space such as a garage. Exhaust fumes contain carbon monoxide which is extremely poisonous. If you need to run the engine, always do so in the open air or at least have the rear of the vehicle outside the workplace.

If you are fortunate enough to have the use of an inspection pit, never drain or pour petrol, and never run the engine, while the vehicle is standing over it; the fumes, being heavier than air, will concentrate in the pit with possibly lethal results.

The battery

Never cause a spark, or allow a naked light, near the vehicle battery. It will normally be giving off a certain amount of hydrogen gas, which is highly explosive.

Always disconnect the battery earth (ground) terminal before working on the fuel or electrical systems.

If possible, loosen the filler plugs or cover when charging the battery from an external source. Do not charge at an excessive rate or the battery may burst.

Take care when topping up and when carrying the battery. The acid electrolyte, even when diluted, is very corrosive and should not be allowed to contact the eyes or skin.

If you ever need to prepare electrolyte yourself, always add the acid slowly to the water, and never the other way round. Protect against splashes by wearing rubber gloves and goggles.

Mains electricity

When using an electric power tool, inspection light, etc., which works from the mains, always ensure that the appliance is correctly connected to its plug and that, where necessary, it is properly earthed (grounded). Do not use such appliances in damp conditions and, again, beware of creating a spark or applying excessive heat in the vicinity of fuel or fuel vapour.

Also, before using any mains powered electrical equipment, take one more simple precaution – use an RCD (Residual Current Device) circuit breaker. Then, if there is a short, the RCD circuit breaker minimises the risk of electrocution by instantly cutting the power supply. Buy from any

electrical store or DIY centre. RCDs fit simply into your electrical socket before plugging in your electrical equipment.

Ignition HT voltage

A severe electric shock can result from touching certain parts of the ignition system, such as the HT leads, when the engine is running or being cranked, particularly if components are damp or the insulation is defective. Where an electronic ignition system is fitted, the HT voltage is much higher and could prove fatal. Consult your handbook or main dealer if in any doubt. Risk of injury while working on running engines, e.g. adjusting the timing, can arise if the operator touches a high voltage lead and pulls his hand away on to a projection or revolving part.

Welding and bodywork repairs

It is so useful to be able to weld when carrying out restoration work, and yet there is a good deal that could go dangerously wrong for the uninformed – in fact more than could be covered here. **For safety's sake** you are strongly recommended to seek tuition, in whatever branch of welding you wish to use, from your local evening institute or adult education classes. In addition, all of the information and instructional material produced by the suppliers of materials and equipment you will be using must be studied carefully. You may have to ask your stockist for some of this printed material if it is not made available at the time of purchase.

In addition, it is strongly recommended that *The Car*

Bodywork Repair Manual, published by Haynes, is purchased and studied before carrying out any welding or bodywork repairs. Consisting of 292 pages, around 1,000 illustrations and written by Lindsay Porter, the author of this book, *The Car Bodywork Repair Manual* picks the brains of specialists from a variety of fields, and covers arc, MIG and 'gas' welding, panel beating and accident repair, rust repair and treatment, paint spraying, glass-fibre work, filler, lead loading, interiors and much more besides. Alongside a number of projects, the book describes in detail how to carry out each of the techniques involved in car bodywork repair with safety notes where necessary. As such, it is the ideal complement to this book.

Compressed gas cylinders

There are serious hazards associated with the storage and handling of gas cylinders and fittings, and standard precautions should be strictly observed in dealing with them. Ensure that cylinders are stored in safe conditions, properly maintained and always handled with special care and make constant efforts to eliminate the possibilities of leakage, fire and explosion.

The cylinder gases that are commonly used are oxygen, acetylene and liquid petroleum gas (LPG). Safety requirements for all three gases are: Cylinders must be stored in a fire resistant, dry and well-ventilated space, away from any source of heat or ignition and protected from ice, snow or direct sunlight. Valves of cylinders in store must always be kept uppermost and closed, even when the cylinder is empty. Cylinders should be handled with care and only by personnel who

are reliable, adequately informed and fully aware of all associated hazards. Damaged or leaking cylinders should be immediately taken outside into the open air, and the supplier and fire authorities should be notified immediately. No one should approach a gas cylinder store with a naked light or cigarette. Care should be taken to avoid striking or dropping cylinders, or knocking them together. Cylinders should never be used as rollers. One cylinder should never be filled from another. Every care must be taken to avoid accidental damage to cylinder valves. Valves must be operated without haste, never fully opened hard back against the back stop (so that other users know the valve is open) and never wrenched shut but turned just securely enough to stop the gas. Before removing or loosening any outlet connections, caps or plugs, a check should be made that the valves are closed. When changing cylinders, close all valves and appliance taps, and extinguish naked flames, including pilot jets, before disconnecting them. When reconnecting ensure that all connections and washers are clean and in good condition and do not overtighten them. Immediately a cylinder becomes empty, close its valve.

Safety requirements for acetylene: Cylinders must always be stored and used in the upright position. If a cylinder becomes heated accidentally or becomes hot because of excessive backfiring, immediately shut the valve, detach the regulator, take the cylinder out of doors well away from the building, immerse it in or continuously spray it with water, open the valve and allow the gas to escape until the cylinder is empty. If necessary, notify the emergency fire service without delay.

Safety requirements for oxygen are:
No oil or grease should be used on valves or fittings. Cylinders with convex bases should be used in a stand or held securely to a wall.

Safety requirements for LPG are:
The store must be kept free of combustible material, corrosive material and cylinders of oxygen.
Cylinders should only ever be carried upright, securely strapped down, preferably in an open vehicle or with windows open. Carry the suppliers safety data with you. In the event of an accident, notify the Police and Fire Services and hand the safety data to them.

Dangerous liquids and gases

Because of flammable gas given off by batteries when on charge, care should be taken to avoid sparking by switching off the power supply before charger leads are connected or disconnected. Battery terminals should be shielded, since a battery contains energy and a spark can be caused by any conductor which touches its terminals or exposed connecting straps.

When internal combustion engines are operated inside buildings the exhaust fumes must be properly discharged to the open air. Petroleum spirit or mixture must be contained in metal cans which should be kept in a store. In any area where battery charging or the testing of fuel injection systems is carried out there must be good ventilation, and no sources of ignition. Inspection pits often present serious hazards. They should be of adequate length to allow safe access and exit while

a car is in position. If there is an inspection pit, petrol may enter it. Since petrol vapour is heavier than air it will remain there and be a hazard if there is any source of ignition. All sources of ignition must therefore be excluded.

Lifting equipment

Special care should be taken when any type of lifting equipment is used. Lifting jacks are for raising vehicles; they should never be used as supports while work is in progress. Jacks must be replaced by adequate rigid supports before any work is begun on the vehicle. Risk of injury while working on running engines, e.g. adjusting the timing, can arise if the operator touches a high voltage lead and pulls his hand away on to a projection or revolving part. On some vehicles the voltage used in the ignition system is so high as to cause injury or death by electrocution. Consult your handbook or main dealer if in any doubt.

Work with plastics

Work with plastic materials brings additional hazards into workshops. Many of the materials used (polymers, resins, adhesives and materials acting as catalysts and accelerators) readily produce very dangerous situations in the form of poisonous fumes, skin irritants, risk of fire and explosions. Do not allow resin or 2-pack adhesive hardener, or that supplied with filler or 2-pack stopper to come into contact with skin or eyes. Read carefully the safety notes supplied on the tin, tube or packaging.

Jacks and axle stands

Special care should be taken when any type of lifting equipment is used. Any jack is made for lifting the car, not for supporting it. NEVER even consider working under your car using only a jack to support the weight of it. Jacks are only for raising vehicles, and must be replaced by adequate supports before any work is begun on the vehicle; axle stands are available from many discount stores, and all auto parts stores. These stands are absolutely essential if you plan to work under your car. Simple triangular stands (fixed or adjustable) will suit almost all of your working situations. Drive-on ramps are very limiting because of their design and size.

When jacking the car from the front, leave the gearbox in neutral and the brake off until you have placed the axle stands under the frame. Make sure that the car is on level ground first! Then put the car into gear and/or engage the handbrake and lower the jack. Obviously DO NOT put the car in gear if you plan to turn over the engine! Leaving the brake on, or leaving the car in gear while jacking the front of the car will necessarily cause the jack to tip (unless a good quality trolley jack with wheels is being used). This is unavoidable when jacking the car on one side, and the use of the handbrake in this case is recommended.

If the car is older and if it shows signs of weakening at the jack tubes while using the factory jack, it is best to purchase a good scissors jack or hydraulic jack – preferably trolley-type (depending on your budget).

Workshop safety – summary

1 Always have a fire extinguisher at arm's length whenever welding or when working on the fuel system – under the car, or under the bonnet.

2 NEVER use a naked flame near the petrol tank.

If you do have a fire, DON'T PANIC. Use the extinguisher effectively by directing it at the base of the fire.

Paint spraying

NEVER use 2-pack, isocyanate-based paints in the home environment or home workshop. Ask your supplier if you are not sure which is which. If you have use of a professional booth, wear an air-fed mask. Wear a charcoal face mask when spraying other paints and maintain ventilation to the spray area. Concentrated fumes are dangerous!

Spray fumes, thinners and paint are highly flammable. Keep away from naked flames or sparks.

Paint spraying safety is too large a subject for this book. See Lindsay Porter's *The Car Bodywork Repair Manual* (Haynes) for further information.

6.1 Invest in a workshop-sized fire extinguisher. Choose the carbon dioxide type or preferably, dry powder but never a water type extinguisher for workshop use. Water conducts electricty and can make worse an oil or petrol-based fire, in certain circumstances.

Fluoroelastomers – Most Important! Please Read This Section!

Many synthetic rubber-like materials used in motor cars contain a substance called fluorine. These substances are known as fluoroelastomers and are commonly used for oil seals, wiring and cabling, bearing surfaces, gaskets, diaphragms, hoses and 'O' rings. If they are subjected to temperatures greater than 315°C, they will decompose and can be potentially hazardous. Fluoroelastomer materials will show physical signs of decomposition under such conditions in the form of charring of black sticky masses. Some decomposition may occur at temperatures above 200°C, and it is obvious that when a car has been in a fire or has been dismantled with the assistance of a cutting torch or blow torch, the fluoroelastomers can decompose in the manner indicated above.

In the presence of any water or humidity, including atmospheric moisture, the by-products caused by the fluoroelastomers being heated

can be extremely dangerous. According to the Health and Safety Executive, 'Skin contact with this liquid or decomposition residues can cause painful and penetrating burns. Permanent irreversible skin and tissue damage can occur.' Damage can also be caused to eyes or by the inhalation of fumes created as fluoroelastomers are burned or heated.

If you are in the vicinity of a vehicle fire or a place where a vehicle is being cut up with cutting equipment, the Health and Safety Executive recommend the following action:

1 Assume unless you know otherwise that seals, gaskets and 'O' rings, hoses, wiring and cabling, bearing surfaces and diaphragms are fluoroelastomers.

2 Inform firefighters of the presence of fluoroelastomers and toxic and corrosive fume hazards when they arrive.

4 All personnel not wearing breathing apparatus must leave the immediate area of a fire.

After fires or exposure to high temperatures:

1 Do not touch blackened or charred seals or equipment.

2 Allow all burnt or decomposed fluoroelastomer materials to cool down before inspection, investigation, tear-down or removal.

3 Preferably, don't handle parts containing decomposed fluoroelastomers, but if you must, wear goggles and PVC (polyvinyl chloride) or neoprene protective gloves whilst doing so. Never handle such parts unless they are completely cool.

4 Contaminated parts, residues, materials and clothing, including protective clothing and gloves, should be disposed of by an approved

contractor to landfill or by incineration according to national or local regulations. Original seals, gaskets and 'O' rings, along with contaminated material, must not be burned locally.

Symptoms and clinical findings of exposure:

A Skin/eye contact
Symptoms may be apparent immediately, soon after contact or there may be considerable delay after exposure. Do not assume that there has been no damage from a lack of immediate symptoms; delays of minutes in treatment can have severe consequences:

1 Dull throbbing ache.
2 Severe and persistent pain.
3 Black discoloration under nails (skin contact).

4 Severe, persistent and penetrating burns.
5 Skin swelling and redness.
6 Blistering.
7 Sometimes pain without visible change.

B Inhalation (breathing) – immediate
1 Coughing.
2 Choking.
3 Chills lasting one to two hours after exposure.
4 Irritation.

C Inhalation (breathing) – delays of one to two days or more
1 Fever.
2 Cough.
3 Chest tightness.
4 Pulmonary oedema (congestion).
5 Bronchial pneumonia.

First aid

A Skin contact
1 Remove contaminated clothing immediately.
2 Irrigate affected skin with copious amounts of cold water or lime water (saturated calcium hydroxide solution) for 15 to 60 minutes. Obtain medical assistance urgently.

B Inhalation
Remove to fresh air and obtain medical supportive treatment immediately. Treat for pulmonary oedema.

C Eye contact
Wash/irrigate eyes immediately with water followed by normal saline for 30 to 60 minutes. Obtain immediate medical attention.

2 Tools and Working Facilities

Introduction

A selection of good tools is a fundamental requirement for anyone contemplating the maintenance and repair of a motor vehicle. For the owner who does not possess any, their purchase will prove a considerable expense, offsetting some of the savings made by doing-it-yourself. However, provided that the tools purchased are of good quality, they will last for many years and prove an extremely worthwhile investment.

To help the average owner to decide which tools are needed to carry out the various tasks detailed in this book, we have compiled three lists of tools under the following headings: *Maintenance and minor repair, Repair and overhaul,* and *Special.* The newcomer to practical mechanics should start off with the *Maintenance and minor repair* tool kit and confine himself to the simpler jobs around the vehicle. Then, as his confidence and experience grow, he can undertake more difficult tasks, buying extra tools as, and when, they are needed. In this way, a *Maintenance and minor repair* tool kit can be built up into a *Repair and overhaul* tool kit over a considerable period of time without any major cash outlays.

The experienced do-it-yourselfer will have a tool kit good enough for most repair and overhaul procedures and will add tools from the *Special* category when he feels the expense is justified by the amount of use to which these tools will be put.

It is obviously not possible to cover the subject of tools fully here. For those who wish to learn more about tools and their use there is a book entitled *How to Choose and Use Car Tools* available from the publishers of this book.

Maintenance and minor repair tool kit

The tools given in this list should be considered as a minimum requirement if routine maintenance, servicing and minor repair operations are to be undertaken. We recommend the purchase of combination spanners (ring one end, open-ended the other); although more expensive than open-ended ones, they do give the advantages of both types of spanner.

> *Combination spanners – as full a range of metric sizes as you can afford.*
> *Adjustable spanner – 9 inch*

Engine sump/gearbox/rear axle drain plug hexagonal key (where applicable)
Spark plug spanner (with rubber insert)
Spark plug gap adjustment tool
Set of feeler gauges
Brake adjuster spanner (where applicable)
Brake bleed nipple spanner
Screwdriver – 4 in long x $^1/4$ in. dia. (plain)
Screwdriver – 4 in long x $^1/4$ in. dia. (crosshead)
Combination pliers – 6 inch
Hacksaw (junior)
Tyre pump
Tyre pressure gauge
Grease gun
Oil can
Fine emery cloth (1 sheet)
Wire brush (small)
Funnel (medium size)

Repair and overhaul tool kit

These tools are virtually essential for anyone undertaking any major repairs to a motor vehicle, and are additional to those given in the Basic list. Included in this list is a comprehensive set of sockets. Although these are expensive they will be found invaluable as they are so versatile – particularly

if various drives are included in the set. We recommend the 1/2 inch or, for better accessibility, a good quality 3/8 inch square-drive type, as this can be used with most proprietary torque wrenches. If you cannot afford a socket set, even bought piecemeal, then inexpensive tubular box spanners are a useful alternative. Note that cheap socket sets are made of carbon steel which will give way and break when tightening or undoing some of the high-torque bolts found on Porsches. Chrome vanadium steel or some other high-grade steel should be selected.

The tools in this list will occasionally need to be supplemented by tools from the Special list.

Sockets (or box spanners)
Reversible ratchet drive (for use with sockets)
Extension piece, 10 inch (for use with sockets)
Universal joint (for use with sockets)
Torque wrench (for use with sockets)
'Mole' wrench – 8 inch
Ball pein hammer
Soft-faced hammer, plastic or rubber
Screwdriver – 6 in long x 5/16 in. dia. (plain)
Screwdriver – 2 in long x 5/16 in. square (plain)
Screwdriver – 1 1/2 in. long x 1/4 in. dia. (crosshead)
Screwdriver – 3 in. long x 1/8 in. dia. (electrician's)
Pliers – electrician's side cutters
Pliers – needle noses
Pliers – circlip (internal and external)
Cold chisel – 1/2 inch
Scriber
Scraper. (This can be made by flattening and sharpening one end of a piece of copper pipe)
Centre punch
Pin punch
Hacksaw
Valve grinding tool

Steel rule/straight-edge
Allen keys
Selection of files
Wire brush (large)
Axle-stands
Jack (strong scissor or hydraulic type)

Special tools

The tools in this list are those which are not used regularly, are expensive to buy, or which need to be used in accordance with their manufacturers' instructions. Unless relatively difficult mechanical jobs are undertaken frequently, it will not be economical to buy many of these tools. Where this is the case, you could consider clubbing together with friends (or joining a motorists' club) to make a joint purchase. or borrowing the tools against a deposit from a local garage or tool hire specialist.

The following list contains only those tools and instruments freely available to the public, and not those special tools produced by the vehicle manufacturer specifically for its dealer network.

Valve spring compressor
Piston ring compressor
Balljoint separator
Universal hub/bearing puller
Impact screwdriver
Micrometer and/or vernier gauge
Carburettor flow balancing device (where applicable)
Dial gauge
Stroboscopic timing light
Dwell angle meter/ tachometer
Universal electrical multi-meter
Cylinder compression gauge
Lifting tackle
Trolley jack
Light with extension lead

Buying tools

For practically all tools, a tool

factor is the best source since he will have a very comprehensive range compared with the average garage or accessory shop. Having said that, accessory shops often offer excellent quality tools at discount prices, so it pays to shop around.

Remember, you don't have to buy the most expensive items on the shelf, but it is always advisable to steer clear of the very cheap tools. There are plenty of good tools around at reasonable prices, so ask the proprietor or manager of the shop for advice before making a purchase. Avoid carbon-steel spanners, because they are inherently weaker than those of the chrome-vanadium or otherhigh-quality steel alloy variety. However, some cheaper tools are also billed as being 'chrome vanadium' whilst being poor quality and liable to break. Stick to a top-class name such as Sykes-Pickavant which cost more to buy but last for many years.

Care and maintenance of tools

Having purchased a reasonable tool kit, it is necessary to keep the tools in a clean serviceable condition. After use, always wipe off any dirt, grease and metal particles using a clean, dry cloth, before putting the tools away. Never leave them lying around after they have been used. A simple tool rack on the garage or workshop wall, for items such as screwdrivers and pliers is a good idea. Store all normal wrenches and sockets in a metal box. Any measuring instruments, gauges, meters, etc, must be carefully stored where they cannot be damaged or become rusty.

Take a little care when tools are used. Hammer heads inevitably become marked and screwdrivers lose the keen edge on their blades from time to time. A little timely attention with

emery cloth or a file will soon restore items like this to a good serviceable finish.

Working facilities

Not to be forgotten when discussing tools, is the workshop itself. If anything more than routine maintenance is to be carried out, some form of suitable working area becomes essential.

It is appreciated that many an owner mechanic is forced by circumstances to remove an engine or similar item, without the benefit of a garage or workshop. Having done this, any repairs should always be done under the cover of a roof.

Wherever possible, any dismantling should be done on a clean, flat workbench or table at a suitable working height.

Any workbench needs a vice: one with a jaw opening of 4 in (100 mm) is suitable for most jobs. As mentioned previously, some clean dry storage space is also required for tools, as well as for lubricants, cleaning fluids, touch-up paints and so on, which become necessary.

Another item which may be required, and which has a much more general usage, is an electric drill with a chuck capacity of at least $5/16$ in. (8mm). This, together with a good range of twist drills, is virtually essential for fitting accessories such as mirrors and reversing lights.

Last, but not least, always keep a supply of old newspapers and clean, lint-free rags available, and try to keep any working area as clean as possible.

Spanner jaw gap comparison table

Jaw gap (in)	Spanner size
0.625	$5/8$ in. AF
0.629	16 mm AF
0.669	17 mm AF
0.687	$11/16$ in. AF
0.708	18 mm AF
0.710	$3/8$ in. Whitworth/$7/16$ in. BSF
0.748	19 mm AF
0.750	$3/4$ in. AF
0.812	$13/16$ in. AF
0.820	$7/16$ in Whitworth/$1/2$ in. BSF
0.866	22 mm AF
0.875	$7/8$ in. AF
0.920	$1/2$ in. Whitworth/$9/16$ in. BSF
0.937	$15/16$ in. AF
0.944	24 mm AF
1.000	1 in.AF
1.010	$9/16$ in.Whitworth/$5/8$ in.BSF
1.023	26 mm AF
1.062	$1 1/16$ in. AF/27 mm AF
1.100	$5/8$ in. Whitworth/$11/16$ in. BSF
1.125	$1 1/8$ in. AF
1.181	30 mm AF
1.200	$11/16$ in. Whitworth/$3/4$ in. BSF
1.250	$1 1/4$ in. AF
1.259	32 mm AF
1.300	$3/4$ in. Whitworth/$7/8$ in. BSF

Jaw gap (in)	Spanner size
1.312	$1 5/16$ in. AF
1.390	$13/16$ in. Whitworth;/$15/16$ in. BSF
1.417	36 mm AF
1.437	$1 7/16$ in. AF
1.480	$7/8$ in. Whitworth/1 in. BSF
1.500	$1 1/2$ in. AF
1.574	40 mm; AF/$15/16$ in. Whitworth
1.614	41 mm AF
1.625	$1 5/8$ in. AF
1.670	1 in. Whitworth/$1 1/8$ in. BSF
1.687	$1 11/16$ in. AF
1.811	46 mm AF
1.812	$1 13/16$ in. AF
1.860	$1 1/8$ in. Whitworth/$1 1/4$ in. BSF
1.875	$1 7/8$ in. AF
1.968	50 mm AF
2.000	2 in. AF
2.050	$1 1/4$ in. Whitworth/$1 3/8$ in/ BSF
2.165	55 mm AF
2.362	60 mm AF

3 Specifications

These are some of the technical specifications of the Porsche 911 as they appeared at some of the main change points.

911, 911L, 911T, 911E, 911S from 1965 to 1968

Engine
Type   6-cylinder horizontally opposed air-cooled

Bore, stroke & displacement   80 mm bore x 66 mm stroke, 1991 cc

BHP
  911, 911L, 911E   130 DIN/148 SAE at 6100 rpm
  911S   160 DIN/180 SAE at 6600 rpm
  911T   110 DIN/125 SAE at 5800 rpm

Carburation
  911   Six Solex 40 PI
  911T, 911L, 911E   Two Weber 40 IDA
  911S   Two Weber 40 1DS

Transmission final-drive
911T, 911E (with Sportomatic)   3.86:1
**911T, 911E (with standard four-speed
or 911S five-speed)**   4.43:1
**911T, 911E, 911S (optional with
four or five-speed transmission)**   4.833 or 4.38:1

Suspension
Rear
  911, 911T   Independent, semi-trailing link on each side with transverse torsion bars and telescopic shock absorbers
  911S   With anti-roll bar

Front
  911T   MacPherson telescopic shock strut and triangulated wishbone on each side with longitudinal torsion bars
  911, 911S   With anti-roll bar

Wheels and tyres
Wheels
    911, 911T, 911E   Bolt on steel disc
    911S   Pressure-cast alloy

Tyres
    911T   165 HR 15
    911, 911S   185/70 VR 15
    911E (US version)   185 HR 14

Brakes
    911T   ATE solid disc
    911, 911L, 911S   Ventilated disc

Dimensions
Wheelbase   87.1 inches

Front track   53.8 inches

Rear track
    911L, 911S   52.7 inches
    911T   52.5 inches

Length   13 ft 8 ins

Unladen weight
    911 (1965), 911US, 911L, 911T,
    911S (1967), 911L-US   2314.44 lbs
    911, 911S (1966)   2207.29 lbs
    911T, 911E   2185.86 lbs
    911S (1968)   2132.29 lbs

911T, 911E, 911S from 1969 to 1971

Engine

Type   6-cylinder horizontally opposed air-cooled

Bore, stroke & displacement: 1970-71   84 mm bore x 66 mm stroke, 2195 cc

BHP
    911T (1970-71)   125 DIN/145 SAE at 5800 rpm
    911E (1969)   140 DIN/160 SAE at 6500 rpm
    911E (1970-71)   155 DIN/175 SAE at 6200 rpm
    911S (1969)   170 DIN/190 SAE at 6800 rpm
    911S (1970-71)   180 DIN/200 SAE at 6500 rpm

Carburation
    911T (1969)   Two Weber 40 IDT
    911T (1970-71)   Two Zenith 40 TIN
    911E, 911S   Bosch timed fuel injection

Transmission final-drive
    911T, 911E (with Sportomatic)   3.86:1
    911T, 911E (with standard four-
    speed or 911S five-speed)   4.43:1
    911T, 911E, 911S (optional with
    four or five-speed transmission)   4.833 or 4.38:1

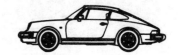

Suspension
Rear
    Except 911S — Independent, semi-trailing link on each with transverse torsion bars & telescopic shock absorbers

    911S — With anti-roll bar

Front
    911T, 911S — Independent MacPherson telescopic shock strut and triangulated wishbone on each side with longitudinal torsion bars and anti-roll bar

    911E — Boge hydro-pneumatic gas/oil shock strut and triangulated wishbone on each side and anti-roll bar

Wheels & Tyres
Wheels
    911T, 911E — Bolt on steel disc
    911S — Pressure-cast alloy

Tyres
    911T — 165 HR 15
    911, 911S — 185/70 VR 15
    911E (US version) — 185 HR 14

Brakes
    911T, 911E, 911S — ATE solid disc

Dimensions
Wheelbase — 89.3 inches

Front track — 54.1 inches

Rear track — 53.3 inches

Length — 13 ft 8 ins

    1971 — 13 ft 7 ins

Unladen weight — 2185.86 lbs

    1971 — 2250.15 lbs

911T, 911E, 911S, Carrera 2.7 from 1972 to 1973

Engine

Type — 6-cylinder horizontally opposed air-cooled

Bore, stroke & displacement
    911T, 911E, 911S — 84 mm bore x 70.4 mm stroke, 2341 cc
    Carrera (1973 only) — 90 mm bore x 70.4 mm stroke, 2687 cc

BHP
    911T (to mid 1973) — 130 DIN/150 SAE at 5600 rpm
    911T (from mid 1973) — 140 DIN/157 SAE at 5600 rpm
    911E — 165 DIN/185 SAE at 6200 rpm
    911S — 190 DIN/210 SAE at 6500 rpm
    Carrera 2.7 — 210 DIN/230 SAE at 6300 rpm

Carburation
    911T (to mid 1973)   Two Zenith 40
    911T (from mid 1973)   Bosch CIS fuel injection
    911E, 911S, Carrera   Bosch timed fuel injection

Transmission final-drive   3.87:1 or 4.43:1

Suspension
Rear   Independent, semi-trailing link on each side with transverse torsion bars, telescopic shock absorbers and anti-roll bar

Front   Independent, MacPherson telescopic shock strut and triangulated wishbone on each side with longitudinal torsion bars and anti-roll bar

Wheels & tyres
Wheels   Pressure-cast alloy

Tyres   185/70 VR 15

Dimensions
Wheelbase   89.4 inches

Front track   54.0 inches

Rear track   53.3 inches

Length   13 ft 6 ins
    911S   13 ft 7 ins

Unladen weight
    911T   2250.15 lbs
    911E, 911S   2303.72 lbs

911, 911S, Carrera, Carrera RS

Engine
Type   6-cylinder horizontally opposed air-cooled

Bore, stroke & displacement
    911, 911S, Carrera   90 mm bore x 70.4 mm stroke, 2687 cc

BHP
    911   150 DIN/143 SAE at 5700 rpm
    911S, Carrera   175 DIN/167 SAE at 5800 rpm
    Carrera RS   230 DIN/220 SAE at 6500 rpm

Carburation   Bosch CIS timed fuel injection

Transmission final-drive
    With four or five speed   4.429:1
    With Sportomatic   3.857:1

Suspension
Rear   Independent, semi-trailing link on each side with transverse torsion bars, telescopic shock absorbers

   Carrera   With anti-roll bar

Front   Independent, MacPherson telescopic shock strut and triangulated wishbone on each side, with longitudinal torsion bars and anti-roll bar

Wheels & tyres
Tyres
   911   165 HR 15
   911S   185/70 VR 15
   Carrera front   185/70 VR 15
   Carrera rear   215/60 VR 15

Dimensions
Front track
   911 (with 5 1/2J-15 wheel)   53.5 inches
   911S, Carrera (with 6-15 wheel)   54.0 inches

Rear track
   911 (with 5 1/2J-15 wheel)   52.8 inches
   Carrera (with 7J wheel)   54.3 inches

Length   14 ft 1 ins

Unladen weight
   911, 911S, Carrera   2303.72 lbs
   911, 911S, Sportomatics   2335.87 lbs

911, 911S, 911S/C, Carrera 3.0, Turbo 1975

Engine
Type   6-cylinder horizontally opposed air-cooled

Bore, stroke & displacement
   (911, 911S)   90 mm bore x 70.4 mm stroke, 2687 cc
   (Carrera 3.0, Turbo)

Turbo   95 mm bore x 70.4 mm stroke, 2993 cc

BHP
   911   150 DIN/143 SAE at 5700 rpm
   911S   175 DIN/167 SAE at 5800 rpm
   Carrera 3.0   210 DIN/200 SAE at 6300 rpm
   Carrera 3.0 (U.S. spec) 165 DIN/157 SAE at 5800 rpm
   Turbo   260 DIN/248 SAE at 5500 rpm

Carburation   Bosch K-Jetronic fuel injection

Transmission final-drive 3.87:1

Suspension
Rear   Independent, semi-trailing link on each side with transverse torsion bars, telescopic shock absorbers and anti-roll bar

Front	Independent, MacPherson telescopic shock strut and triangulated wishbone on each side with longitudinal torsion bars and anti-roll bar

Wheels & Tyres
Tyres

911 Turbo front and rear	185/70 VR 15 and 215/60 VR 15

Dimensions
Wheelbase 89.4 inches

Front track	54.0 inches
Turbo	56.6 inches

Rear track	
911, 911S	53.3 inches
Carrera	54.3 inches
Turbo	59.5 inches

Length 14 ft 1 ins

Unladen weight	
911, 911S, Carrera	2303.72 lbs
911, 911S Sportomatic	2335.87 lbs
911S-US, Carrera-US	2357.30 lbs
911S-US Sportomatic	2389.44 lbs

911, Carrera 3.0, Turbo, Turbo Carrera from 1976 to 1977

Engine
Type 6-cylinder horizontally opposed air-cooled

Bore, stroke & displacement	
911	90 mm bore x 70.4 mm stroke, 2687 cc
Carrera 3.0,	
Turbo, Turbo Carrera – US	95 mm bore x 70.4 mm stroke, 2993 cc

BHP	
911	165 DIN/157 SAE at 5800 rpm
Carrera 3.0	200 DIN/191 SAE at 6000 rpm
Turbo	260 DIN/248 SAE at 5500 rpm
Turbo (Japan, US)	245 DIN/234 SAE at 5500 rpm

Carburation	
911, Carrera 3.0	Bosch K-Jetronic fuel injection
Turbo, Turbo Carrera	KKK Turbocharger and Bosch K-Jetronic fuel injection

Dimensions
Wheelbase 89.4 inches

Front track	
911, Carrera 3.0	53.9 inches
Turbo, Turbo Carrera	56.6 inches

Rear track	
911	53.3 inches
Carrera 3.0	54.3 inches
Turbo, Turbo Carrera	59.5 inches

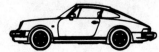

Length	14 ft 1 ins
Unladen weight	
911	2303.72 lbs
911 (1977), Carrera 3.0 Turbo,	
Turbo (Carrera)	2400.16 lbs

These specifications are only on models up to and including 1977 models. Because of the complexity of later cars and because, since 1975, they have been fitted with rust resistant zinc coated body panels they will not be likely candidates for restoration. Yet!

4 Production Modifications

The following production changes details are the most complete set of production change information on the 911 and 912 to be found anywhere. Remember that Porsche produced production changes on the 'Model Year' basis. New models were, and are, introduced after the annual holiday in September and the new model is regarded as the following year's model. So, for instance, a 911 introduced in September of 1972 would be a 1973 Model Year car. All change points shown here are calendar and not necessarily model year change points.

See 'Specification' section for details of spec. on introduction. Please note that Porsche 912 Chassis Number change points as shown here are the best available but are not necessarily reliable. Porsche themselves are secretive about releasing such details on an official basis.

Sometimes, modifications have been made by the factory themselves before the change point given and there are very many cars that have been modified by their owners. Use the facts given here to check their relevance to the model in question.

1963
September

New model announced at Frankfurt Motor Show to replace 356C known as 901. Wheelbase up from 2,100 mm to 2,211 mm (82.7 in to 87.04 in.), overall length up by 153 mm (5.8 in) but width down 60 mm (2.4 in.). New 6-cylinder engine, one overhead camshaft per bank. 1991 cc. 'Racing' pattern gear change: 2nd, 3rd, 4th and 5th in normal 'H' pattern; 1st to the left and down. Reverse high above 1st.

1964
September

Chassis No. 300001. Introduced in Germany. Nomenclature changed to 911 to avoid clashing with Peugeot style of model numbering. '901' cast into engine. All models 'De Luxe'. 912 introduced in Germany as *new model.* 4-cylinder 1582 cc pushrod engine developed from the 356C unit but with power down 5 bhp to 90 bhp and more torque. 4-or 5-speed gearbox. 12 volt electrics. Basically a cost-reduced 911 but facia different with 3 instrument dials instead of 5. '912' motif on rear. Chassis No: K-Coupe, 450001, Coupe, 350001. Initially available in mainland Europe only.

1965
April
July

356C production ended in Germany.
4-speed becomes standard production unit with lower gearing and maximum speed at 6,700 instead of 6,500 rpm.

August
September

911 Chassis No 301929. First imported to UK in r.h.d. form.
'Targa' announced as *new model* at Frankfurt show. Intended originally in a choice of four versions. Detachable targa top with

a very safe roll-over structure. 912 available for export markets and 912 Targa introduced as *new model.* Export Coupe Chassis No. 350800; Targa, 450001 in Germany, not available in UK.

1966
February

Weber 40 IDA 3C carbs replace flat-spot-prone, floatless Solex carbs. One Bendix fuel pump replaces twin pumps formerly used. Later, adjustable accelerator pump rods added to Webers to cure more flat spots.

Spring

Deliveries of 911 and 912 Targa begin.

June

Chassis No. 305101. Type 911S announced as *new model.* Chassis numbers in normal pattern with 'S' suffix. 160 bhp at 6,600 rpm, Chassis No. 305101. Type 911S announced as *new model.* Chassis numbers in normal pattern with 'S' suffix.160 bhp at 6,600 rpm, forged pistons, larger valves, constantly revolving clutch release bearing. Koni shock absorbers, thicker ventilated discs, rear anti-roll bar in addition to front. 50 kg (110 lb) lighter and 9 mph (15 kph) faster than standard. Speed limiter fitted to engine. Leather covered steering wheel and dashboard, tachometer red-lined at 7,200–7,400 rpm. New handles fitted to ashtray and glovebox, silver covered typescript, gearchange pattern engraved in gearknob, carpets in place of rubber mats. Bumper over-riders with rubber protection strip. 5-spoke Fuchs road wheels (5 lb lighter) used for first time. 912 models with safety door locks for German market. Chassis Nos. Coupe, 354001; Targa, 45801. Modifications introduced to UK in August, Chassis No. 354131. Chassis No. 305101. 911N announced as *new model* (base model) for German market. Plastic steering wheel instead of wood rim, alloy dash and painted wheels instead of chrome.

September

Chassis No. 305328S. 911S first imported to UK.

October

Chassis No. 305419. Base model 911N first imported to UK.

1967
August

'A'-series models introduced. More 'safety conscious' spec. to all cars. 'A'-series models introduced. More 'safety conscious' spec. to all cars. Recessed door pushbuttons, slimmer outside door handles, matt black wiper arms, twin-circuit braking, front seat belt anchorage points, anti-glare deformable dash with matt black rims, rubber ashtray handle, wider (5.5 in.) wheel rims, quartz-halogen fog lamps U.S. cars fitted with emission control equipment (air injection pump) which caused backfire. (Porsche produced rectification kit: most of these cars have them fitted.)

September

Chassis No. 11810001 (Fixed Head) and 11860001 (Targa). 911L introduced. *New model.* Interior trim and spec. similar to 911S. Anti-roll bar diameter reduced from 13 mm to 11 mm. Replacement for 911 and 911N.

Chassis No. 11820001 (Fixed Head) and 11870001 (Targa). 911T introduced as *new model.* Similar to 912 chassis and equipment specs. but still 6-cylinder. Cast iron cylinders instead of aluminium alloy. No counterweights on crank, cast iron rockers instead of steel, lower.C.R., solid steel brake discs instead of vented, interior similar to 912.

912 with dual circuit brakes, black rims to dials instead of chrome, slimmer door handles, chrome lettering on exterior and 5.5 in. road wheel instead of 4.5 in. Chassis Nos: Coupe 12820001; Targa, 12870001.

Chassis No. 11800001 (Fixed Head) and 11850001 (Targa). 911S continued as before. Grained leathercloth on dash. Not available in USA: failed to meet US emsion regs.

'Sportomatic' semi-automatic (clutchless) gearchanging available on all 6-cylinder models.
911 'De Luxe' Chassis No. 304173 and 911N Chassis No. 308459 discontinued in UK.
First imports to UK of: 911T, Chassis No. 11820133; 911L, Chassis No. 11810056; 911S, Chassis No. 11800107.

1968

June

Chassis No. 11800912. Last 'Sportomatic' 911S imported to UK. No longer an 'S' option.

August

So-called 'B'-programme put into production for 1969 model year. The wheelbase was lengthened by 57 mm (2.24 in.) to 2,268 mm (7 ft 5.3 in.) by moving the back wheels back whilst leaving the power unit in its original position giving better weight distribution. Rzeppa constant velocity joints (as re-incarnated by Issigonis for Austin Mini) used with new half-shafts and stronger torsion bars plus longer semi-trailing arms. All models received larger rear brake callipers and larger (6 in. wide, 15 in. dia.) wheels, except 911T 'Comfort' and 911E 'Sportomatic' – see below. Front and rear wheel arches slightly flared, more powerful generator fitted, twin batteries (35 amp hr. each) mounted ahead of front wheel arches, quartz-halogen main lights, hazard warning lights, glove box lamp and heated rear screen became standard. A hand throttle was fitted between the seats, dipping mirror, larger door pockets and door opening catch recessed into arm rest. Smaller steering wheel with padded centre. Seat backrests locked into position, reversing lights modified and Targa roll over structure gained air extractors. All models with spec. as for 'Comfort' 911T, as shown below, except hydro-pneumatic struts optional only on S and standard wheel size as shown above.

September

Chassis No. 119200094. 911E *new model* introduced. 911L dropped. (Last Chassis No. 11810685). Bosch mechanical fuel injection system fitted along with electronic ignition system, shared by 911S. 911E gave 140 bhp at 6,500 rpm and 911S gave 170 bhp at 6,800 rpm. Also with self-levelling front suspension and alloy wheels. Wider track from thicker discs. 911S also received larger front brake callipers made of light alloy and E model received thicker ventilated discs all round, widening track by 0.4 in. Independent petrol-electric heating system and quartz-halogen fog lamps dropped. Hydro-pneumatuc self-levelling front struts optional. Now with tinted windows and rear wiper. 5-speed only. Bosch mechanical fuel injection and electronic ignition.
911T (Chassis No. 119100006) now with flared wheel arches, smaller diameter steering wheel, through-flow ventilation, fixed quarter lights and heated rear window as standard. Two Weber 40 IDT carbs.
911T Lux (Chassis No. 119100037) now available with 'Comfort' kit comprising self-levelling front struts, air horns, pile carpets, oil pressure and level gauge, leather covered steering wheel, bumper over-riders with rubber insert and larger 'Porsche' script. 5.5 in. wide by 14 in. alloy wheels.
'Sportomatic' 911E fitted with 5.5 in. wide by 14 in. alloy wheels.
Targa now with wrap-around glass rear window in place of leak-prone zip out plastic.

1969

August

Last Chassis Nos. of 'B'-spec. cars: 911T, 911T Lux, 119100331;

	911E, 119200874; 911S, 119301404.
September	Last 912. Final Chassis Nos: Coupe, 129023450; Targa, 129010801. 'C' programme embarked upon. 2.2 litre versions of 911 announced and production begun for 1970 model year. All models with bore increase from 80 to 84 mm giving 2.2 litres giving more torque and more power to cope with American emission constraints. Compression ratios down on all engines. Front suspension strut mountings modified making steering lighter and reducing kick-back. Underfloor areas galvanised and PVC undercoat used. Instruments now fitted and removed from front of dash. External door handles now of trigger type and new, lighter Targa top fitted. Magnesium alloy replaces aluminium as material for crankcase. Larger valves fitted but port size varied with state of tune of model type. USA models fitted with fuel tank venting system. Larger diameter clutch used. ZF limited slip diff. available as optional extra. Steering column stalks carried controls and instruments placed directly in front of driver. Illuminated ashtray and steering wheel lock introduced and USA cars fitted with warning buzzer to remind driver to remove ignition key before leaving vehicle. Chassis Nos: 911T, 9110100088; 911T Lux, 9110100086; 911E, 9110200037; 911S, 9110300108.
1971 **January**	Chassis Nos: 911T and 911T Lux, 9111100174; 911E, 911120000; 911S, 9111300140. Minor modifications to fuel injection and ignition to comply with emission control regs. Identified by movement of fuel pump from front suspension cross-member to rear left-hand side of car. Last 2195 cc Chassis Nos: 911T, 9111102042; 911T Lux, 9111102441; 911E, 9111201052; 911S, 9111301359.
September	Chassis Nos: 911T, 9112500001; 911T Lux, 911250070; 911E, 9112200001; 911S, 9112300001. 'E' programme models introduced. Wheelbase increased by three millimetres to 2,271 mm. Engine capacity increased to 2.4 litres (2341 cc) by lengthening the stroke from 66 to 70.4 mm. Engine now runs on 'regular' grade fuel: compression ratios lowered, new cam timing and larger ports on all engines. Noticeably faster but thirstier than predecessors. Dry-sump oil tank now made of stainless steel. Model change identified by matt black air intake grille and 'Porsche' script on rear and oil filler flap fitted just behind and to the rear of the right-hand door. All models fitted with softer Boge shock absorbers (Bilstein or Koni available to special order). Rear seat squabs moved back. Gear change pattern made conventional on all 5-speed gearboxes but 4-speed now standard with 5-speed as option. (5-speed standard for UK market E and S models.) Gearbox mountings now bolt-on. Optional larger fuel tank with deflated 'space saver' spare fitted. Plasic bag supplied for carrying punctured tyre in car! Plastic used for air filter housing and intake pipes. Marelli or Bosch distributors used. 911E produced 160 bhp at 6,200 rpm. Engine bay cover and central part of bumpers made of aluminium. No anti-roll bars as standard, 6J x 15 steel wheels but alloys optional. 185/70VR tyres. No bumper over-riders fitted. Spoiler optional. 911S produced 190 bhp at 6,500 rpm. Engine bay cover and central part of bumpers made of aluminium. 'Sportomatic' not an option. 15 mm anti-roll bars front and rear. 6J x 15 alloy wheels standard, 185/70VR tyres. Front bumper integral with front air dam, or spoiler. 15 mm anti-roll bars front and rear.

911T 130bhp at 5,600 rpm for European markets with
Solex-Zenith carbs. 140 bhp at 5,600 rpm for American market
with mechanical fuel injection. Fitted with cast iron callipers all
round. Later, used 914-type steering gear. No anti-roll bars as
standard. 5.5J x 15 steel wheels and 165 HR 15 tyres standard
but 911E wheel and tyres optional. No bumper over-riders fitted.
Spoiler optional.

1972
October

External oil filler flap deleted for 1973 model-year and oil tank
(now of stainless steel) moved back to original position behind
right-hand rear wheel. More robust oil cooler fitted. Crankcase
strengthened in main bearing area. Gear change made more
precise. Rear trailing arm brackets modified to allow removal
without having first to remove power unit from car. Larger fuel
tank, previously an option, now standard along with 'space
saver' spare wheel but now with an electric compressor for
inflation instead of air can previously offered. Combined bumper
and air dam now standard on all models. Exhaust silencer now
of stainless steel. UK models with black horn grilles and side and
rear light surrounds.
911S Chassis No. 9113300001.
911E Chassis No. 9113200001. Cast alloy wheels as standard.
Lux model with 911S-type front spoiler.
91T Chassis No. 9113500001. Above wheels available as
optional equipment. 911T Lux. Chassis No. 9113500075.
911 Carrera. 2.7RS available as *new model*. Available in three
stages: Sport, Touring or Racing. 911 body style but lightened
with thinner steel, glass, etc. Greatly modified 911 with 2.7 litre
engine, with bore increased by 6 mm to 90 mm from 2.4 litre
spec. and giving 210 bhp at 6,300 rpm. Most engine
components common with 911S except flatter forged pistons
and aluminium cylinders (11 fin instead of the former engine's
15 fin). Gearbox included an oil pump. 6J x 15 front wheels
with 185/70 VR15 tyres and rear wheels of 7J x 15 with 215/60
VR tyres. Rear track widened by 4 mm. The Touring version was
given similar trim to that of the 911S and the standard steel front
bumper, while the RS Sport had no clock, glovelocker door or
soundproofing, the rear side windows were fixed and there were
no rear seats while the front seats were lightweight Recaros and
the engine cover was held down with rubber fasteners. The
whole of the interior was much more austere. A single twelve
bolt battery was fitted and a single horn. Both the Sport and
Racing models had a fibreglass front bumper/spoiler while all
three cars' engine cover and 'duck's tail' spoiler were of
fibreglass. Suspension substantially reinforced on all three
models. All standard colour options available but usual colour
scheme was 'Grand Prix White'. If white, red, blue or green was
chosen, an ostentatious 'Carrera' script was added to the side of
the car and enamelled wheels were fitted. Chassis Nos: RS Sport
and Touring 9113600001. Not available in USA for road use.
Carrera originally planned for 500 production run to qualify car
for Group 4 Special GT category, but demand from European
drivers led to semi-production.

1973
January

Targa first imported to UK in r.h.d. form. Chassis Nos. in Coupe
sequence. Special order only. Carrera first imported to UK.
Chassis Nos. RS Sport 9113600342; RS Touring 9113600061.

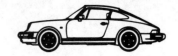

September	Final 2341 cc engine Chassis Nos: 911T and 911T Lux, 9113501746; 911T Targa, 9113511448; 911E Lux, 9113201283; 911E Targa, 9113211013; 911S, 9113301364; 911S Targa, 9113310893. 'G' programme models introduced. 2.7 litre engine fitted to all models giving startling performance, better economy and extra torque and flexibility. 'T' and 'E' suffixes dispensed with. New 'base' model reverted to 911 designation. 911 and 911S now fitted with K-Jetronic fuel injection to cope with emission control regs. while Carrera models continued with mechanical fuel injection. Protruding aluminium bumpers fitted with 'shock absorber' mountings (not re-usable). Bumpers with concertina pleated rubber 'joints' with the bodywork and thick rubber inserts identify the model change. 2-gallon (9-litre) windscreen washer reservoir fitted beneath from l.h. wing. Interior trim substantially redesigned, headrests fitted to seats. New, simpler one-piece 16mm anti-roll bar; Carrera-type rear anti-roll bar available. Front wheels now centred on the hub. Cast iron calliper now used. Forged aluminium alloy rear trailing arms in place of welded steel. Clutch pedal made lighter and brake pedal lengthened. New silencer system dictated by new bumper positions. Higher backed lightweight seats, redesigned steering wheel with extra padding. Inertia reel seat belts as standard. 'Safety conscious' dash and instrument layout, clock now quartz-electric, tacho. now electronic. Chassis Nos: 911, 9114100001; 911 Targa, 9114110001; 911S, 9114300001; 911S Targa, 9114310001.
September	Carrera Sport and Touring discontinued in favour of Carrera Coupe (Chassis No. 9114600001) and Carrera Targa (Chassis No. 9114610001). Introduced into US market. Standard 911 body used. Carrera not fitted with full power mechanically fuel injected engine for USA market but still fuel injected elsewhere. Fitted with 20mm front and 18mm rear anti-roll bar. Now in full series production. Alloy callipers as previously fitted to 911S. Steering wheel of 380mm diameter. Still with ducktail spoiler and distinctive lettering on side.
	911 & 911S. Light alloy cylinders in 'Nikasil' now fitted, shortly changed to 'Alusil'. Cast pistons used. Camshafts modified to give 'softer' timing than Carrera. 400 mm dia. steering wheel fitted. Electrically-operated windows as standard. 16 mm anti-roll bars fitted to front suspension.
	Swedish market cars with headlamp washers (optional in other markets).
	USA cars with ignition interlock.
1974	
	912 briefly introduced as 912E, Coupe only. Chassis Nos. 9126000001 – 9126002099. Body and trim basically similar to 911 but a little simpler. 2-litre 4-cylinder engine as used in VW-Porsche 914-4. L-Jetronic fuel injection. Exhaust thermal reactors. 5-speed gearbox. 90 bhp. Fixed rear windows (opening lights optional). Pressed steel 5.5J x 15 in. wheels, 165 HR 15 tyres. $3,000 less than 911S in USA. Not sold in Europe where VW/(Audi) designed 924 took its place.
September	Basic 911 (Chassis No. 9115100251; Targa 9115110996) with 6J x 15 cast alloy wheels and 185/70 VR tyres. Carrera: external mirror and headlamp surrounds finished in body colour. Also with rubber edges to front and rear spoilers. (Chassis Nos. Coupe, 9115600001; Targa, 9115610001.
	First imports into UK: Coupe, 9115600096; Targa, 9115610049). Targa: matt black roll-over frame, 911S: (Chassis No.

9115300068S; Targa 9115310082S) top two gears in both 4-speed and 5-speed 'boxes made higher. General improvements in comfort: blower on heater, heat output adjustable for l.h. and r.h. sides of cockpit and sound insulation improved. Rear anti-roll bar mounting brackets fitted to all cars and alternator output increased to 980 Watts. Export model with stainless steel door sills and wheel arch surrounds.

October

Type 930 Turbo announced at Paris Motor Show. Interior little different from other 911s but for 'Tempostat' thermostatically controlled heating. 0-50 mph (0-80 kph) in 3.6 secs! Wider rear wings with plastic skirt protector. 18 mm anti-roll bars front and rear. 4 ventilated (but not perforated) discs. 7 in. front wheels; 8in. rears. First example of turbocharging combined with fuel injection. (Still K-Jetronic.) Strengthened 4-speed gearbox. Black body trim, tinted glass, electrically heated windscreen and 2-stage rear screen heating. Leather and cloth upholstery. 'Turbo' logo on backrest of left rear seat. Electric aerial, quadrophonic stereo.

1975

January.

Coupe Turbo Type 930 production started.

March.

Coupe Turbo introduced to special order. Similar to Carrera, with flared wheel arches, leather trim, sun roof, stereo, power windows and heated front and rear screens.

August.

Carrera Coupe and Targa discontinued. Final Chassis Nos. Coupe, 9115600518 in Germany & UK, 9115400395 in USA; Targa, 9115610197 but 9115610194 in UK. 911S and 911S Targa discontinued. Final Chassis Nos. 9115300380 and 9115310265 respectively.

September.

Model range changed for the 1976 model year. 911 still 2.7 litres but Carrera (new model) of 3-litres with K-Jetronic fuel injection. Chassis Nos: Carrera 3 Coupe, 9116600001; Carrera 3 Targa, 9116610001; Carrera 3 Sports Coupe, 9116600253; Carrera 3 Sport Targa, 9116610028. Sport distinguished from 'basic' Carrera by front and rear spoilers. (None on 'basic'), 7in. front and 8in. rear alloy wheels and Recaro seats. Power outputs of 911, Carrera and Turbo 165 bhp, 200 bhp and 260 bhp respectively. Significant change in body production: entire body constructed of zinc-coated steel (except fixed-head roof on early cars only) and far more rust resistant. Door locks and Targa's quarter-light pivoting window vents with improved locking systems. External mirror in matching body colour, with heated glass and electrically adjustable. Electronic speedo. New 'A'-type cast iron front brake calipers. One-piece carpet, thicker rear bulkhead padding, padded leather-like door trim panels. Engine fan with 5 blades instead of 11. Three-speed Sportomatic gearbox replaced four-speed type. Front suspension struts inclined inwards to make camber adjustment simpler. Turbo. Sophisticated thermostatic heater control standard. Cruise control as standard. 'S'-type alloy callipers still used. Carrera. Thermostatic heater and cruise control as standard. Turbo-style camshaft housings. 8in. wide rear wheels available at no extra cost. Now only with 4-speed gearbox. Heated driver's door mirror. 205/50 VR 15 front and 225/50 VR 15 rear tyres now standard, i.e. 50 series tyres now fitted. 911 Lux Fixed Head and Targa, Chassis Nos. 9116300001 and 9116310001. Thermostatic heater and cruise control optional extras. Engine similar to previous year's 911S, with unlinered aluminium cylinders. Turbo-style camshaft housing. Better hot starting – air slide operated by thermostatic control.

911N introduced for European market to replace base 911 model. Fixed head only. Chassis No. 9116300001. Without recoil bumpers, wheel-arch trims, tinted glass or power windows. US market had 3.0 Turbo and 911S 2.7 available for 1976. Turbo as described above but 911S similar to 1975 Carrera. Options included oil cooler located in front right wing (fender), forged alloy wheels, sports seats, electric sunroof, electric wheels, air conditioning, Bilstein gas/oil shock absorbers or Koni adjustables. Standard included tinted glass, 2-speed plus intermittent wipers, two-stage rear window heating, front and rear anti-roll bars and 5-speed transmission.

1976
September.

For the 1977 model year: USA, Canada and Japanese market cars fitted with potentially strangulatory emission control equipment: extra air pump, twin thermal reactors and exhaust gas recirculation. All Sportomatic cars fitted with brake servo. Pivoting quarter lights omitted from Targa but electric windows standard. Shorter door opening pushes, retracted into surround when locked. Fuel pump now with a return pipe. Cars fitted with 'Comfort' kit (which included 130 mph-rated 'HR' tyres, fitted with an automatic speed governor cutting the fuel supply momentarily if the road speed reached 130 mph (210 km/h). Gearbox fitted to 911 and Carrera improved in several ways including first gear selection at rest. Optional centre console with shelf offered to include a wide range of sophisticated electronic equipment. Face-level vents fitted in centre of dash and brake fluid warning light fitted. Rear ride height adjustment made easier to carry out.
911N discontinued, reversion to 911. Chassis No. 9117300069. 5-speed gearbox or 3-speed Sportomatic available at no extra cost over standard 4-speed 'box.
911 Lux and Targa. Chassis Nos. 9117300008 and 9117310006. Carrera. Carrera 3 has cast alloy wheels. Sport has forged alloy wheels and all-rubber front spoiler. Chassis Nos: 9117600001 and 9117610001.
Turbo. Mods. as 911 plus centre console as standard. 16 in. rims replace 15 in. still with 50 series tyres. Twin fuel pumps and improvements to the fuel supply system. 20mm simplified-type anti-roll bar fitted, as 911. Chassis No. 9307700001.

1977
August

Last Carrera Chassis Nos: Carrera 3 Coupe, 9117601472; Carrera Targa, 9117600641; Carrera 3 Coupe Sport, 9117601470; Carrera Sport Targa, 9117610644.
Final Turbo Chassis No. 9307700694.

September.

911 3.3 Coupe Turbo *new model* introduced. Similar to 3 litre Turbo but with servo assisted brakes, new rear spoiler, leather upholstery, air conditioning and sun roof. Chassis No. 9308700001.
Chassis Nos. 911 SC Coupe and Sports Coupe, 9118300001; 911 SC Targa and Sports Targa, 9118310001. New 'base' model for 1978 model year was 911 SC. Both 911 and Carrera nomenclature deleted. Fitted with 3-litre engine with new, stronger crankshaft and larger bearings. Engine develops 180 bhp at 5,500 rpm. Carrera-style rear wings and 7 in. rear wheels fitted. 11-blade cooling fan re-fitted, exhaust system made quieter and contactless electronic ignition fitted. Air pump fitted to European spec. engines in advance of possible tightening in emission control regs. Interior trim to Carrera standards. 5-speed

gearbox and brake servo now standard. Clutch operation made lighter and characteristic Porsche low speed gear chatter now eliminated. Front and rear anti-roll bars standard. Gearbox housing of aluminium instead of magnesium alloy. 16 in. 50 series tyres an option. This model also made as Targa. Virtually a 'Carrera' without the name although bhp down 20 to 180 but torque improved. Sportomatic no longer available.
Sports Coupe and Sports Targa models with front and rear spoilers and sports seats.

1978
Thermostatic heater control standardised.

1979
January.   911 SC still only model of 911 built. Power increased to 188 bhp through ignition improvements which bring greater fuel economy improvements. Engine compartment illuminated, new interior, black window frames, electrically operated windows and 15 in. three-spoke steering wheel. 911 Turbo-type oil cooler fitted. Rear torsion bars increased by 1 mm to 24 mm dia. Chassis Nos. 911 SC and Sports Coupe 9119300001; 911 SC Targa and Sports Targa, 9119310001. 911 3.3 Coupe Turbo Chassis No. 9309700001.

1980
January.   Chassis No. Change of numbering system. All models 91A013000-on. Except Turbo 3.3, 93A0070000.
July.   Compression ratio increased from 8.6 to 9.8:1. New pistons with squish area and combustion recess near sparking plug. Valve timing, fuel and ignition settings revised to give 204bhp and remarkably good fuel economy. Indicator side marker lamps fitted to body. Sports seats, berber cloth and leather upholstery are options for the interior. Another change in Chassis Number types: 911 SC Coupe and Sports Coupe, 91ZBS100001; 911 SC Targa and Sports Targa, 91ZBS140001.

1981
January.   Turbo 3.3 Chassis No. 93ZBS000001

1982
January.   Chassis Nos. 911 SC Coupe and Sports Coupe, 91CS100001; 911 SC Targa and Sports Targa, 91CS140001. Turbo 3.3, 93CS000001.
August.   Turbo 3.3 Chassis No. 93DS000001. Impoved heating system.

1983
January   Cabriolet introduced. R.h.d. Chassis Nos. (Cabriolet and Cabriolet Sports Equip.), 91DS150001.

911 SC Coupe, Sports Coupe, Targa and Sports Targa in above Chassis No. sequence.
July.   SC range discontinued. Replaced by Carrera. Final Chassis Nos: 911 SC Coupe and Sports Coupe, 91DS102992; SC Targa and Sports Targa, 91DS141252, 911 SC Cabriolet and Cabriolet Sport, 91DS152404.
September.   911 Carrera introduced as new model. Chassis Nos. 911 Carrera fhc and Sport, 91ES100001; 911 Carrera Targa and Sport Targa, 91ES140001; 911 Carrera Cabriolet and Cabriolet Targa, 91ES150001. Now with 3.2 litre (3164 cc) engine. Similar to previous 911 but with fog lamps in front spoiler, light alloy

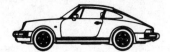

wheels with styling holes and 'Carrera' script on boot lid. New auto. heating system with 3-speed blower. 2-stage tinted rear window (not Cabriolet). Wheel anti-theft device on Sport. 5-speed gearbox standard, optional tonneau on Cabriolet, air conditioning optional. Turbo 3.3 continued with above changes and thief-proof wheel nuts. Chassis No. 93ES0001.

5 Clubs and Specialists

Clubs

Listed below are the major clubs in the English-speaking world. Should you wish to know the address of a club in any other country (and there is a club in virtually every town in Germany), contact Porsche Clubs Co-ordinator at Dr. Ing. hc F Porsche AG, porschestrasse 15-19, D-7140, Ludwigsberg, Germany.

When running a well restored, unrestored or original Porsche, there's little that can give more satisfaction than meeting lots of like-minded people. You'll find comradeship, shared experiences and hints and tips galore by joining your Porsche Club, reading the publications and taking part in events.

Australia

Porsche Club New South Wales, PO Box 183, Lindfield, NSW 2070, Sydney, Australia.

Porsche Club Queensland, PO Box 584, Brisbane 4001, Australia.

Porsche Club Victoria, PO Box 222, Kew, Victoria 3101, Australia.

Porsche Club Western Australia, PO Box 447, South Perth 6151, Western Australia.

Great Britain

Porsche Club Great Britain, Ayton House, West End, Northleach, Glos. GL54 3HG, England.

The Porsche Club Great Britain is now the second largest in the world. They are in close contact with the factory at Stuttgart and with other Porsche Clubs throughout the world. The PCBG organises a variety of events each year on both a local and national basis to suit all tastes. These include race meetings, weekend mixed events, film shows, 'natter & noggins', dinner dances, factory visits and circuit driving tuition, etc. There is also an annual Concours d'Elegance and numerous invitations are received to participate in overseas Porsche Club activities. The PCGB is divided into regions covering the UK and members can participate in any event, local or national.

A professional club magazine, 'Porsche Post', is produced four times a year and, together with regular newsletters, is posted free of charge to members. Club insignia is available at reasonable cost to members only. Technical information is available; equipment and workshop manuals are loaned free of charge. Parts discounts are available from many authorised dealers and there are special insurance arrangements for members.

Hong Kong

Porsche Club Hong Kong, No 1, Yip Fat Street, PO Box 24539, Aberdeen, Hong Kong.

New Zealand

Porsche Club New Zealand, PO Box 39-074, Auckland 9, New Zealand.

United States

Porsche Club of America, 243 McMane Avenue, Berkeley Heights, NJ 07922, USA.

Specialists

Restoration

Three specialists contributed enormously to the content of this book and without them, there would have been no Porsche 911 'Restoration Guide'. It is

unfortunately true that some folk who set themselves up as Porsche restorers don't manage to achieve very high standards. Lindsay Porter visited a number of specialists whose work he refused to use until he came across those specialists featured here. All produced a high standard of work for the photographs shown in this book and each has something a little different to offer. In alphabetical order they are:

Autofarm, Cowroast, London Road, Nr Tring, Hertfordshire, HP23 2RE, Tel. 0442 827922. Autofarm sell Porsches and Porsche parts and carry out servicing, conversions and restorations to Porsches. They are undoubtedly the largest independent Porsche specialist in the UK.

Classic Car Restorations, The Green, Tedstone Wafre, Bromyard, Herefordshire, Tel. 0885 82330. Classic Car Restorations top panel beater Ken Wright can be seen carrying out much of the work featured in this book and his work has been featured in many books and magazine articles. Their charges are known to be moderate.

David Felton, Brook Farm, Rushton Spencer, Nr Macclesfield, Cheshire, Tel. 0260 226451. David and Peter, who works with him, are quite simply the best there is. There is no vast emporium or stores (in fact there are no stores!); just the finest panel beating that Lindsay Porter has ever seen. You can't pin David down to a time; he's a perfectionist and won't let anyone have less!

Insurance

Clarkson Puckle West Midlands Limited, PO Box 27, Falcon House, The Minories, Dudley DY2 8PF, Tel. 0384 455011. Clarksons offer 'Agreed Value' insurance schemes whereby a 911 will be covered for a value agreed in advance with the insurers. Where mileage per annum is limited, the cost is much less than for conventional insurance.

Tools and equipment

Black & Decker manufacture probably the widest range of power tools available for the amateur and professional alike. Favourites for restoration include the cordless drill, random orbit sander, single grinder and 'Workmate' portable work bench.

Corroless produce rust proofing fluid for spraying into a car's enclosed steel sections, using aerosol propellant, so no compressor is required; rust inhibiting body filler and rust inhibiting paint. The latter two items incorporate a rust killing chemical within the primer and the filler, while both top coat

paints, suitable for underbody and chip-prone areas, include microscopic glass beads which makes the paint incredibly tough.

S.I.P. manufacture a full range of compressors and arc and MIG welding sets to suit all pockets. Priced considerably lower than the most expensive 'professional' items (although they sell those too!), S.I.P's equipment is definitely a cut above the average and is known to last longer.

Sykes-Pickavant/Speedline are ranges of hand tools covering every conceivable use in the workshop from panel beating to top quality socket sets and diagnostic equipment. You can buy cheaper than Sykes-Pickavant and Speedline but you can't buy better when it comes to hand tools.

6 British and American Technical Terms

As this book has been written in England, it uses the appropriate English component names, phrases, and spelling. Some of these differ from those used in America. Normally, these cause no difficulty, but to make sure, a glossary is printed below. In ordering spare parts remember the parts list may use some of these words:

English	American	English	American
Accelerator	Gas pedal	Leading shoe (of brake)	Primary shoe
Aerial	Antenna	Locks	Latches
Anti-roll bar	Stabiliser or sway bar	Methylated spirit	Denatured alcohol
Big-end bearing	Rod bearing	Motorway	Freeway, turnpike etc
Bonnet (engine cover)	Hood	Number plate	License plate
Boot (luggage compartment)	Trunk	Paraffin	Kerosene
Bulkhead	Firewall	Petrol	Gasoline (gas)
Bush	Bushing	Petrol tank	Gas tank
Cam follower or tappet	Valve lifter or tappet	'Pinking'	'Pinging'
Carburettor	Carburetor	Prise (force apart)	Pry
Catch	Latch	Propeller shaft	Driveshaft
Choke/venturi	Barrel	Quarterlight	Quarter window
Circlip	Snap-ring	Retread	Recap
Clearance	Lash	Reverse	Back-up
Crownwheel	Ring gear (of differential)	Rocker cover	Valve cover
Damper	Shock absorber, shock	Saloon	Sedan
Disc (brake)	Rotor/disk	Seized	Frozen
Distance piece	Spacer	Sidelight	Parking light
Drop arm	Pitman arm	Silencer	Muffler
Drop head coupe	Convertible	Sill panel (beneath doors)	Rocker panel
Dynamo	Generator (DC)	Small end, little end	Piston pin or wrist pin
Earth (electrical)	Ground	Spanner	Wrench
Engineer's blue	Prussian blue	Split cotter (for valve spring cap)	Lock (for valve spring retainer)
Estate car	Station wagon	Split pin	Cotter pin
Exhaust manifold	Header	Steering arm	Spindle arm
Fault finding/diagnosis	Troubleshooting	Sump	Oil pan
Float chamber	Float bowl	Swarf	Metal chips or debris
Free-play	Lash	Tab washer	Tang or lock
Freewheel	Coast	Tappet	Valve lifter
Gearbox	Transmission	Thrust bearing	Throw-out bearing
Gearchange	Shift	Top gear	High
Grub screw	Setscrew, Allen screw	Trackrod (of steering)	Tie-rod (or connecting rod)
Gudgeon pin	Piston pin or wrist pin	Trailing shoe (of brake)	Secondary shoe
Halfshaft	Axleshaft	Transmission	Whole drive line
Handbrake	Parking brake	Tyre	Tire
Hood	Soft top	Van	Panel wagon/van
Hot spot	Heat riser	Vice	Vise
Indicator	Turn signal	Wheel nut	Lug nut
Interior light	Dome lamp	Windscreen	Windshield
Layshaft (of gearbox)	Countershaft	Wing/mudguard	Fender

Miscellaneous points

An oil seal is fitted to components lubricated by grease!

A 'damper' is a shock absorber, it damps out bouncing and absorbs shock of bump impact. Both names are correct, and both are used haphazardly.

Note that British drum brakes are different from the Bendix type that is common in America, so different descriptive names result. The shoe end furthest from the hydraulic wheel cylinder is on a pivot, interconnection between the shoes as on Bendix brakes is most uncommon. Therefore the phrase 'Primary' or 'Secondary' shoe does not apply. A shoe is said to be 'Leading' or 'Trailing'. A 'Leading' shoe is one on which a point on the drum, as it rotates forward, reaches the shoe at the end worked by the hydraulic cylinder before the anchor end. The opposite is a 'Trailing' shoe and this one has no self-servo from the wrapping effect of the rotating drum.

Lindsay Porter

Lindsay, once an apprentice at John Thompson Motor
Pressings near Wolverhampton escaped to the world of
the classroom after taking a teacher training course. He
specialised in English and Design Studies. However, in
1979 he started to write on a part-time basis for DIY
Magazine and Practical Classics. Before long he was
also a regular contributor to many other magazines and
had written a number of books for Haynes. At the start
of 1984, he left teaching and now spends his time
writing, pointing his camera at cars, working on them
and even driving them on occasion.

Peter Morgan

Peter's interest in motoring stems from the time he was
given a go-kart at the age of twelve. After terrorising
his family's neighbours, the interest led him to kart
racing and later to club level motor racing, designing
his own car in the process. His first Porsche was a
911T, which he acquired after a succession of sports
cars including a Mini Marcos and various Lotus Elans
and Europas. He has owned or driven most 911 models
at some time or other and at the time of writing owns a
1972 911S and a 1981 924 Turbo. He is 35 and
married to Anne, with two children. By profession he is
a Chartered Engineer and a Member of the Institution
of Mechanical Engineers. He is formal Technical Editor
of Porsche Post and looks after the organization of the
Porsche Club Great Britain National Concours.

*Rear panel photos by
Chris Harvey*